T0318418

Monetisation and Commercialisation in the Baltic Sea, 1050–1450

Monetisation and Commercialisation in the Baltic Sea, 1050–1450 explores the varied uses of silver and gold in the Baltic Sea zone during the medieval period.

Ten original contributions examine coins and currencies, trade, economy, and power, taking care to avoid an out-of-date approach to economic history which assumes a progression from 'primitive' forms to 'developed' structures. Combining a variety of methodological approaches, and drawing on written sources, archaeological and numismatic evidence, and anthropological perspectives, the book considers the various ways in which silver and gold were used as monetary currency, fiscal instruments of power, and gifts in the High and Late Medieval societies of the Baltic Sea.

This book will appeal to scholars and students of medieval European history, as well as those interested in economic history, and the history of trade and commerce.

Dariusz Adamczyk is Associate Professor at the University of Hannover, Germany.

Beata Możejko is Professor at the Institute of History, University of Gdańsk, Poland.

Studies in Medieval History and Culture

Recent titles include

Margaret's Monsters
Women, Identity, and the Life of St Margaret in Medieval England
Michael E. Heyes

Supernatural Encounters
Demons and the Restless Dead in Medieval England, c. 1050-1450
Stephen Gordon

Ancestor Worship and the Elite in Late Iron Age Scandinavia
A Grave Matter
Triin Laidoner

Warfare and the Making of Early Medieval Italy (568-652)
Eduardo Fabbro

Rethinking Medieval Margins and Marginality
Edited by Ann E. Zimo, Tiffany D. Vann Sprecher, Kathryn Reyerson and Debra Blumenthal

English Readers of Catholic Saints
The Printing History of William Caxton's *Golden Legend*
Judy Ann Ford

Early Medieval Venice
Cultural Memory and History
Luigi Andrea Berto

Heresy and Citizenship
Persecution of Heresy in Late Medieval German Cities
Eugene Smelyansky

From Justinian to Branimir
The Making of the Middle Ages in Dalmatia
Danijel Džino

The Triumph of an Accursed Lineage
Kingship in Castile from Alfonso X to Alfonso XI (1252–1350)
Fernando Arias Guillén

Franks and Lombards in Italian Carolingian Texts
Memories of the Vanquished
Luigi Andrea Berto

The Bible and Jews in Medieval Spain
Norman Roth

The Cursed Carolers in Context
Edited by Lynneth Miller Renberg and Bradley Phillis

Women in the Medieval Common Law c.1200–1500
Gwen Seabourne

Jews and Converts in Late Medieval Castile
Breaking with the Past
Cecil D. Reid

Mobile Saints
Relic Circulation, Devotion, and Conflict in the Central Middle Ages
Kate M. Craig

Monetisation and Commercialisation in the Baltic Sea, 1050–1450
Edited by Dariusz Adamczyk and Beata Możejko

For more information about this series, please visit: https://www.routledge.com/Studies-in-Medieval-History-and-Culture/book-series/SMHC

Monetisation and Commercialisation in the Baltic Sea, 1050–1450

Edited by Dariusz Adamczyk and Beata Możejko

LONDON AND NEW YORK

First published 2021
by Routledge
2 Park Square, Milton Park, Abingdon, Oxon OX14 4RN

and by Routledge
52 Vanderbilt Avenue, New York, NY 10017

Routledge is an imprint of the Taylor & Francis Group, an informa business

British Library Cataloguing-in-Publication Data
A catalogue record for this book is available from the British Library

Library of Congress Cataloging-in-Publication Data
Names: Adamczyk, Dariusz, editor.
Title: Monetisation and commercialisation in the Baltic Sea, 1050-1450 / edited by Dariusz Adamczyk and Beata Możejko.
Description: Abingdon, Oxon ; New York, NY : Routledge, [2021] | Series: Studies in medieval history and culture | Includes bibliographical references and index.
Subjects: LCSH: Money--Baltic Sea--History. | Money--Baltic States--History--To 1500. | Commercialism--Baltic Sea--History. | Baltic Sea--Commerce--History.
Classification: LCC HG1089.6 .M67 2021 (print) | LCC HG1089.6 (ebook) | DDC 332.4/94850902--dc23
LC record available at https://lccn.loc.gov/2020051446
LC ebook record available at https://lccn.loc.gov/2020051447

ISBN: 978-0-367-89856-4 (hbk)
ISBN: 978-0-367-74244-7 (pbk)
ISBN: 978-1-003-02147-6 (ebk)

Typeset in Times
by SPi Global, India

Contents

Figures

Tables

Notes on the Contributors

Dariusz Adamczyk is a Researcher at the Deutsches Historisches Institut Warschau and Associate Professor in History at Leibniz University, Hannover. Publications include *Monetarisierungsmomente, Kommerzialisierungszonen oder fiskalische Währungslandschaften? Edelmetalle, Silberverteilungsnetzwerke und Gesellschaften in Ostmitteleuropa (800–1200)* (2020) and *Silber und Macht. Fernhandel, Tribute und die piastische Herrschaftsbildung in nordosteuropäischer Perspektive (800–1100)* (2014; Polisch translation 2018). His research interests focus on Viking Age silver flows, the history of trade and money and the state building in Eastern Europe.

Ulf Christian Ewert is a trained historian (Doctorate in Medieval and Modern History, University of Kiel 1999; Habilitation including a Venia legendi in Medieval History as well as in Economic and Social History, Chemnitz University of Technology 2008), economist and econometrician (Diploma in Business Administration and Econometrics, University of Kiel 1994). He has taught medieval and economic history at Chemnitz University of Technology, Helmut-Schmidt-University Hamburg, Free University of Berlin and the universities of Munich, Münster, Halle and Regensburg. His research emphasis has always been on long-term developments in the pre-modern era and particularly covers the medieval Hanse, the Portuguese overseas expansion, the political economy of princely courts, and living standards. He published numerous articles on these issues, and his work also encompasses economic theoretical approaches to the historical analysis of medieval and early-modern rules, institutions and organisations, thereby extensively drawing upon concepts of the New Institutional Economics, game theory and statistics. Currently, he is working at the University of Erfurt in an international research project on fairs in late medieval and early-modern Europe.

Marcin Grulkowski is Assistant Professor at the Institute of History, Polish Academy of Sciences, interested in: codicology, the chancelleries of Hanseatic cities in the late Middle Ages and the early modern era, the history of Gdańsk finances. He also took part in research projects dealing with publishing Gdańsk account book of the 14th–15th century. Since 2019 he has been a member of the Group of Urban History at the Committee of Historical Sciences of the Polish Academy of Sciences.

Piotr Guzowski is Assistant Professor at the University of Białystok, Poland. He specialises in research in the field of economic history, historical demography and environmental history of the preindustrial period. He is the author of books published in Polish: *Peasants and money at the turn of the Middle Ages and modern times* [*Chłopi i pieniądze na przełomie średniowiecza i czasów nowożytnych*, Kraków: Avalon 2008] and *Gentry Family in Pre-Partition Poland. A Demographic Study* [*Demografia rodziny szlacheckiej w Polsce przedrozbiorowej*, Białystok: Polskie Towarzystwo Historyczne 2019].

Carsten Jahnke is Associate Professor for Medieval history at the Saxo-Institute of the University of Copenhagen. He is an expert in the economic and social history of Northern Europe, especially the Hanseatic League and the economies of the Baltic- and Northern Sea Areas from the pre-hanseatic times to the 16th century. He has i.a. written books about the Hanseatic League and the History of Denmark.

Krzysztof Kopiński is Professor at Nicolaus Copernicus University in Toruń; in the years 1998–2007 he was employed at the State Archives in Toruń; since 2007 he has been working at the Institute of History and Archival Studies of Nicolaus Copernicus University, where he has been deputy director since 2015. He has been the secretary general of the Scientific Society in Toruń – the oldest Polish scientific society in Pomerania – since 2018. Within the scope of his academic work, he has published sources on the history of medieval Toruń and Gdańsk, along with reports of the General Assembly of Royal Prussia from the first half of the 16th century; he also published works on the patriciate of the city of Toruń, and is also a co-author of a textbook on editing historical sources.

Beata Możejko is Professor at the Faculty of History at the University of Gdańsk, specialises in medieval history and the auxiliary sciences of history. Author of over 130 papers and articles, 6 monographs, including "Peter von Danzig. The story of Great Caravel 1462–1475" (Brill 2020). Member of the Bureau of Committee on Historical Sciences of the Polish Academy of Sciences (2020–2023). Member of the Knowledge Committee of the Gdańsk Encyclopedia (Gedanopedia).

Anna Paulina Orłowska studied history at Warsaw University and Christian-Albrecht-University in Kiel, afterwards she studied history of arts and prepared her PhD thesis on a medieval merchant in Gdańsk at Christian-Albrecht-University in Kiel. Her first post-doc project, at the Institute of History Polish Academy of Science and financed by MSCA, utilised the methods of digital humanities to analyse the network of periodic fairs in Greater Poland in the late Middle Ages and early modernity.

Grzegorz Śnieżko is archaeologist and numismatist. Previously worked in The Royal Castle in Warsaw and National Bank of Poland. Now he is an employee of The Institute of Archaeology and Ethnology of Polish Academy of Sciences, where under prof. Stanisław Suchodolski's supervision he prepared his PhD. thesis entitled *Coin in Poland under the reign of Bolesław III Wrymouth*.

Roman Zaoral is Senior Lecturer in Medieval History in the Faculty of Humanities, at Charles University, Prague, Czech Republic. His research in the field of monetary and financial history concerns medieval trade and cultural exchange between Venice and Bohemia, papal collections management in Central Europe, credit and taxation of late medieval towns, pilgrims´ money and circulation of gold in Italy. He is a main editor of the volume *Money and Finance in Central Europe during the Later Middle Ages* published in 2016 in the series Palgrave Studies in the History of Finance. He also participated in the projects regarding the analysis of the medieval coin and jewellery hoards of Fuchsenhof (2004) and Levínská Olešnice (2018).

Introduction

Dariusz Adamczyk and Beata Możejko

It is generally accepted that the level of monetisation and commercialisation constitutes an appropriate indicator of economic development in pre-modern societies. The term "monetisation" reflects the use of precious metals, silver and gold, as means of payment, medium of exchange, currency on different markets: not only in long-distance trade, but also in regional and local commerce. Under this terminus, we grasp all forms of metal money containing coins and ingots as well as their fragments. "Commercialisation", in turn, refers to an extension of the market and economic logic into various social segments. According to some historians, one can distinguish between two forms of commercialisation. In the "weaker" sense it was a growth of economic activity over a period of time. This type of commercialisation would include the increase of trading institutions, the growth of towns and the expansion of the quantity of money in circulation. The "strong" commercialisation, on the other hand, assumes that economic activity was growing faster than the population. Consequently, different social strata used the market mechanisms for buying and selling goods for their livelihood.[1] Additionally, we should bear in mind other indicators like the quality of the division of labour and of agrarian structures, the velocity of circulation of coins, the development of transport and communication, the usage of credits or literacy and numeracy skills.[2]

The point of departure of this volume, relying on a conference that took place in Warsaw on 13th and 14th September 2018, is the fact that around the Baltic Sea in the course of the later eleventh and twelfth centuries occurred an economic, social and political transformation. The raiding economy and long-distance trade typical of the Viking Age were replaced by social forms based upon stronger local structures and bulk goods commerce. Parallel to this phenomenon, domestic production of coins in several regions began or was augmented. Such evidence we note in Denmark, Norway, among the Elbe Slaves, in Pomerania, in the Piast realm south of Pomerania, beyond in Latvia, Estonia, Sweden and Rus' – even when the minting of deniers was not always and anywhere continually. The issuing of coins is believed to have been traced to the making of local markets, which stimulated and created demand for precious metals. On the other hand, and this seems lesser examined, the minting policy reflects efforts of political authorities directed against traditional social hierarchies. The "old" networks based upon the kinship loyalties were supplanted by emerging states and power centres, which became the dominating geo-political and geo-economic element. Thus, the rulers did not only try to get access to the existing markets, but also to take control over the circulation of silver having enormous strategic importance.

This raises several questions: Was the issuing of coins a consequence of economic processes or of the fiscal need conducted by emerging monarchies and political centres? Which sectors of the economy and which parts of society were commercialised? Where and in what extent can we speak of an integration of market? And last but not least, was the monetisation a linear process or characterised by social, political or economic disruptions?

In order to answer these questions, we need interdisciplinary indicators including different sources and methods. Firstly, we have to interpret the written sources, chronicles and charters as well as custom regulations and city account books. Secondly, we should use the archaeological and numismatic material, contextualising the location of hoards as well as single coin finds and determining where and when the deniers were struck. However, the image would be too simple if we do not consider anthropological configurations, for example various social attitudes to precious metals containing the gift and potlatch cultures. As Laurence Fontaine points out in reference to Early Modern economies:

> The border between gift and market was far from watertight, with the two categories constantly overlapping each other in modern Europe. Second-hand objects were used as an alternative currency to feed multiple markets. Everywhere, monetary practices, which led people to hoard their money rather than to let it circulate, as well as the lack of cash, had allowed an economy based on the circulation of goods to develop. In urban exchanges, bartering was still largely prevalent not only among traders, as we saw in Chapter 4, but also among peasants because there were many who paid peddlers with their harvest or the produce of their home-based industry.[3]

Evidently, we cannot speak of a linear development of monetisation between the post-Viking Age and the late Medieval Ages.

Dariusz Adamczyk proposes a non-linear approach including several methods, which may help to explain the circulation of precious metals in the post-Viking Age. He explores the quantity of coin stray finds in settlements as well as the composition of hoards regarding the origin of coins and the structure of hoards concerning the existence of silver, particularly in the form of jewellery. In the next step, he tries to establish evidence in the written sources available and to relate them as far as possible with the archaeological and numismatic data. Thus, in the post-Viking Age several coin types circulated around the Baltic Sea, among others pennies imported from western Europe, primarily Germany, as well as deniers struck in domestic mints. It does not mean, however, that the prime mover of issuing coins was the demand for currency on local markets. Rather, fiscal and political needs driven by kings, dukes and warlords may have decided about striking deniers, particularly as the remuneration for a retinue or client was the crucial element for exercising power. Additionally, the redistribution of valuable goods (reflected in numerous pieces of jewellery in hoards) and the giving of gifts belonged to the major social principles allowing an intensification of relations within various elite groupings or creating bonds between people. On the other hand, several communities around the Baltic Sea were involved into the long-distance and regional trade. They constituted monetarised and commercialised enclaves where silver was used as money in the form of coins and ingots. In rural societies living more away from trading centres precious metals may have served as fiscal instrument, prestige good and raw material for making jewellery. These people paid their obligations in kind and in coins – the latter they could gain at commercial places exchanging their agrarian surplus for silver. Therefore, in reference to the post-Viking Age we can speak of hybrid political economies reflecting different forms of social structure and different levels of cultural attitudes.

The influx of deniers from Germany into several regions around the Baltic Sea collapsed in the early twelfth century. Consequently, a transformation from an import-oriented economy to a domestic circulation of silver took place. Grzegorz Śnieżko contextualises this development using the example of Poland: he distinguishes between eight types of coins, six two-sided and two bracteates, minted by Bolesław the Wrymouth between 1097–1099 and 1138, and discusses their commercial, fiscal and political functions. The finds of oldest coins come mainly from Silesia, Kraków and Sandomierz Lands (Lesser Poland), while pennies of the following types have been also found in Mazovia, Kuyavia and Wielkopolska (Greater Poland). Thus, their presence there suggests a geographical spreading of domestic deniers. Moreover, they appear in central strongholds as well as in smaller forts. Numismatic evidence, the number of hoards as well as the quantity of single coin finds, shows that there was less silver available than in the last decades of the eleventh century when large amounts of Saxon cross-deniers flowed to Wielkopolska and other regions ruled by the Piasts. According to conservative estimation based on the interpretation of coin dies, it would have been four or five domestic pennies per head for several decades of coinage.

As concluded from written sources, most people in Poland participated only rudimentarily in money economy until the early thirteenth century. An expansion of circulating silver by wider social strata happened first as consequence of the German colonisation and the resulting agrarian revolution. In this context, Roman Zaoral introduces two other categories: By combining textual evidence with numismatic data, he discusses the usage of coins as a monetary tax in the form of periodic renewal of money (the so-called *renovatio monetae*) and coin debasement. In the Czech lands, the system of re-coinage evolved gradually during the reign of prince Vratislaus II (1061–1092, since 1085 the first king of Bohemia) and was replaced by the debasement strategy around 1300. The monetary policy based on a renewal of deniers, bracteates or pfennigs (the so-called short-lived coins) was common in the less developed economic systems of central and northern Europe. However, the process of monetisation did not occur lineally during the thirteenth and early fourteenth centuries, but overlapped parallel with phases of demonetisation, reflected in the use of un-minted metal and fragmented bracteates. Evidently, Zaoral defines monetisation narrowly as circulating coins (and not generally precious metals). The short-lived money of regional type became obsolete with the growing volume of trade and towns, the increase of peasants paying feudal rent in money and the interconnection of the local and supra-regional market. This process coincided with the circulation of two new coin forms in the Czech lands – silver Prague groschen and gold Bohemian florins.

As Zaoral points out, it was trade accompanied by cultural exchange, which helped to link different regions of Europe and to reduce differences among them. According to Fritz Rörig, in the thirteenth and fourteenth centuries a *Mittelalterliche Weltwirtschaft*, a medieval world economy was created. Its outer corners were Novgorod, London, Lisbon and Constantinople.[4] Thereby, the most important silver mines supplying this system lay in Central Europe. This is why the editors of this volume have decided to include in the examination some Central European lands like Bohemia.

Let us come back to the North. During the economic boom period of the later twelfth and thirteenth centuries, several settlers from the Roman-German Empire came into the Baltic Sea region and established a dense network of towns along its southern shore. Beyond, local rulers granted privileges to groups of Low German merchants at some important markets at various places of the Baltic Sea and North Sea (Bergen, London, Bruges, Novgorod).

The trade around the Baltic Sea, generally conducted by the so-called Hanse, included an exchange between crafted goods such as linen and cloth provided by the West for raw materials coming from eastern and northern Europe like wax, timber and ore alongside with furs, honey and foodstuffs like grain, herrings or dried cod. However, the Hanse system worked within kinship and friendship networks existing until the late fifteenth century. We may describe this commerce, following Ulf Christian Ewert in this volume, as "reciprocal trade" based upon bilateral relationships, which distributed goods extremely effective across space without paying with silver. So, we can speak of a high level of commercialisation, but low level of monetisation. This raises further questions. Which role did credit play? And why did the Hanse not adopt the more modern techniques of trade and finance known already in Italy? Ewert argues that a single merchant could not simply quit the Hanse's system of trade and adopt instead trading habits and financing techniques of other European competitors, because this would have meant losing all connections within the Hanse network and all benefits coming from it. A second reason was the negative impact of "reciprocal trade" on the economic development of capital market. This resulted in "lock-in" effects – a path dependence. Nevertheless, the Hanse traders used the existing currencies to fix the value of their goods mostly paid with the goods sent in return by the trading partner.

In contrast to Ewert, Carsten Jahnke conceives the extension of using coins in Hanse cities more optimistic, as he states that by 1250 the world of international trade was fully monetised (after the proto-monetary and the pre-monetary stages during the earlier Middle Ages). As he shows, the system of the mark as monetary unit reached the commercial outposts of the Hanse in the East. The usage of metal money along the southern shores of the Baltic Sea between Slesvig or Lübeck and Novgorod, however, only encompassed the Latin Christian areas. Inside of the kontor business was done in *equum pro equo dare*, in barter, while outside of the same commercial transactions were paid per *emere pro pecunia*, by money. Thus, regarding the transaction-cost-theory, the monetisation of the Hanse quarter in Novgorod was just rudimentarily developed. It is evidently that the trade of German merchants with Novgorod did not base upon trust, security and common language. In Jahnke's opinion, this mutual distrust impeded the emergence of a more sophisticated monetisation of the trade in the eastern periphery of the Baltic.

Nonetheless, besides the barter-trade precious metals were still in circulation. We should add, in their trade with Novgorod German merchants used silver, as dukes of Moscow Rus' paid tributes to the Golden Horde (Tatars) since the early fourteenth century in the form of precious metals, probably ingots, which they had to import.[5] Thus, for the Rus' the disposal of silver coming from mines in Central Europe had an essential political importance.

We have evidence that the domestic markets in late medieval Prussian towns such as Gdańsk (Danzig), Elbląg (Elbing) and Toruń (Thorn) were monetised to some extent. Minted coinage existed, and a money of account system based on the Prussian mark was also in use. Accounting and bookkeeping were developing. Money played a leading role in the transactions of merchants, shippers and craftsmen. Sophisticated mechanisms had also been developed for concluding and settling financial transactions, both among individual merchants and at the level of municipal authorities (the introduction of city account books).[6]

In the first half of the fifteenth century Gdańsk was still ruled by the Teutonic Order, and the city's merchants already had extensive commercial contacts with other Hanseatic towns as well as with England and Flanders. As highlighted by Anna P. Orłowska, an invaluable source dating from this period is the account book of the Gdańsk merchant Johan Pyre, active from 1421 to 1455, which documents the use of gold and silver in commercial practice. Written in Middle Low German, the book contains detailed notes relating to business partners, goods, transactions and payments made in various currencies – in both actual money (coinage) and in money of account. At that time, the money of account in Prussia was the Prussian mark; however, Orłowska's analysis shows that the payments recorded in Pyre's merchant book were made in various gold and silver coins and settled using various systems. Notably, during the first ten years of his career, gold coins played a significant role in the transactions conducted by Pyre. One hypothesis is that he made use of differences in the price of gold between Gdańsk and Riga, where he sent the majority of the gold coins. We also know that Pyre used offsetting of liabilities and promissory notes in his payments. This enabled him to settle his accounts without using cash, hence without using minted currencies. For late medieval merchants who, like Johan Pyre, had numerous networks of connections in different cities and different parts of Europe, it was vital to be able to pay in different currencies without losing money on their exchange. In addition to monetary transactions, Pyre's account book reveals that a barter system based on the exchange of goods was also used. This pertained especially to trade with Lithuania.

In the fifteenth century cities such as Gdańsk invested money in land, granaries and ships, but even wars provided an investment opportunity of sorts. In 1454, along with other towns and noble estates of Prussia, Gdańsk and the local nobility renounced obedience to the Teutonic Order and surrendered themselves to the king of Poland, Kazimierz Jagiellończyk (Casimir IV Jagiellon). The king's subsequent incorporation of Prussia into Poland led to the Polish-Teutonic Thirteen Years' War (1454–1466).[7] Poland's military and political endeavours were financed by the city of Gdańsk (the city council), which raised the necessary funds from its inhabitants. Marcin Grulkowski points out that the municipal authorities of Gdańsk were already borrowing money from their citizens to pay for the war effort during the very first years of this conflict. An example from 1454 shows that the individuals who granted these loans were issued with a type of promissory note (*Schuldbriefe*) acknowledging the debt. In 1457 the city council introduced new taxes on goods and exacted a "tenth pfenning" (*den zehenden pfennig*) loan from burghers on their properties. Other important means of securing additional funds included pledges and taking over the former revenues of the Teutonic Order in Prussia. The financial and credit operations conducted by Gdańsk during the war were about to have far-reaching consequences. The loans taken out by the city were not repaid until the late 1470s.

Toruń was another major Prussian town undergoing an intensive process of circulating and hoarding precious metals. Krzysztof Kopiński shows that to better understanding the particulars of this process it is worth examining the quantity of gold and silver items in Toruń and their use, as recorded in the city's mid-fifteenth century sources. Mention is made, among other things, of silver jewellery and vessels; however, these objects not only had a practical purpose but, more importantly, they were used as security. Silver buttons, possibly the equivalent of coins, are particularly noteworthy. The sources also refer to silver in melted form (*lotiges silber*). Silver was used by the burghers of Toruń in financial and property settlements; it was also the subject of loans and their collateral. Kopiński provides numerous examples of transactions of this type. Although there are far fewer records concerning gold articles in the Toruń sources, we do know about the work of the city's goldsmiths. Coins circulating in Prussia, including Toruń, also contained silver. As noted by Kopiński, after the defeat of the Teutonic Order at Grunwald in 1410 the silver content in coins was reduced due to inflation. Restrictions were imposed on trade in silver and old coins. The Teutonic Order also regulated the price of silver goods and tried to prevent the circulation of counterfeit coins. The silver used in Toruń came from Hungary (present-day Slovakia) via Wrocław and Kraków.

Thus, money played an important role among the societies of medieval cities on the southern coast of the Baltic Sea. In contrast to urbanised centres, the situation in rural areas shows deviating patterns. Their economic structure is examined by Piotr Guzowski, who focuses his attention on medieval Poland, where peasants constituted the most numerous social strata. His analysis addresses the process of commercialisation and the question how it led to increasing economic inequality among medieval peasants. Guzowski states that a more complex stage of monetisation took place only during the thirteenth and fourteenth centuries as a result of German colonisation. Changes were introduced in land management and cultivation systems, which had an impact on economic development as a whole. Money played an increasingly significant role in relations between peasants, dukes and landowners, and numerous obligations were paid in monetary form. The thirteenth and fourteenth centuries marked an increase in the monetisation of the agrarian economy, though not necessarily in the everyday lives. These processes became more entrenched in the fifteenth century, during the reign of the Jagiellon dynasty. Extant court records indicate that land transactions were concluded between peasants using primitive forms of credit. Guzowski's examination clearly shows that the so-called Gini coefficient was much higher for people living near towns than for those living in villages far away from urban centres. In this way, more intensive usage of coins as means of payment on local markets led to a growing economic inequality in rural communities.

Finally, we would like to note that the velocity of money in pre-modern societies varied and depended on a plenty of factors. Wars and fiscal needs of rulers caused debasements and destabilised monetary systems. Occasionally, they could have restricted access to precious metals among ordinary people. The Teutonic Order, for example, had to pay after the battle of Grunwald to the Polish Kingdom the enormous sum of eleven tons silver, more than double that its annual revenues.[8] This ransom obviously affected the fiscal policy in Prussia in the subsequent years. Thus, the quality of monetisation was influenced by political disruptions. In this regard, the primacy of politics over economics remained also in the later Middle Age an important feature around the Baltic.

Our sincerest thanks go to Małgorzata Sparenberg and Gregor Christiansmeyer, and in particular to Stewart Beale, Taylor & Francis's Editorial Assistant. All of his editorial work was invaluable. We are very grateful to him for all this.

Notes

1 Piotr Guzowski, "Money Economy and Money Growth: The Case of Medieval and Early Modern Poland", in *Quaestiones Medii Aevi Novae* 18 (2013), 235–256, particularly 236; Richard Britnell, *The Commercialisation of English Society, 1000–1500* (Manchester-New York 1996), XIII–XIV.
2 Jim L. Bolton, *Money in the Medieval English Economy, 973–1489* (Manchester: Manchester University Press, 2012), 133; Sławomir Gawlas, "Komercjalizacja jako mechanizm europeizacji peryferii na przykładzie Polski", in *Ziemie polskie wobec Zachodu. Studia nad rozwojem średniowiecznej Europy*, edited by Roman Czaja a.o. (Warszawa: DIG, 2006), 25–116, particularly 71.
3 Laurence Fontaine, *The Moral Economy. Poverty, Credit, and the Trust in Early Modern Europe* (New York: Cambridge University Press, 2014), p. 254.
4 Fritz Rörig, "Mittelalterliche Weltwirtschaft", in *Wirtschaftskräfte im Mittelalter*, edited by Paul Kaegbein (Wien etc. 1971), pp. 351–91.
5 Janet Martin, *Medieval Russia, 980–1584*, (Cambridge: Cambridge University Press, 2003), p. 211.
6 Henryk Samsonowicz, *Badania nad kapitałem mieszczańskim Gdańska w II połowie XV wieku*, (Warsaw: Uniwersytet Warszawski, 1960). A good example of sources concerning monetisation are the city account books of Gdańsk, see: *Najstarsze księgi kamlarskie Głównego Miasta Gdańska z XIV–XV wieku*, edited and annotated by Marcin Grulkowski, Studia i materiały do dziejów kancelarii w Gdańsku, Vol. 2 (Warsaw: Instytut Historii PAN, 2016); see also Grulkowski "Gdańsk chancellery and registers in the fourteenth to fifteenth centuries", in *New Studies in Medieval and Renaissance Poland and Prussia. The Impact of Gdańsk*, edited by Beata Możejko (London and New York: Routledge, 2017), pp. 47–59.

7 Marian Biskup, *Wojna trzynastoletnia z Zakonem krzyżackim 1454–1466*, (Warsaw: Wydawnictwo Ministerstwo Obrony Narodowej, 1967) remains the seminal work on the Thirteen Years' War. However, no separate study has ever been made of the financial aspects of this war.
8 Oliver Volckart, *Die Münzpolitik im Ordensland und Herzogtum Preußen von 1370 bis 1550*, (Wiesbaden: Harrassowitz, 1996), p. 68.

Bibliography

Primary sources

Marcin Grulkowski (edited and annotated) *Najstarsze księgi kamlarskie Głównego Miasta Gdańska z XIV–XV wieku (Studia i materiały do dziejów kancelarii w Gdańsku, vol. 2) [The earliest city account books of Gdańsk's Main Town from the 14th–15th centuries]*. Warsaw: Instytut Historii PAN, 2016.

Secondary literature

Biskup, Marian. *Wojna trzynastoletnia z Zakonem krzyżackim 1454–1466 [The Thirteen Years' War with the Teutonic Order 1454–1466]*. Warsaw: Wydawnictwo Ministerstwo Obrony Narodowej, 1967.

Bolton, Jim L. *Money in the Medieval English Economy, 973–1489*. Manchester: Manchester University Press, 2012.

Britnell, Richard. *The Commercialisation of English Society, 1000–1500*. New York: Manchester University Press, 1996.

Fontaine, Laurence. *The Moral Economy. Poverty, Credit, and the Trust in Early Modern Europe*. New York: Cambridge University Press, 2014.

Gawlas, Sławomir. "Komercjalizacja jako mechanizm europeizacji peryferii na przykładzie Polski," [Commercialization as an Europeanization mechanism of the periphery on the example of Poland] in *Ziemie polskie wobec Zachodu. Studia nad rozwojem średniowiecznej Europy [Polish lands and the West. Studies on the development of medieval Europe]*, edited by Sławomir Gawlas, pp. 25–116. Warszawa: Wydawnictwo DIG, 2006.

Grulkowski, Marcin. "Gdańsk chancellery and registers in the fourteenth to fifteenth centuries", in *New Studies in Medieval and Renaissance Poland and Prussia. The Impact of Gdańsk*, edited by Beata Możejko, pp. 47–59. London and New York: Routledge, 2017.

Guzowski, Piotr. "Money Economy and Money Growth: The Case of Medieval and Early Modern Poland", in *Quaestiones Medii Aevi Novae 18* (2013), 235–256.

Martin, Janet. *Medieval Russia, 980–1584*. Cambridge: Cambridge University Press, 2003.

Rörig, Fritz. "Mittelalterliche Weltwirtschaft. Blüte und Ende einer Wirschaftsperiode", in *Wirtschaftskräfte im Mittelalter*, edited by Paul Kaegbein, pp. 351–391. Wien, Graz and Köln: Böhlau, 1971.

Samsonowicz, Henryk. *Badania nad kapitałem mieszczańskim Gdańska w II połowie XV wieku [Research into bourgeois capital in Gdańsk in the latter half of the fifteenth century]*. Warszawa: Uniwersytet Warszawski, 1960.

Volckart, Oliver. *Die Münzpolitik im Ordensland und Herzogtum Preußen von 1370 bis 1550*, Wiesbaden: Harrassowitz, 1996.

1   Money, gift or instrument of power? Hybrid (political) economies in the post-Viking age around the Baltic Sea

Dariusz Adamczyk

The second half of the eleventh century is believed to have marked the end of the Viking Age. At this time occurred a transition of economies based on loot, plunder and long-distance trade to social and political forms established stronger in regional structures.[1] In several areas of the Baltic Sea there began significant production of coins. At first glance, they served as money on regional and local markets, which may have stimulated demand for precious metals. At second glance, however, this explanation seems too simple as it ignores the political, fiscal and cultural context. Archaeological evidence, in particular the existence of bullion (ingots, jewellery, undefined scrap and hacksilver, fragmented pieces of silver) found in hoards from lands around the Baltic, suggests functions other than purely commercial use. Silver could fulfil different roles: a means of payment for market transactions, rents, tributes or taxes; remuneration for a retinue or a client potentate; or, more generally, as a way of establishing relationships within a society. Precious metals could also be served as prestige objects, for cult or magic.[2]

This raises several questions. What was the prime mover of issuing coins within the Baltic area: demand for money on the domestic market or needs driven by authorities like kings, dukes and warlords? Which political and fiscal forms of silver payment can be distinguished? Which segments of a society were monetised and commercialised? Finally, how can we quantify and measure the scale and intensity of monetisation and commercialisation?

In order to answer these questions, we need a bunch of interdisciplinary indicators including different sources and methods. This involves three steps:

1. establishing the archaeological contexts of hoards and stray coin finds. This includes, amongst other things, the find-spot (such as a trading place, settlement or stronghold); density of hoards; density of stray finds; the volume of hoards; the appearance of ingots and jewellery;
2. locating the hoards and determining where and when their coins were struck; and
3. contextualising them and the structure of division of labour using the written sources, chronicles and charters as well as custom regulations, available.

Last but not least, we have to take political and anthropological contexts, for example the emergence of power structures and various social attitudes to precious metals comprising the gift and potlatch cultures, into account. Let us start with monetary aspects.

Silver as money (but where?)

It is evident that silver in the form of coins and ingots was a common means of payment at various trading places around the Baltic Sea. Clusters of deniers scattered throughout such settlements and the existence of weights or balance scales would indicate this. In contrast to hoards, clusters of stray deniers found inside a settlement suggest that they were not intentionally lost and may have used for commercial purpose. Such coin finds dating to the eleventh or twelfth century are known from several sites, among others, Hedeby, Lund, Parchim-Löddigsee, Jaromarsburg at Kap Arkona, Wolin, Szczecin, Kołobrzeg-Budzistowo, Gdańsk and Kałdus, around 140 km south of Gdańsk.

Judging from the quantity of finds, the fortified cultic site at Kap Arkona on the island of Rügen is very impressive. It is possible that the area of the whole complex amounted to nearly 5 ha. Here about 500 coins have been unearthed to date: 219 Arab dirhams, mostly fragmented, struck from the eighth through early tenth century, and 252 cross-deniers minted during the eleventh and early twelfth centuries. Just 15 coins dated after 1168, the year of looting the Rani-treasure by the Danes.[3] It is striking that the chronology of coins covers more than 300 years. However, *Chronica Slavorum*, "The Chronicle of the Slavs" written in about 1170 by Helmold of Bosau, does not confirm a commercial circulation of silver. According to him, the Rani did not possess minted money; they used, instead, linen cloths as currency.[4] On the other hand, Helmold's reference reflects the economic and cultural conditions of the mid-twelfth century, so we should be cautious of projecting them onto a time before 1100. More on this later.

Around 500 coins have been unearthed also inside the Gdańsk settlement, in layers located in the Tartaczna and Panieńska streets and believed to have originated from the twelfth century. Additionally, a small hoard known as Gdańsk X turned up in the Zamczysko (old castle ruin). This find contained eight imitations of Anglo-Saxon, Danish and German deniers and may have been buried after 1119. Commercial use of these coins is suggested by the fact that they were struck from brass.[5]

Let us move around 200 km southwest of Arkona and 70 km south of the Baltic shore. In Parchim-Löddigsee during the eleventh century there existed a significant trading place. From the whole settlement complex of ca. 1.8 ha are known more than 120 coins: 48 have been found in the form of two small (26 and 22 deniers) hoards dating around 1060. Other coins, among others the so-called Agrippiner from the Lower Elbe area, appeared as stray finds and were issued between 1060–1080 and 1080–1100, as well as in the period 1100–1120. A group of 48 counterfeit and imitated specimen including Frisian pennies and German cross-deniers illustrates that the indigenous Slavs minted their own coins. They were made of copper and covered with a thin silver layer. 188 weights and at least

20 scales of balance clearly show that precious metal was weighted. Furthermore, we note 420 carnelian and rock crystal beads alongside items from Scandinavia, western Germany and the Kievan Rus'. Three shackles suggest the existence of slave trade. Consequently, the finds of silver as well as of various goods indicate that Parchim-Löddigsee was a nodal point of the cross-continental trade linking the Baltic Sea with various parts of Europe.

Finally, the stronghold complex of Kałdus including adjacent settlement and burial ground is worth mentioning. We count here around 140 stray finds of coins, mainly struck in the second half of the eleventh century, and two small hoards dating to 1065 or 1090.[6] Kałdus' localisation on the lower/middle Vistula, 140 km south of Gdańsk, shows it as an important marketplace where commercial functions may have been combined with the collection of tolls.

All these aforementioned sites had much in common. Lying on strategic routes along the Baltic shore or the inland waterways, they fulfilled a notable role in the cross-continental trade. Thus, it is quite possible the people living there used coins as currency. It does not mean, however, that this was the only form of money in circulation. In Novgorod, for example, archaeological evidence indicates the existence of an ingot-based system.[7] As one silver grivna was made of ca. 200 g silver (in contrast one coin of ca. 0.5–1 g), they must have been redistributed in the long-distance trade, where greater market transactions were common. The hoard from Burge (Gotland) dated to ca. 1140 contained 32 such ingots, produced in Novgorod and perhaps Kiev. As small change on the market of Novgorod served probably bunches of old worn-out squirrel furs.[8] Accordingly, in several settlements around the Baltic Sea we observe a currency dualism: on one hand, there were precious metals in the form of coins and ingots; on the other, fur bunches or linen cloths like in Kap Arkona.

Table 1.1 Hoards with recent coins minted in the late eleventh or early twelfth century from Pomerania[9]

Find-spot and terminus post quem of the hoard (the recent coin)	*Number of imported coins (in percent)*	*Number of imitated coins (in percent)*
Bonin (Koszalin) 1080	96	4
Horniki (60 km southwest of Gdańsk) 1088	98	2
Pommern VII 1088	99	1
Malczkowo (Słupsk) 1092–1114	100	–
Gdańsk X 1119?	–	100
Łupawa (Słupsk) 1120	25	75
Pommern XIII 1120	15	85
Gliszcz (Bydgoszcz) 1047–1100?	5	95
Włynkowo (Słupsk) 1050–1100?	7	93
Pommern XI 1050–1100?	74	26
Pommern XV 1050–1100?	31	69
Pommern XVI 1050–1100?	9	91

In order to explain the extent of monetisation in areas lying in greater distance from cross-continental routes, we have to change the method and try to examine the content of hoards. Let me take, for instance, Pomerania. The following table illustrates several late eleventh/early twelfth century finds from this region.

First of all, we have to regard that the terminus *post quem* (recent coin) of the Gdańsk X, Gliszcz and Włynkowo hoards as well as of the finds known as Pommern XI, XV, XVI could be determined only approximately, as many imitations of German, Anglo-Saxon, Bohemian or Scandinavian deniers do not allow a precise dating. The indication of the year 1047 or 1050 in these finds illustrates the recent datable coin being struck abroad. The year 1100 constitutes a chronological endpoint when the imitations of abroad deniers may have been issued. Second, five hoards cannot be attributed to their find-spots, so they have been declared as "Pommern".

It is striking, however, that Pomeranian hoards constitute two various structures containing, generally speaking, overwhelmingly either imported deniers or the domestic imitations of foreign coins, minted by the indigenous Slavic chieftains or warlords. Even within the same region remarkable differences occur. The local imitations of western specimen prevailed in the finds from Łupawa and Włynkowo, while German, Bohemian and Hungarian deniers were dominant in the Malczkowo-hoard. In the vicinity of Gdańsk the find known as Gdańsk X consisted exclusively of imitations, in contrast to the Horniki-hoard comprising almost entirely of imported coins. If local markets in Pomerania had been, at least in some extent, monetised, these different coin types would have been circulated together and reflected in hoards which would be strong mixed and their structure similar. It seems to be opposite: the smallest ratio between imitations and imports, 69% to 31%, occurs in the hoard Pommmern XV. Obviously, in the Pomeranian interior precious metals were redistributed and used for other purposes rather than as means of payment at local markets.

In Denmark, among the finds with at least ten coins dated between 1079 and 1130, eight hoards contain only domestic products (or in one case, also Norwegian deniers), while in seven hoards several foreign specimens appear.[10] Finally, ten Polabian hoards dated between 1077 and ca. 1100 consist exclusively of German pennies, including, in three cases, the cross-deniers.[11] So, around the Baltic Sea various silver circles can be distinguished.

Precious metals as gifts

Besides huge number of coins, several Pomeranian finds contain jewellery and raw silver. From those illustrated in Table 1.1, just two, Bonin and Gdańsk X, have not included ornaments. The hoard from Łupawa in Middle Pomerania, nearly 50 km from the Baltic coast, appears very impressive in this regard. It consists of 473 armrings, wires, pendants, Kaptorgas (small decorated boxes worn on the chest), beads, earrings and neck rings. We should add that most of them appear in fragments. Similar to the hoard from Gliszcz we note more than 350 fragments of jewellery and raw silver. Furthermore, some finds known as "Pommern" comprise jewellery; for example: Pommern XV (1050–1100), 372 pieces of ornaments, wires, rods and melts/lumps, mainly in the form of hacksilver; and Pommern XIII (1120) 239 fragments of silver items, among others rings.[12]

Obviously, there are other possibilities beyond market needs why silver in Pomerania was cut and fragmented. The settlements along the south shore of the Baltic may have served both as centres for tribute collection by the elite, and as places for various forms of exchange. Some of the hacked coins and rings could have been gifts to express friendship and ensure political alliances. "Baugbroti" (ring-breaker) is the name in the sagas for these chieftains and warlords who were lavish and gave pieces of armrings to their followers. Accordingly, fragmented ornaments reflect not necessarily the commercial logic of silver using. They may have held prestige and ritual functions we know as the potlach. During such gift-giving ceremony, members of the elite would redistribute or destroy their property in order to maintain or strengthen their own social status. By redistributing goods, symbolic and political ties with the retinue could be reinforced.[13]

Let me come back to Arkona. Helmold of Bosau describes the social functions of precious metals as follows:

> Gold and silver they [the Rani] gain through robbery or capturing people or in any other way, they use either as jewellery for their women, or they put it in treasure of their god.[14]
>
> People who were subjected by their [the Rani] weapons must pay tribute to their temple; [...] By drawing lots they decide where their army should be sent. After victory they put gold and silver in treasure their god, and what there is left over, they divide up.[15]

This passage suggests the existence of a temple-fiscality, combining raiding and imposing tributes with ritual habits and prestige roles.[16] Thus, coins found on Rügen circulated at this time, not necessarily as money on local markets, but as tools of cult and raw material for making jewellery, both fulfilled important social functions. The redistribution of valuable goods was one of the major social principles and allowed an intensification of relations by circulation of silver within members of kinships and between them. The giving of gifts accumulated social prestige and created bonds between people. The gifts from treasuries served Slavic warlords and chieftains to strengthen the social ties with their retinue, helping in this way to create a symbolic capital necessary for the reproduction of power. By the redistribution of precious metals, prestige and authority could be consolidated.

Silver as instrument of power and fiscalism

Tolomeo da Lucca (1236–1327) recognised around seven hundred years ago that king cannot adequately reign without gold, silver and coins minted from them. Money, furthermore, would be very important for the kingdom as it regulates the life of people and affects rulership through collecting various revenues in the form of coins. Additionally, money exemplifies the importance of sovereignty by regulating and measuring the commerce, particularly as the image of king supervises trade in his absence.[17]

Evidently, Tolomeo distinguishes between political and fiscal aspects of using precious metals: as political instrument of power and as fiscal tool of rulership. Silver served as a means of remuneration for a retinue or a client potentate. The Chronicle of Gallus Anonymus appears very impressive when it is composed around 1113. He describes the political economy of the Piast realm in Wielkopolska (Greater Poland), just south of Pomerania, at the beginning of the twelfth century:

> Eight days before wedding and as much thereafter the belligerent Bolesław [Wrymouth] did not stop to distribute gifts. Some got pelts and furs covered with clothes and fringed with gold, the princes received coats, gold and silver vessels, others obtained towns and strongholds, villages and manors.[18]

This quotation clearly shows that the logic of political economy at the turn of the eleventh and twelfth centuries can be described as hybrid. Bolesław Wrymouth distributed moveable goods like silver, gold and luxury pelts as well as immoveable goods such as strongholds and villages. However, the Annalist does not mention coins which seem to have been "preserved" of the lower level of social echelon and used to pay a retinue and soldiers. We should bear in mind that the Piast duke, particularly between 1102 and 1121, conducted several wars and tried to conquer Pomerania (on Bolesław Wrymouth's monetary and fiscal politics more Grzegorz Śnieżko in this volume). Conversely, some imitated coins struck by Pomeranian chieftains at this time may have been redistributed among their warriors trying to fend off the Piast expansion. Nevertheless, Bolesław Wrymouth succeeded in imposing a modest tribute on Pomerania amounting to 300–500 mark of silver.[19]

Other rulers around the Baltic used silver to redistribute it among their followers, too. Some time before 1123, for example, the Danish king conveyed the right to collect the Bornholm-tribute of ten marks of silver to the Archbishop of Lund.[20]

Precious metals were significant for sovereigns as they imposed and collected taxes in the form of coins. We have some evidence in written sources. The tribe of the Circipanes in eastern Mecklenburg, for instance, paid 1114 in their levy in *nomismata Bardenwiccensis monetae simillima vel propria*, deniers similar to those from Bardowick.[21] Helmold of Bosau also points out that several West Slavs paid tithes in deniers:

> And the duke imposed upon the Slavs, who stayed in the lands of the Wagrians, the Polabians, the Obotrites and the Kessinians, the same tithe to be paid to the bishopric as the Poles and the Pomeranians had to give: from each plow three bushels wheat and twelfth usual coins [...] and one Slavic plow is reckoned with two oxen and as much horses.[22]

Was the existence of monetised local markets a necessary condition for collecting rents and taxes in coins? According to Roger Svensson, there were two reasons why this constellation would have emerged and worked. Firstly, peasants must have been able to sell some of their output in a local market in order to obtain coins. Secondly, the landowner could only have accepted monetary rents if the local markets had already developed. Svensson concludes:

> Then, but not before, he could more efficiently purchase what he demanded. Generally, it is reasonable to claim that the division of labour and the development of local markets must be in place before the landlord and other authorities require taxes and rents in coins.[23]

But did that pertain to the West Slavic area at the turn of the eleventh and twelfth centuries? It is very unlikely that every farm disposed of two oxen and two horses and, as consequence, was able to give as tax twelve coins. Perhaps this system worked through other mechanisms encompassing the barter of silver equivalents and values. For example, higher authorities like tribal elders collected agricultural surplus from every farm and then exchanged it (along with salt and herrings) at long-distance and regional centres for silver. A range of such trading places appeared along the West Slavic Baltic coast (mentioned in the first section of this paper). Thus, deniers were a fiscal instrument without the existence of a monetised local market.

In the Polish interior, foundation charters dating only from the early thirteenth century onwards reflect a more sophisticated division of labour. In 1204, Duke Henry the Bearded issued the foundation charter for the Cistercian monastery in Trzebnica, near Wrocław (Silesia). It describes all revenues for the monastery comprising labour, payment in kind and payment in coins. 120 families paid their levies in kind, 20 in money and ten in a mixed form. Every crocker, baker and cottager as well as tenants in the village at Węgrzynów who possessed two oxen or one horse had to give 20 deniers. Peasants who sow their own or other field by third parties paid twelve coins. The highest tax amounting to 60 deniers had to pay fox hunters from the village in Kliszów (if they possessed four oxen).[24] Fox pelts may have been brought to Wrocław, an important centre of regional and long-distance trade. When some groups of ordinary people in rural areas disposed of money they had to obtain on local markets like Trzebnica, a more complex commercial activity must have existed. We should add that according to numismatic evidence the import of foreign coins to Poland collapsed by the early twelfth century, and from this time onwards, most deniers circulating there were domestic products. Thus, the increasing use of coins during the thirteenth century was traced back to the evolution of local markets driven by ducal entrepreneurship.

In Scandinavia and Novgorod Rus' tributes imposing on foreign tribes rather than tithes levying on "own" population seem to have been the most prevalent form of redistributing silver. After the conquest of Arkona in 1168, the Danish King transformed the tribute being paid to the temple from one coin to 40 deniers from each plough. Further information originates from the first half of the thirteenth century. A survey dated to 1231, again in context of Arkona, mentions 200 mark of silver in the form of deniers. The tribute levied from the Sylt-island by the same year amounted to 40-mark pure silver, from entire Friesland subject to the Danish King 400–500 marks per year. Similar, the inhabitants of the Fehmarn-island were obliged to pay 500 mark of silver. However, the form of taxes within Denmark was mixed and could include payments in kind. King Valdemar II (1202–1241) collected for his retinue consisting of 400 men, besides coins, honey, corn, malt, meat, butter, cheese, fish and oat. According to Bjørn Poulsen, in Denmark transition from a society based upon tributes to a society based upon taxes took place from around 1200 onwards.[25]

Regarding Sweden, too, we know of taxes paid in silver. The Guta Saga records:

> Sixty marks of silver in respect of each year is the Gotlanders' tax, divided so that the king of Sweden should have forty marks of silver out of the sixty, and the jarl twenty marks of silver [...] In this way, the Gotlanders submitted to the king of Sweden, of their own free will, in order that they might travel everywhere in Sweden free and unhindered, exempt from toll and all other charges. Similarly, the Swedes also have the right to visit Gotland, without ban against trade in corn, or other prohibitions. The king was obliged to give the Gotlanders protection and assistance, if they should need it and request it. In addition, the king, and likewise the jarl, should send messengers to the Gotlanders' general assembly and arrange for their tax to be collected there. The messengers in question have a duty to proclaim the freedom of Gotlanders to visit all places overseas that belong to the king in Uppsala and, similarly, to such as have the right to travel here from that side.[26]

Unfortunately, we do not know to what time-span this quotation applies. Quite possible, the Gotland-tax was imposed as early as ninth century and was levied through the eleventh century. Archaeological and numismatic evidence clearly shows that the Gotlanders had access to coins from around 800 through the time after 1100 (see section 1.1 on silver as money). Obviously, the right to collect the Gotland-tribute based upon reciprocity as the islanders were allowed to travel to Sweden and overseas and to trade for goods, which were not available on Gotland.

Finally, a passage from the Chronicle of Novgorod referring to the year 1193 mentions a Novgorod expedition against the tribe of Yugra:

> The same year they went from Novgorod with armed force to the Yugra country with the *Voyevoda* Jadrei, and they came to the Yugra country and took a town; and they came to another town and they shut themselves up in the town, and they stood by the town five weeks; and the Yugra people used to send out to them saying with deceit thus, that: "We are gathering silver and sables, and other precious goods [...]"[27]

It is very impressive that people living around the Arctic Ocean more than 1,200 km east of Novgorod possessed silver. The hoard from Arkhangelsk found on the Northern Dvina River lends credence to the Chronicle. This hoard, buried around 1125, contained about 1,900 coins, of which nearly 1,800 were issued in Germany, along with jewellery and hacksilver.[28] However, most tributes the Novgorod levied in the far north on regularly basis were paid in the form of furs.[29] On the other hand, the above quotation clearly shows that collecting taxes could take a form of raids characteristic for roving bandits, term coined by Mancur Olson.[30]

Summary: A plea for non-linear research and methods

At the beginning of this paper, I have addressed some questions and proposed several methods applicable to explain the use of precious metals around the Baltic in the post-Viking Age. In order to quantify and measure the scale and intensity of monetisation and commercialisation, only applying a range of methods seems to be fruitful. Accordingly, I have examined the quantity of stray coin finds in settlements as well as the composition of hoards regarding the origin of coins and the structure of hoards concerning the existence of unminted silver, particularly in the form of jewellery. Thereafter, I have tried to establish our evidence in the written sources available and related them as far as possible with the archaeological and numismatic data.

In the post-Viking age, several coin types circulated around the Baltic Sea: pennies imported from Western Europe, primarily Germany, as well as deniers struck in domestic mints. The latter could have been imitations of western specimen (like in Pomerania) or "official" silver pieces issued by the monarchs (like in Denmark or Polish interior). It is unlikely that the prime mover of issuing coins was the demand for currency on local markets. Rather, fiscal and political needs driven by kings, dukes and warlords have decided about striking deniers, particularly as the remuneration for a retinue or clients was the crucial element for exercising power. The fragility of the local circulation of minted money seems to be due to a manorial mode described by John Lie as "an intraregional trading system in which buying and selling are restricted to or controlled by local elites." He concludes, "The greater the concentration of political and economic power in a dominant class, the less autonomous economic activity by the bulk of the populace."[31]

Additionally, the redistribution of valuable goods (reflected in numerous pieces of jewellery in hoards) and the giving of gifts belonged to the major social principles allowing an intensification of relations within various elite groupings or creating bonds between people. However, some segments of a community were involved in the long-distance and regional trade. In these monetarised and commercialised enclaves, silver was used as money in the form of coins and ingots. In rural societies living more away from trading centres precious metals may have served as fiscal instrument, prestige good and raw material for making jewellery. These people paid their obligations in kind as well as in coins. Consequently, we can speak of hybrid political economies reflecting different forms of social structure and different levels of cultural attitudes.

Notes

1 Dariusz Adamczyk, "Pommern und das Ende der Wikingerzeit: Bruch oder Kontinuität?," *Studia Maritima* 32 (2019), 13–27.
2 Dariusz Adamczyk, *Silber und Macht: Fernhandel, Tribute und die piastische Herrschaftsbildung in nordosteuropäischer Perspektive (800–1100)* (Wiesbaden: Harrassowitz, 2014).
3 For this information I would like to thank Fred Ruchhöft who heads archaeological excavations at Kap Arkona.
4 Helmoldi *Presbyteri Bozoviensis Cronica Slavorum* (Monumenta Germaniae Historica XXXII), edited by Sydoniusz Apolinary, Johann Martin Lappenberg, and Bernhard Schmeidler (Hannover: Hahn, 1937), p. 77.

5 *Frühmittelalterliche Münzfunde aus Polen*, vol. 2: *Inventar Pommern*, edited by Genowefa Horoszko, et al. (Warszawa: IAE PAN, 2016), Gdańsk X.
6 Ibid., Kałdus I–VII; hoards: Kałdus VIII and IX.
7 Nikolaj P. Bauer, "Die Silber- und Goldbarren des russischen Mittelalters," *Numismatische Zeitschrift* N. F. 22 (1929), 77–120, (1931), 61–100.
8 Carsten Goehrke, *Russischer Alltag: Eine Geschichte in neun Zeitbildern*, vol. 1: *Vormoderne* (Zürich: Chronos, 2003), pp. 155–156.
9 According to data contained in *Frühmittelalterliche Münzfunde*, vol. 2: *Inventar Pommern*.
10 Cecilia von Heijne, *Särpräglat: Vikingatida och tidigmedeltida myntfynd från Danmark, Skåne, Blekinge och Halland (ca. 800–1130)* (Stockholm: Tryckt av Elanders Gotab, 2004), p. 219.
11 Adamczyk, *Silber und Macht*, p. 238.
12 *Frühmittelalterliche Münzfunde*, vol. 2: *Inventar Pommern*, finds: Łupawa, Pommern XIII, Pommern XV.
13 Dariusz Adamczyk, "The Use of Silver by the Norsemen of Truso and Wolin: The Logic of the Market or Social Prestige?" in *Social Norms in Medieval Scandinavia*, edited by Jakub Morawiec, Aleksandra Jochymek, and Grzegorz Bartusik (Leeds: ARC Humanities Press, 2019), pp. 27–28.
14 Helmold, *Chronik der Slaven*, edited by Alexander Heine, Johann C. M. Laurent, and Wilhelm Wattenbach (Essen and Stuttgart: Phaidon, 1986), p. 128.
15 Ibid., p. 120.
16 Leszek P. Słupecki, "Temple Fiscality of Pagan Slavs and Scandinavians," in *Economies, Monetisation and Society in the West Slavic Lands 800–1200 AD*, edited by Mateusz Bogucki and Marian Rębkowski (Szczecin: Wydawnictwo IAE PAN, 2013), pp. 109–113.
17 Hendrik Mäkeler, *Reichsmünzwesen im späten Mittelalter*, vol. 1: *Das 14. Jahrhundert* (Stuttgart: Franz Steiner Verlag, 2010), pp. 29–30.
18 Gallus Anonymus, *Chronik und Taten der Herzöge und Fürsten von Polen*, edited by Josef Bujnoch (Graz, Wien and Köln: Styria, 1978), p. 129.
19 Dariusz Adamczyk, "Pieniądz czy strategiczny instrument władzy? Obieg kruszcu w społeczeństwie piastowskim przełomu XI i XII wieku, załamanie w dopływie denarów z Saksonii a ekspansja Bolesława Krzywoustego na Pomorze," *Przegląd Zachodniopomorski* 32 (2017), no. 2, 160–161.
20 Bjørn Poulsen, "Tribute as part of the financial system of the medieval Danish King," in *Taxes, Tributes and Tributary Lands in the Making of the Scandinavian Kingdoms in the Middle Ages*, edited by Steinar Imsen (Trondheim: Tapir Academic Press, 2011), p. 286.
21 Ralf Wiechmann, "Kupfer und Messing statt Silber: Münzimitationen des 11. und 12. Jahrhunderts aus Nordostdeutschland," in *Economies, Monetisation and Society in the West Slavic Lands 800–1200 AD*, edited by Mateusz Bogucki and Marian Rębkowski (Szczecin: Wydawnictwo IAE PAN, 2013), pp. 267–312, here 287.
22 Helmold, *Chronik der Slaven*, pp. 254–255.
23 Roger Svensson, "Coinage Policies in Medieval Sweden," *Wiadomości Numizmatyczne* 59 (2015), no. 1–2, 135.
24 *Kodeks dyplomatyczny Śląska*, edited by Karol Maleczyński, vol. 1 (Wrocław: Societas Scientiarum et Litterarum Wratislaviensis 1951), no. 104, pp. 260–268.
25 Poulsen, "Tribute as Part," pp. 282–285, 288–289.
26 *Guta Saga: The History of the Gotlanders*, edited by Christine Peel (Exeter: Short Run Press Limited, 1999), p. 7.
27 *The Chronicle of Novgorod 1016–1471*, edited by Robert Michell and Nevill Forbes (London: South Square Gray's Inn, W.C., 1914), p. 36.
28 Evgenij N. Nosov, Oleg V. Ovsyannikov, and Vsevolod Potin, "The Arkhangelsk Hoard," *Fennoscandia archaeologica* 9 (1992), 3–21.

29 *Russian Primary Chronicle: Laurentian Text*, edited by Samuel Hazard Cross and Olgerd P. Sherbowitz-Wetzor (Cambridge, MA: Crimson Printing Company, 1953), p. 184; Roman K. Kovalev and Thomas S. Noonan, "'The Furry 40s': Packaging Pelts in Medieval Northern Europe," in *States, Societies, Cultures: East and West: Essays in Honor of Jaroslaw Pelenski*, edited by Janusz Duzinkiewicz, Natalia Jakovenko, Myroslav Popovych, and Vladyslav Verstiuk (New York: Ross Publishing, 2004), pp. 655–656.
30 Mancur Olson, *Power and Prosperity: Outgrowing Communist and Capitalist Dictatorship* (New York: Basic Books, 2000).
31 John Lie, "The Concept of Mode of Exchange," *American Sociological Review* 57 (1992), no. 4, 513

Bibliography

Primary sources

Robert Michell and Nevill Forbes (eds.), *The Chronicle of Novgorod 1016–1471*. London: South Square Gray's Inn, W. C., 1914.

Genowefa Horoszko, Peter Ilisch, Dorota Malarczyk, Tomasz Nowakiewicz, and Jerzy Piniński (eds.), *Frühmittelalterliche Münzfunde aus Polen*, vol. 2, Warszawa: IAE PAN, 2016.

Gallus Anonymus. *Chronik und Taten der Herzöge und Fürsten von Polen*, edited by Josef Bujnoch. Graz, Wien and Köln: Styria, 1978.

Guta Saga. *The History of the Gotlanders, edited by Christine Peel*. Exeter: Short Run Press Limited, 1999.

Heijne, Cecilia von. *Särpräglat: Vikingatida och tidigmedeltida myntfynd från Danmark, Skåne, Blekinge och Halland (ca. 800–1130)*. Stockholm: Tryckt av Elanders Gotab, 2004.

Helmold *Chronik der Slaven*, edited by Alexander Heine, Johann C. M. Laurent, and Wilhelm Wattenbach. Essen and Stuttgart: Phaidon, 1986.

Helmoldi *Presbyteri Bozoviensis Cronica Slavorum (Monumenta Germaniae Historica XXXII)*, edited by Sydoniusz Apolinary, Johann Martin Lappenberg, and Bernhard Schmeidler. Hannover: Hahn, 1937.

Karol Maleczyński (ed.). *Kodeks dyplomatyczny Śląska [The diplomatic codex of Silesia]*, vol. 1. Wrocław: Societas Scientiarum et Litterarum Wratislaviensis, 1951.

Samuel Hazard Cross and Olgerd P. Sherbowitz-Wetzor(ed.). *Russian Primary Chronicle: Laurentian Text*. Cambridge, MA: Crimson Printing Company, 1953.

Secondary literature

Adamczyk, Dariusz. "Pommern und das Ende der Wikingerzeit: Bruch oder Kontinuität?," *Studia Maritima* 32 (2019a), 13–27.

Adamczyk, Dariusz. "The Use of Silver by the Norsemen of Truso and Wolin: The Logic of the Market or Social Prestige?," in *Social Norms in Medieval Scandinavia*, edited by Jakub Morawiec, Aleksandra Jochymek, and Grzegorz Bartusik, pp. 19–34. Leeds: ARC Humanities Press, 2019b.

Adamczyk, Dariusz. "Pieniądz czy strategiczny instrument władzy? Obieg kruszcu w społeczeństwie piastowskim przełomu XI i XII wieku, załamanie w dopływie denarów z Saksonii a ekspansja Bolesława Krzywoustego na Pomorze" [Money or a strategic instrument of power? The circulation of precious metals in the Piast society at the turn of the 12th century, the collapse of the inflow of deniers from Saxony and Bolesław's Wrymouth expansion to Pomerania], *Przegląd Zachodniopomorski* 32 (2017), no. 2, 143–167.

Adamczyk, Dariusz. *Silber und Macht: Fernhandel, Tribute und die piastische Herrschaftsbildung in nordosteuropäischer Perspektive (800–1100)*. Wiesbaden: Harrassowitz, 2014.

Bauer, Nikolaj P. "Die Silber- und Goldbarren des russischen Mittelalters", *Numismatische Zeitschrift N. F.* 22 (1929), pp. 77–120, (1931), pp. 61–100.

Goehrke, Carsten. *Russischer Alltag: Eine Geschichte in neun Zeitbildern, vol. 1: Vormoderne*. Zürich: Chronos, 2003.

Kovalev, Roman K., and Thomas S. Noonan. "'The Furry 40s': Packaging Pelts in Medieval Northern Europe," in *States, Societies, Cultures. East and West. Essays in Honor of Jaroslaw Pelenski*, edited by Janusz Duzinkiewicz, Natalia Jakovenko, Myroslav Popovych, and Vladyslav Verstiuk, pp. 653–682. New York: Ross Publishing, 2004.

Lie, John. "The Concept of Mode of Exchange," *American Sociological Review* 57 (1992), no. 4, 508–523.

Mäkeler, Hendrik. *Reichsmünzwesen im späten Mittelalter, vol. 1: Das 14. Jahrhundert*. Stuttgart: Franz Steiner Verlag, 2010.

Nosov, Evgenij N., Oleg V. Ovsyannikov and Vsevolod Potin, "The Arkhangelsk Hoard," *Fennoscandia archaeologica* 9 (1992), 3–21.

Olson, Mancur. *Power and Prosperity: Outgrowing Communist and Capitalist Dictatorship*. New York: Basic Books, 2000.

Poulsen, Bjørn. "Tribute as Part of the Financial System of the Medieval Danish King," in *Taxes, Tributes and Tributary Lands in the Making of the Scandinavian Kingdoms in the Middle Ages*, edited by Steinar Imsen, pp. 279–292. Trondheim: Tapir Academic Press, 2011.

Słupecki, Leszek P. "Temple Fiscality of Pagan Slavs and Scandinavians," in *Economies, Monetisation and Society in the West Slavic Lands 800–1200 AD*, edited by Mateusz Bogucki and Marian Rębkowski, pp. 109–113. Szczecin: Wydawnictwo IAE PAN, 2013.

Svensson, Roger. "Coinage Policies in Medieval Sweden," *Wiadomości Numizmatyczne* 59 (2015), no. 1–2, 129–187.

Wiechmann, Ralf. "Kupfer und Messing statt Silber: Münzimitationen des 11. und 12. Jahrhunderts aus Nordostdeutschland," in *Economies, Monetisation and Society in the West Slavic Lands 800–1200 AD*, edited by Mateusz Bogucki and Marian Rębkowski, pp. 267–312. Szczecin: Wydawnictwo IAE PAN, 2013.

2 Coin circulation in Poland under the rule of Bolesław III Wrymouth (1102–1138)

Grzegorz Śnieżko

Bolesław III Wrymouth was a son of Władysław I Herman and Judith, daughter of the King of Bohemia Wratislaus II. He was descended from the dynasty, in later tradition named Piasts. In the eyes of later generations his image as a tireless warrior and heathens' conqueror solidified. Largely, it was a result of an apologetic account of the Anonymous called Gallus, author of the first Polish chronicle – Deeds of the Princes of the Poles which has been wrote at Bolesław's court. It is the most precious source to the first several years of his long rule that can be divided into several periods. The first begins at the end of the eleventh century when his father passed on part of the reins in South Poland to hands of a young prince. The second lasted from the death of Władysław Herman in 1102 to 1107 when Bolesław defeated his stepbrother Zbigniew, who ruled in Northern Poland. So, these five years were a period of diarchy. The third stage lasted until the death of Bolesław in 1138 and it was a sovereign rule.[1]

With regards to the latest state of the research, at each of these stages, Bolesław were minting coins. Lack of written sources about his coinage makes numismatic and physicochemical analyses of coins the only possibility of obtaining information on the subject. In the years 1097(1099)–1138 the prince issued eight types of coins. Pennies called *Silesian* (from the most likely place of their being struck) are actually considered the oldest. They divide into the two main types of similar iconography (mainly head motif) and inscriptions (names of a prince and St John the Baptist as a patron of the Wrocław Cathedral), but different coin blanks conform (Figure 2.1a, b). They were probably issued already during Władysław Herman's lifetime.[2] Next were pennies with an image of a standing prince and his name on the obverse, and a building with three towers on the reverse (Figure 2.1c). These were presumably struck consecutively in 1107, when Bolesław defeated Zbigniew and became the only ruler. It may be indicated by the depiction – a prince on the throne with a sword in his right hand, and the left raised in a commanding gesture. On the reverse side there is an equal-armed cross. They can be divided into two main inscription groups: *DVCIS BOLEZLA – DENARIVS* and *BOLEZLAVS – BOLEZLAVS* (Figure 2.1d). Pennies of the following type have the images of the standing prince, who was shown as a knight once again, and of St Wojciech on the throne. Both figures are captioned in the two-line legend on the reverse: *ADALBIBTVS* (erroneous form of name *Adalbertvs*, given to Wojciech Slavnik when he was confirmed)/*BOLEZLAV*. However, Bolesław's

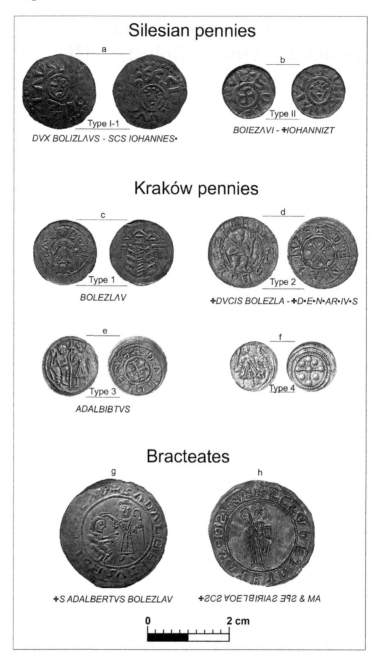

Figure 2.1 Coins issued by Bolesław III Wrymouth. Source: a–c, g – private collection of Mr. Filip Wartacz from Wrocław, Poland;[4] d–f, h – collections of the National Museum in Warsaw (in sequence Inv. nos.: NPO 8386; NPO 8388; NPO 5214; 115856), graphic design by Grzegorz Śnieżko.

name disappears from younger coins (Figure 2.1e). Two-sided pennies of the last type are anepigraphic. On their obverse a knight beating the dragon with a spear is depicted (Figure 2.1f).[3] Wrymouth also issued the oldest Polish bracteates. On the older type (in my opinion), an expressive scene with a prince praying to the St Adalbert of Prague can be seen (Figure 2.1g). Next, were coins with frontal figures of this martyr (Figure 2.1h).

Despite the great variety of his coinage, still not enough attention was paid to the problem of a coin circulation in Poland in the first half of the twelfth century.[5]

Dispersion and coin finds categories

The first map of finds of Bolesław Wrymouth's coins was published by Stanisław Suchodolski – it contained 16 of them.[7] In the last 50 years their number increased more than three times and reached 58[8] (Figure 2.2). They occurred definitely in the provinces that were earlier poorly represented or even completely lacking: Pomerania (then none), Greater Poland (there was one find) or Silesia (two). The occurrence of finds of Bolesław's III coins outside the borders of his principality also increased – earlier one was known, while now four are available. Actually, recorded coin finds cluster mainly in Sandomierz and Kraków Lands (13 and 6), Greater Poland (14) and Silesia (12). The vast majority of hoards and monetary grave goods come from the southern provinces, while in Greater Poland pieces from the settlement sites dominate. The fewest finds are from Mazovia, Kuyavia and Central Poland (in total, eight). First find from Pomerania is a penny registered in hoard from Stolpe auf Usedom on the Baltic Sea island called Usedom. This is also the northernmost find of Wrymouth's coins now (Figure 2.2: no. 56, Table 2.1).[9]

All finds come from 43 localities. Four of them in the twelfth century were (and still are) located beyond the Polish borders. Among 20 hoards, 13[10] were deposited after the Bolesław's death. From the other seven, five were hidden before year 1120 (two abroad) and two more (one in Moravia) in the last several years of Wrymouth's life. His coins in hoards hidden outside Poland are individual pieces. Among domestic deposits from the years of prince's rule, the most numerous are from the localities: Kopacz, Sędziszowice and Karczmiska in particular (Figure 2.2: nos. 6, 19, 29). None of them contained Silesian and Kraków pennies together.

Single coin finds were also recorded – in total 38 of different categories. The most numerous are pieces from settlements (15). Part of them are losses. Coins deposited as grave goods and originally probably related to the funeral practices are by two finds less numerous. In case of eight finds, location of the pennies in relation to the burials allows to interpret them as obol of the dead. They were found in the mouth or between the finger bones.[11] Five more at first could also had such character, but now we cannot be absolutely sure. These are the pieces registered at the sepulchral sites, in grave pits or outside them.[12] When it comes to the coin finds without context (9), it is hard to tell anything about the circumstances of their loss or deposition. Archaeological context of the last one piece points its connection with the church house.[13]

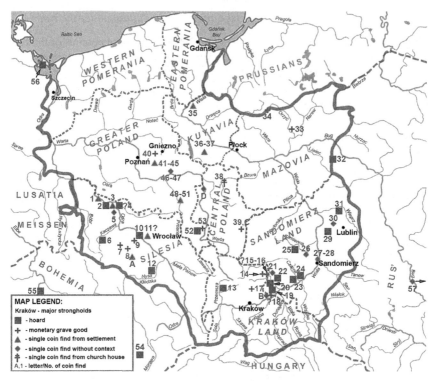

Figure 2.2 Finds of Bolesław III Wrymouth's coins and finds of single foreign coins from the years of his rule:[6] 1. Bytom Odrzański, Dolnośląskie Voivodeship; 2. Głogów, Dolnośląskie Voivodeship; 3. Głogów, Dolnośląskie Voivodeship; 4. Głogów – environs? (known also as Śląsk XII), Dolnośląskie Voivodeship; 5. Krzydłowice, Dolnośląskie Voivodeship; 6. Kopacz, Dolnośląskie Voivodeship; 7. Osiek, Dolnośląskie Voivodeship; 8. Stary Zamek, Dolnośląskie Voivodeship; 9. Mokronos Dolny, Dolnośląskie Voivodeship; 10. Wrocław, capital of Dolnośląskie Voivodeship; 11. Wrocław, capital of Dolnośląskie Voivodeship; 12. Smolice, Opolskie Voivodeship; 13. Dąbrowa Górnicza, Śląskie Voivodeship; 14. Prząsław, Świętokrzyskie Voivodeship; 15–16. Jedrzejów, Świętokrzyskie Voivodeship; 17. Prandocin, Małopolskie Voivodeship; 18. Witów, Małopolskie Voivodeship; 19. Sędziszowice, Świętokrzyskie Voivodeship; 20. Pełczyska, Świętokrzyskie Voivodeship; 21. Korytnica, Świętokrzyskie Voivodeship; 22. Busko-Zdrój, Świętokrzyskie Voivodeship; 23. Ruszcza, Świętokrzyskie Voivodeship; 24. Rudniki, Świętokrzyskie Voivodeship; 25. Nietulisko Małe, Świętokrzyskie Voivodeship; 26. Ćmielów, Świętokrzyskie Voivodeship; 27–28. Gierlachów, Świętokrzyskie Voivodeship; 29. Karczmiska, Lubelskie Voivodeship; 30. Klementowice, Lubelskie Voivodeship; 31. Wola Skromowska, Lubelskie Voivodeship; 32. Włodki, Mazowieckie Voivodeship; 33. Bazar, Mazowieckie Voivodeship; 34. Pokrzywnica Wielka, Mazowieckie Voivodeship; 35. Kałdus, Kujawsko-Pomorskie Voivodeship; 36–37. Zgłowiączka, Kujawsko-Pomorskie Voivodeship; 38. Tum, Łódzkie Voivodeship; 39. Lubień, Łódzkie Voivodeship; 40. Dziekanowice, Wielkopolskie Voivodeship; 41–45. Giecz, Wielkopolskie Voivodeship; 46–47. Ląd, Wielkopolskie Voivodeship; 48–51. Kalisz, Wielkopolskie Voivodeship; 52. Urbanice, Łódzkie Voivodeship; 53. Dębina, Łódzkie Voivodeship; 54. Víceměřice, The Czech Republic; 55. Bílá Hora (now in Prague), The Czech Republic; 56. Stolpe auf Usedom, Germany; 57. Boryspol near Kiev, Ukraine. Single finds of foreign coins issued between 1102–1138: A. Niemcza, Dolnośląskie Voivodeship; B. Hebdów, Małopolskie Voivodeship; C. Lubień, Łódzkie Voivodeship; D. Uniejów – environs, Łódzkie Voivodeship. Hoards deposited after the death of Bolesław III are underlined above. Drawn by Grzegorz Śnieżko.

Table 2.1 Number of coin finds of individual categories

	Hoards	Single finds			
		Settlement coin finds	Monetary grave goods	Coin finds without context	Coin from church house
Silesian pennies	3	2	3	–	–
Kraków pennies and bracteates	17	13	10	9	1

Structure of finds and coin circulation

There are two written mentions about tributes paid in pelts referring to the first half of the twelfth century. Older information is from the document listing incomes of the Benedictine abbey in Tyniec (now in Kraków), allegedly from 1105, but in fact issued in the twenties of the twelfth century[14]. It is stated there that local peasants have to give to the monastery one pot of honey and four squirrel pelts each and every year: *item de qualibet curia quolibet anno una urna melis et quator asperioli monasterio suprascripto cedent de ipsisi hominibus.*[15] Also in the Bull of Gniezno issued in the 1136 by Pope Innocent II tithe in marten and fox pelts is mentioned twice: *pellicularum mardurinarum et vulpinarium.*[16]

However, it should be emphasised that we cannot determine if the tribute was paid in kind or in money.[17] This question has a fundamental meaning to interpret pelts as a commodity money that have pecuniary function as means of payment intended to further exchange. Both sources are silent in this matter.[18] It is worth to say that these pelts could also have a value as a semi-finished furrier product what would make them an element of a tribute in kind.[19] In consequence it is impossible to consider them as a commodity money. So, I think it will remain an unsolved issue if these mentions are the oldest known from written sources traces of relics of a fur money or tribute paid in kind. Moreover, in the *Dialogue on the Life of St Otto* by Herbord, the author mentions barrels or vats where Pomeranians kept their clothing, money (*pecuniam*) and valuables.[20] In the subject literature arose the supposition that second kind of goods can mean a linen money.[21] As we can see above, clear evidence for the relic use of non-metallic money in this period do not exist. Therefore, in this text I will discuss the problem of coin circulation.

In Table 2.2 all hoards and single coin finds from the years 1080–1146 were compiled. Chronological periods correspond approximately with years of Władysław Herman's reign (1079–1102), diarchy of Zbigniew and Bolesław (1102–1107),

Table 2.2 Number of finds from particular provinces. The date of their deposition was taken into account[22]

Years of deposition	Silesia		Kraków and Sandomierz Lands		Mazovia, Kuyavia and Central Poland		Greater Poland		Pomerania		in total	
	Hoards	Single finds	hoards	single finds	hoards	single finds	hoards	single finds	hoards	single finds	hoards	single finds
1080–1100	6	23	6	65	14	16	7	80	15	13	48	197
1101–1110	5	8	8	11	6	8	14	13	2	11	35	51
1111–1138	–		2	5	–		–		4		6	
1139–1146	2	6	6		1	9	–	19	–	–	9	39
in total	13	37	22	81	21	33	21	112	21	24	98	287

sovereign Wrymouth's rule (1107–1138) and first years after the fragmentation of Poland in 1138, when Władysław II was a High Duke (1138–1146).

In the scholarship the possibility that many of coins from the eleventh century in fact were deposited later, has been accurately signalised.[23] This would reduce the prevalence of single finds from Władysław Herman's period on the later ones. Inasmuch generally coins are the chronological determinant for its contexts, it is hard to determine precisely which one come from the later layers.

Quite similar observations are on some hoards, especially those with anonymous cross pennies of younger variants (Types VII and VIII according to Marian Gumowski[24]). It is worth noting that *terminus post quem* and moment of deposition are not synonyms, and they do not indicate the same date. The time after which the hoard has been deposited is usually determined by first year of rule of the youngest coins' issuer. This is why some hoards, whose *terminus post quem* is at the turn of the 1080s/1090s, were in fact deposited a little later; i.e., in the first decade of the twelfth century. In the light of current data source, this is the most likely for hoards from Silesia, Mazovia and Greater Poland.[25] Incidentally, cross pennies appeared also in much later hoards from the end of Wrymouth's rule and years of Władysław II reign.[26]

Data presented in Table 2.2 take the above postulate into account. The aim of this collation was to show differences in the distribution of hoards and single finds in particular provinces. Despite the increase of information, earlier statements remain valid. Deposits and single finds from the eleventh century still preponderate over the later ones. In the oldest period finds from Mazovia, Kuyavia, Central Poland, Greater Poland and Pomerania dominate, but the prevalence is visible for the hoards. Without Pomerania, single finds have a similar share throughout Poland.

Disappearance of hoards was dated to the end of the eleventh century, and this phenomenon has been interpreted in two ways. Ryszard Kiersnowski described it as a consequence of ore crisis in the West, when silver deposits in Harz were exhausted.[27] Stanisław Tabaczyński, by contrast, investigates the disappearance of deposits and growth of number of single finds jointly. He noticed that it was a result of increased need for money, that intensified coin circulation and monetisation of the society.[28] As a consequence of my proposal of changing the deposition date of several hoards with cross pennies from the end of the eleventh century to the first decade of the twelfth, we also have to move forward the date of finds' disappearances to the second decade of the twelfth century. The number of hoards from the end of the eleventh century and first decade of the following is outstandingly close (except the Pomerania where it falls). From the whole period of sovereign Bolesław's III rule (30 years) we know of only two hoards. Their number grows again during the rule of Władysław II while hoarding is exceedingly evident. In eight years of his reign nine deposits were hidden.

Comparison of the number of finds from similar period in neighbouring countries provides inconclusive data; e.g., in Denmark and northern parts of Hungary it falls, like in Poland. In each of these countries this phenomenon is explained differently. In Denmark it is explained with the collapse of economic activity or lack of silver for mintage because of smaller mining.[29] In the part of Kingdom of

Table 2.3 Coin finds from Bohemia and Moravia[36]

	1080–1100	1101–1138	1139–1146
Hoard	22	38	6
monetary grave good	42	11	0
single find from settlement site	10	15	6
accidental single find	14	4	1

Hungary adjacent to Poland, it was considered as a growing distrust to debased royal coins.[30] This aspect is completely different for The Holy Roman Empire as well as Bohemia and Moravia, where finds become more frequent; in the Empire almost twice.[31] It is taken there as a symptom of the new stage in German coinage which is described as a period of a regional penny (*Regionalpfennige*).[32] However, opinions appear that already earlier German coins were important both in the internal circulation and as export products.[33] Also, data from Table 2.3 unambiguously show that in Bohemia and Moravia, not only there was no disappearance of hoards, but also that they are even more frequent in the twelfth century.[34] Likewise, the difference in the number of single finds is not as huge as in Poland.[35] These remarks could confirm the above opinion on the chronology being too early on some of the finds from Poland. On the other hand, the possibility that updating the inventory of finds might conform the situation in each of the countries mentioned above, and so cannot be ruled out.

I was mainly looking for earlier causes of the disappearance of finds in Poland in the internal bullion crisis.[37] Now, I think that this is a multi-faceted problem, but we do not have enough information on the volume of Władysław Herman's and cross pennies coinages to make less speculative assessment of the impact of silver insufficiency on finds diminishing. As a consequence, we do not know if the Wrymouth's emission against previous period was smaller or bigger. I have analysed the weight of 1,765 Kraków pennies and bracteates. Moreover, almost 220 pieces had their chemical content examined with the X-ray fluorescence method. These analyses showed that quality of Bolesław's III coins is much better than his father's pennies. Furthermore, his coinage size reached several million pieces. This may contradict the hypothesis of bullion crisis as the most important causative factor of the find's disappearance.

Therefore, the only premise is comparative analysis of hoards composition from discussed period (Table 2.4).[40] Definitely more coins were registered in hoards from the end of the eleventh and the first decade of the twelfth century in Mazovia, Kuyavia, Central Poland, Greater Poland and in Pomerania. At the time of sovereign Bolesław's III rule and following period when Władysław II was a High Duke, number of pieces falls several times and they are clustering on the South. In the light of these observations, it is possible that circulation of the coins was less intensive in the North. It cannot be excluded that in the face of silver insufficiency,[41] inhabitants of Greater Poland, Kuyavia and Mazovia ingested money surrogates, e.g., salt.[42] Falling numbers of coins in hoards from Poland as a whole is accompanied by the proportion reversion between cross pennies and

Table 2.4 Composition of hoards hidden in particular provinces. The date of their deposition was taken into account[38]

Province, years of deposition		Number of pieces	Number of cross pennies	Number of Polish coins	Number of fragments of coins
Silesia	1080–1100	345	162 (47%)	8 (2%)	4 (1%)
	1101–1110	620	314 (51%)	285 (46%)	35 (6%)
	1111–1138	–	–	–	–
	1139–1146	2 333	203 (9%)	2 129 (91%)	0
Kraków and Sandomierz Lands	1080–1100	1 841	834 (45%)	702 (38%)	12 (0,7%)
	1101–1110	3 289	2 131 (65%)	27 (0,8%)	101 (3%)
	1111–1138	5 473	231 (4%)	4 524 (83%)	7 (0,1%)
	1139–1146	547	252 (46%)	291 (53%)	1 (0,2%)
Mazovia, Kuyavia and Central Poland	1080–1100	11 601	9 390 (81%)	2 002 (17%)	149 (1%)
	1101–1110	3 182	2 812 (88%)	3 (0,1%)	208 (7%)
	1111–1138	–	–	–	–
	1139–1146	?[39]	?	?	?
Greater Poland	1080–1100	437	343 (78%)	0	101 (23%)
	1101–1110	18 485	12 608 (68%)	124+4970 cross pennies considered Polish (0,7+27%)	776 (4%)
	1111–1138	–	–	–	–
	1139–1146	–	–	–	–
Pomerania	1080–1100	5 920	2 922 (49%)	0	1 142 (19%)
	1101–1110	4 725	3 808 (81%)	2 (0,04%)	2 574 (55%)
	1111–1138	7 959	80 (1%)	2 (0,03%)	211 (3%)
	1139–1146	–	–	–	–
In total (without Pomerania)	1080–1100	14 224	10 729 (75%)	2 712 (19%)	266 (2%)
	1101–1110	25 576	17 865 (70%)	439+4970 (2%+19%)	1 120 (4%)
	1111–1138	5 473	231 (4%)	4 524 (83%)	7 (0,1%)
	1139–1146	2 880	455 (16%)	2 420 (84%)	1 (0,03%)

ducal coins. While in the earlier period the former were predominant in hoards from each province, later their share falls sharply. Ducal coins dominate in hoards from years 1111–1146 – they form more than 80% of their composition (without Pomerania). In the earlier scholarship, where all cross pennies were considered to be foreign, it was taken as a sign that Polish ducal coins started to dominate in domestic money market under the Wrymouth's rule.[43] Now, however, more often some of the cross pennies are believed to be issued in Poland, which obliges revision of the former opinion. It seems that such Polonization of a circulation was not a breakthrough event, but a gradual process. In hoards from the first decades of the twelfth century, cross pennies still appear, but their share in total do not exceed several percent. So, the proportion reversion between coins of both kinds, would be rather a reflection of the centralisation of the coinage in hands of one issuer – Bolesław III, than sudden increase of indigenous money in the market.

In the last decades of the eleventh century foreign coins were an important component of hoards. Besides the most frequent German and Bohemian pennies, Hungarian, English, Danish, Norwegian, exceptionally Byzantine and fragments of dirhams were also recorded. The younger the hoard is, the lower the percentage of foreign coins in its composition falls. It is also accompanied by a decreasing of their diversity. From the years of Bolesław's III and Władysław's II reigns only German, Bohemian, Hungarian and English pennies appeared. There is no relation between the hoards and coins chronology. Both in the older and younger deposits, pennies from the tenth century[44] appeared with pieces contemporary with the date of hoards hiding. It suggests that they were still in use. Apart from the deposits, four single foreign coins issued in the two last decades of Władysław Herman's reign were found – two German, one Bohemian and one Byzantine.[45] The same can be referred to Wrymouth's rule. In this period to Silesia could arrive Bohemian penny of Bořivoj found in Niemcza (Figure 2.2 and Table 2.5, letter A), to Central Poland Moravian penny of Svatopluk (letter

Table 2.5 Finds of foreign coins issued in the years of Wrymouth's rule

Letter	Locality	Category of find	Coin	Catalogue reference
A	Niemcza, Dolnośląskie Voivodeship	Settlement	Bohemian penny (coin fragment – 1/3), Bořivoj II, 1100–1107 or 1109–1110	Jan Šmerda, *Denáry české a moravské. Katalog mincí českého státu od X. do počátku XIII. století* (Brno: Datel, 1996), no. 172a.
B	Hebdów	Accidental	Polabian penny, 1120–1140	Hermann Dannenberg, *Die deutschen Münzen der sächsischen und fränkischen Kaiserzeit*, vol. 2 (Darmstadt: Scientia Verlag, 1967), no. 1778b.
C	Lubień	Grave good	Hungarian penny, Béla II, 1131–1141	Lajos Huszár, *Münzkatalog Ungarn von 1000 bis heute* (München: Battenberg, 1979), no. 49.
D	Uniejów	Accidental	Moravian penny, Svatopluk, 1095–1107	Jan Videman, Josef Paukert, *Moravské denáry 11. a 12. století* (Kroměříž: Česká numismatická společnost, 2009), no. 104.

D). In two other localities Polabian penny and Hungarian penny of Béla II were recorded (letters B and C).

Composition of the deposits changed not only in the aspect of provenance of hoarding silver, but also its form. Under the rule of Władysław Herman and in the first decade of the twelfth century, coins fragments were more frequent than later. Percentage of fragmented pennies is much higher in hoards from Greater Poland and especially from Pomerania. In deposits from Bonin and Mosiny hidden between 1101–1110 fragments form more than 50% of their composition.[46] Fragmented silver and jewellery in later hoards becomes a marginal component, although it still appears sporadically (e.g., in Sędziszowice and Wola Skromowska).

As to the hoards size and structure comparison, it is impossible to say anything for certain. Admittedly, one huge deposit from Karczmiska is known. It suggests that at the expense of frequency, the size of hoards grows. But subsequent discoveries can make this one seem unusual. Anyway, the composition is somewhat differentiated, even though it was hidden after the first re-coinage in Poland.[47] It is therefore very probable that it was a saving hoard. Its structure is not atypical, because deposits hidden in the years of Władysław's II rule also contain pennies of few types, including coins issued by his predecessors. So, they were purely savings deposits or combined both features, such as bullion,[48] and currency supply (by which I mean the youngest coins). Simultaneously, commonness of multitype hoards may be a result of existing in the twelfth century economic justification, which inclined owners of invalid coins to not exchange them. Maybe it was allowed to deliver them to the mint and exchange for a fee not only in the time of re-coinage?[49] Moreover, silver could be used in private transactions amongst the population. From people's perspective, every next exchange resulted in loss, which could be reduced or postponed by keeping a part of owned silver.

On the coin circulation in Poland under Wrymouth's reign, dispersion of finds taking into account, date of hiding hoards and absolute dating of pennies says a lot (Figure 2.3). On the map of the oldest Bolesław's III coins, deposits without ducal coins were added too.

Silesian pennies of this issuer groups mainly in Silesia (five of eight finds, on the map marked with the letter "s"). Outside this territory, one piece was recorded in hoard from Bohemia (Bílá Hora, now in Prague) and two more in Kraków Land and in Greater Poland. Dispersion of these coins finds and their iconography with St John the Baptist show their local character. Map of finds of Władysław Herman's pennies displayed that in this period his pennies are nearly completely absent in Silesia. So maybe Bolesław (or his father) noticed that and this is why Wrymouth's coinage begun in this province, not in Kraków or Sandomierz Lands where Herman's coins circulated intensively. From the other side, the opposite interpretation is also acceptable – lack of finds of Herman's pennies could be a result of circulation of local coins here.

Geographical distribution of pennies with the standing prince (Figure 2.1: Type 1) is different. They are gathered mainly in Kraków and Sandomierz Lands, moreover in several dozen pieces appeared in the Głogów hoard in Silesia and one copy was recorded in Moravian deposit from Vícemĕřice. Dispersion shows that Silesian and Kraków pennies with standing prince circulated mostly in

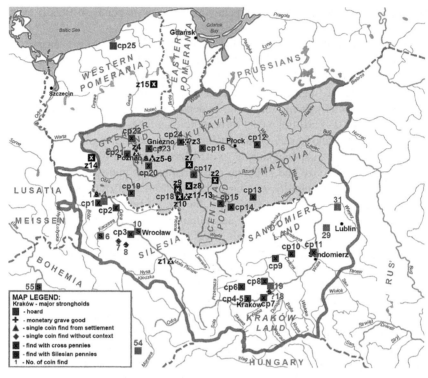

Figure 2.3 Coin finds from the first decade of the twelfth century[50] (approximately period of diarchy of Zbigniew and Bolesław III). Zbigniew's province is distinguished: Figures just numbered[51] – finds of Bolesław's III coins (numbering corresponds to Figure 2.2). Black figures with letter "z" ahead – finds of cross pennies attributed to Zbigniew: z1. Opole, Opolskie Voivodeship; z2. Leźnica Mała, Łódzkie Voivodeship; z3. Kruszwica, Kujawsko-Pomorskie Voivodeship; z4. Poznań, Wielkopolskie Voivodeship; z5–6. Giecz, Wielkopolskie Voivodeship; z7. Konin-Grójec, Wielkopolskie Voivodeship; z8. Słuszków, Wielkopolskie Voivodeship; z9. Żerniki, Wielkopolskie Voivodeship; z10–13. Kalisz Wielkopolskie Voivodeship; z14. Jordanowo, Lubuskie Voivodeship; z15. Mosiny, Pomorskie Voivodeship. Figures with letters "cp" ahead – hoards of cross pennies deposited probably in the first decade of the twelfth century, without ducal coins: cp1. Drożyna, Dolnośląskie Voivodeship; cp2. Chobienia, Dolnośląskie Voivodeship; cp3. Kębłowice, Dolnośląskie Voivodeship; cp4–5. Kraków, Małopolskie Voivodeship; cp6. Ojców, Małopolskie Voivodeship; cp7. Grobla, Małopolskie Voivodeship; cp8. Chruszczyna, Świętokrzyskie Voivodeship; cp9. Górki, Świętokrzyskie Voivodeship; cp10. Stara Łagowica, Świętokrzyskie Voivodeship; cp11. Zawichost-Trójca, Świętokrzyskie Voivodeship; cp12. Naruszewo, Mazowieckie Voivodeship; cp13. Rawa Mazowiecka, Łódzkie Voivodeship; cp14. Wodzin, Łódzkie Voivodeship; cp15. Wodzierady, Łódzkie Voivodeship; cp16. Zgłowiączka, Kujawsko-Pomorskie Voivodeship; cp17. Ogorzelczyn, Wielkopolskie Voivodeship; cp18. Jastrzębniki, Wielkopolskie Voivodeship; cp19. Rokosowo, Wielkopolskie Voivodeship; cp20. Środa Wielkopolska III – environs, Wielkopolskie Voivodeship; cp21. Sędzinko, Wielkopolskie Voivodeship; cp22. Oborniki I – environs, Wielkopolskie Voivodeship; cp23. Rybitwy–Ostrów Lednicki VI, Wielkopolskie Voivodeship; cp24. Kruszwica, Kujawsko-Pomorskie Voivodeship; cp25. Bonin, Zachodniopomorskie Voivodeship. Drawn by Grzegorz Śnieżko.

southern provinces where Bolesław ruled while father passed him on part of the reins. Most likely they did not circulate together, because they have not been registered in the same hoards yet.[52] This allows us to state that pennies with a standing warrior were a kind of starting point for further Wrymouth's coinage. They are present in four hoards with his younger coins, so they had to occur on the money market together.

On the contrary, cross pennies attributed to Zbigniew concentrate mostly in Greater and Central Poland. In these provinces (with Mazovia) hoarding was also much more intense – now we know 18 hoards from there, while from Silesia, Kraków and Sandomierz Lands only 10.[53] Their composition shows that Wrymouth's coins in this period were almost absent in the circulation outside Silesia, Kraków and Sandomierz Lands, since they were not registered in any of numerous hoards. It seems impossible to interpret this observation in the categories of people's unwillingness to use such coins because of worse quality of ducal coins than cross pennies. Anonymous coins were indeed heavier than Władysław Herman's and the oldest Bolesław's III pennies, but at the same time they were struck with silver of similar or even worse quality. So, one of the acceptable reasons for the absence of a more widespread presence of Herman's coins in Central Poland, Mazovia, Kuyavia and Greater Poland could be insufficient size of issue. Justifying this interpretation, we are condemned only to hypotheses, because we do not know even estimated scale of Władysław's I issue. The only premise for a decrease in its size relative to Bolesław II the Generous (1058–1079) coinage is a comparison of the number of their coins finds. From Mazovia, Central and Greater Poland, 26 finds of Bolesław II[54] pennies and 13 of Herman are registered. The decline will also be clear if we include the remaining part of Poland – Generous' coins come from 50 finds, while Herman's from 31.[55] This is why insufficient reachability of Herman's and Wrymouth's oldest coins is a probable reason of such regionalisation of a circulation that is visible especially under the Władysław's I reign.

In the second decade of the twelfth century only one hoard was hidden (from Sędziszowice – Figure 2.4: no. 19), which is an evidence of sudden decrease in hoarding. Finds of pennies of Type 2 with the prince sitting on the throne, compared with the older ones, more often occur in the Mazovia, Central and Greater Poland. In provinces earlier under Zbigniew's reign, they are known from four single finds. The quality of these pennies increased significantly. The average weight of coins with standing prince is 0.72 g and silver content gains 66.53%, while the following is 0.83–0.84 g and 84.75–87.09% Ag. The growth pertains both to the weight and fineness of silver as well as the quality of engravers' work (e.g., better layout of a die surface). Thus, it is indisputable that it was purposeful. It could be an act directed to monopolise the domestic coin circulation and evidence of prince's reaction to changes in the international money market.[56]

It turned out to be effective, because Bolesław's III and Władysław's II pennies of next types are constantly present in the Mazovia, Kuyavia, Central and Greater Poland, and their representation there grows (Figure 2.5). Also, in the years 1120–1138 four hoards from Pomerania[57] are known (three contained cross pennies) and the most northerly find of Bolesław's III penny.

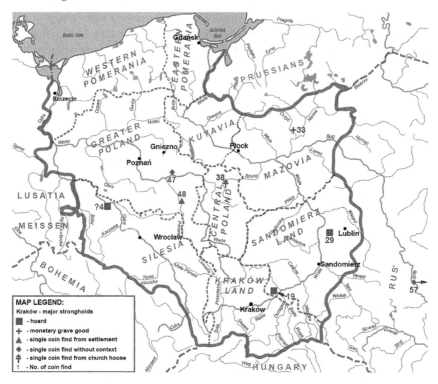

Figure 2.4 Finds of Wrymouth's pennies of Type 2 (numbering corresponds to Figure 2.2). Drawn by Grzegorz Śnieżko.

* * *

Comparison of geographical dispersion of finds from years 1080–1146 shows its movement from the capital centres, called by Gallus Anonymous *sedes regni principales*, and their environs to the main strongholds of provinces and partially also to complete periphery. Territory of Poland under the Wrymouth's rule is not homogenous in this regard (Figure 2.2). Spread of single coin finds and hoards hidden during his reign indicates broader circulation of ducal coins in southern provinces; i.e., in Silesia, Kraków and Sandomierz Lands. Higher numbers of finds not only proves that, but also more frequent representation outside the administrative centres than in them. Besides, southern provinces are differentiated too. As in Silesia Wrymouth's pennies appear both in the main centres of province (Wrocław, Głogów) and outside, in Kraków and Sandomierz Lands they are mostly found in the periphery. It is different in Central Poland, Kuyavia and Greater Poland in particular, where finds tend to group in the main strongholds; e.g., Kałdus (Chełmno before foundation of a town), Giecz, Ląd or Kalisz.[58] Earlier, I considered it as symptom of socio-economic changes without concrete interpretation and paying enough attention to local administrative centre's rank.[59] I think we should leave the platitudes on the growing monetisation of the society. This is only a kind of interpretative skeleton key. The fall of the number of single

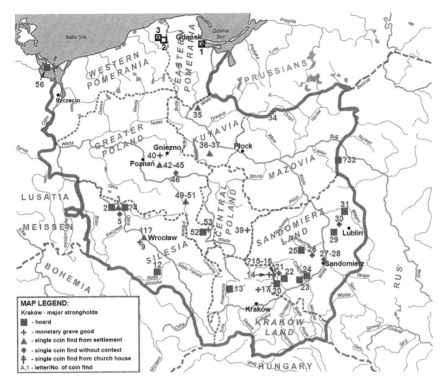

Figure 2.5 Finds of Wrymouth's Kraków pennies of types 3 and 4 and bracteates of both types (with hoards hidden after Bolesław's death; numbering of figures corresponds to Figure 2.2) and hoards from Pomerania deposited in the second and third decade of the twelfth century (black figures with white square inside): 1. Gdańsk X, Pomorskie Voivodeship (*Frühmittelalterliche Münzfunde* 2, no. 53); 2. Łupawa, Pomorskie Voivodeship (*ibid.*, no. 136); 3. Malczkowo, Pomorskie Voivodeship (*ibid.*, no. 137). Drawn by Grzegorz Śnieżko.

coin finds[60] and their dispersion is at odds with that. Already under Władysław Herman's rule and at the beginning of the twelfth century, finds occur outside the main centres. It is also important that in southern Poland, overwhelmingly they are cross pennies (Figure 2.3). Finds of Herman's coins are grouped mostly in the capital centres (Kraków, Płock) and strongholds of smaller rank, but still of huge significance (Opole, Wiślica, Lublin, Czersk). I therefore think that availability of ducal coins, which indicates a disseminating within circulation, is a way to interpret that phenomenon. Wrymouth's pennies replaced or even displaced cross pennies. These anonymous coins were less common in the circulation in South, because of higher widespread of ducal (and earlier royal) coins already under Bolesław II the Generous and Herman's reigns (Table 2.4). Therefore, market's need for coins was easier to meet. In Mazovia, Kuyavia, Central and Greater Poland, the process of dissemination of ducal coins was similar, but delayed or even without a stage of ducal coins' presence in the capital centres. It could be

Table 2.6 Estimated minimal and total volume of Bolesław's III coinage

Minimal	Total volume of a coinage		
	Good 1953	Carter 1983	Esty 2011
4,970,000 pieces	5,782,000 pieces	6,640,000 pieces	7,220,000 pieces

a result of cross pennies domination in circulation there, presumably to the first decade of the twelfth century. Finds of Bolesław's III coins group mostly in the main strongholds of provinces, where they may have appeared with mighty and clerks of Wrymouth's ducal administration.[61] Afterwards, money penetrated the countryside, just like in the South.[62] On the other hand, in many of these centres, markets are documented in the twelfth century.[63] Then, it is possible that coins could also get there in commercial transactions. Besides, both influx routes are likely. More broadly, the phenomenon of disappearance of finds in capital centres reflects changes in the economic balance point, which moved to strongholds of lesser rank.

We may try to calculate the number of Wrymouth's coins *per capita*. It is of course simplified and probably underestimated, because as stated earlier, we do not have any information on the volume of cross pennies coinage, common in circulation at the beginning of the twelfth century. The results cannot be compared with Herman's coinage for the same reason. However, maybe in the future these estimates will prove to be useful.

Table 2.6 shows estimated minimal and total size of Wrymouth's coinage.[64] It could range from nearly 6 to over 7 million pieces. Researchers in the fields of historical demography have estimated that population of Poland around year 1000 was about 1 million people, whereas to the year 1370 it grown up to 2 million.[65] For my estimations, I assumed it was 1.5 million people in the first half of the twelfth century. In that case, it would be four or five pennies per head for several decades of coinage. Analogous calculations were made for Bolesław's II the Generous mintage by Stanisław Suchodolski. He stated that per each inhabitant of Lesser Poland there were seven-eight pennies and for the whole family 35–40.[66] Comparative data are available also for England in the end of the eleventh century. Jim Bolton says that Jim Bolton says that *in 1100 there were probably between two and four silver pennies per head of population.*[67] My estimates pertained to almost 40 years of Wrymouth's reign, which leads to conclusion that the level of monetisation in England was definitely higher. After all, it must be remembered that the result for Poland is underestimated because we do not have similar estimates for the older coinage, especially Herman's and cross pennies, which circulated intensively at the beginning of the twelfth century. In addition, any reliable written sources on the purchasing power in this period are not preserved.[68]

Notes

1 For the newest biography, see Stanisław Rosik, *Bolesław Krzywousty*, (Wrocław: Chronicon, 2013).
2 Witold Nakielski, "Propozycja nowej atrybucji monet śląskich przełomu XI i XII w. w świetle depozytu z miejscowości Kopacz gm. Złotoryja," in *Studia nad Dziejami Pieniądza i Bankowości w Polsce*, vol. 2: *Pieniądz i banki na Śląsku*, edited by Witold Garbaczewski and Roman Macyra (Poznań: Muzeum Narodowe, 2012), pp. 147–184.
3 Typology of the Kraków pennies after Stanisław Suchodolski, *Mennictwo polskie w XI i XII wieku* (Wrocław: Ossolineum, 1973), pp. 44–47, 109–111; idem, "Kult św. Wacława i św. Wojciecha przez pryzmat polskich monet z wczesnego średniowiecza," in idem, *Numizmatyka średniowieczna. Moneta źródłem archeologicznym, historycznym i ikonograficznym* (Warszawa: Trio, 2012), pp. 397–402.
4 I am grateful to their owner for providing photographs for publication.
5 Present text is a synthesized chapter of my doctoral thesis entitled *Moneta w Polsce za panowania Bolesława III Krzywoustego* [Coin in Poland under the reign of Bolesław III Wrymouth], prepared under prof. Stanisław Suchodolski's supervision. To carry out the research I have obtained the grant from the National Science Centre, Poland (research project no. 2014/13/N/HS3/04588) realized in The Institute of Archaeology and Ethnology of Polish Academy of Sciences between 2015 and 2017.
6 After *Frühmittelalterliche Münzfunde aus Polen*, vols 1–5, edited by Mateusz Bogucki, Peter Ilisch, and Stanisław Suchodolski (Warszawa: IAE PAN, 2013–2017).
7 Suchodolski, *Mennictwo polskie*, p. 81.
8 The updated map I published in 2018: Grzegorz Śnieżko, "Znaleziska monet Bolesława Krzywoustego na tle porównawczym," in *Studia nad Dziejami Pieniądza i Bankowości w Polsce*, vol. 4: *Pieniądz i banki w Małopolsce*, edited by Witold Garbaczewski and Roman Macyra (Poznań: Muzeum Narodowe, 2018), pp. 81–112. There were 54 finds included, while now three more are available.
9 Gerd Sobietzky, "Der Denarfund von Stolpe II/Usedom," *Bodendenkmalpflege im Mecklenburg-Vorpommern* 59 (2012), pp. 90, 97, Figure 2.5: 38, 100 (mistakenly as halfpenny – *Halbdenar*), p. 105, no. 14.1.
10 In Figure 2.2 there is 12 hoards underlined. Another one is known but it comes from undetermined place so it could not be marked on the map.
11 Osiek (Figure 2.2: no. 7), Stary Zamek (no. 8), Mokronos Dolny (no. 9), Prząsław (no. 14), Prandocin (no. 17), Bazar (no. 33), Pokrzywnica (no. 34), Dziekanowice (no. 40).
12 Jędrzejów (Figure 2.2: nos. 15–16), Witów (no. 18), Lubień (no. 39); Dębina (no. 53).
13 Tum (Figure 2.2: no. 38).
14 Mariusz Dworsatschek, *Władysław II Wygnaniec* (Kraków: Universitas, 2009), p. 42.
15 *Kodeks dyplomatyczny klasztoru tynieckiego*, published by Wojciech Kętrzyński and Stanisław Smolka, (Lwów: Zakład Narodowy im. Ossolińskich, 1875), no. I, p. 3; on this subject also Marian Gumowski, *O grzywnie i monecie piastowskiej*, Rozprawy Akademii Umiejętności. Wydział Historyczno-Filozoficzny, 2nd series, Vol. 26 (1908), p. 363; Kiersnowski, *Pieniądz kruszcowy*, pp. 441, 451–452; Jacek Adamczyk, *Płacidła w Europie Środkowej i Wschodniej w średniowieczu. Formy, funkcjonowanie, ewolucja* (Warszawa: Neriton, IH PAN, 2004), p. 182; Dariusz Adamczyk, "Pieniądz czy strategiczny instrument władzy? Obieg kruszcu w społeczeństwie piastowskim przełomu XI i XII wieku, załamanie w dopływie denarów z Saksonii a ekspansja Bolesława Krzywoustego na Pomorze", *Przegląd Zachodniopomorski* 32 (2017), no. 2, 152.
16 *Dyplomatyczny Wielkopolski* (Poznań: 1877), no. 7; Gumowski, "O grzywnie," p. 363; Kiersnowski, *Pieniądz kruszcowy*, pp. 451–452; Jacek Adamczyk, *Płacidła*, p. 182; Dariusz Adamczyk, "Pieniądz czy strategiczny," 152.

17 Both possibilities were highlighted accurately by Kiersnowski, *Pieniądz kruszcowy*, pp. 450–451.

18 Jacek Adamczyk, *Płacidła*, p. 182, considers them as relics of commodity money, while Kiersnowski, *Pieniądz kruszcowy*, p. 451, stressed that *such pelts were a product for further exchange for sure.*

19 As such assigns them Dariusz Adamczyk, "Pieniądz czy strategiczny," 152.

20 Herbord *dialogus de vita S. Ottonis episcopi babenbergensis/Herbord. Dialog o życiu św. Ottona biskupa bamberskiego*, translated by Jan Wikarjak, introduction and comments by Kazimierz Liman, Monumenta Poloniae Historica, 2nd series, vol. 7, Part 3 (Warszawa: Państwowe Wydawnictwo Naukowe, 1974), II, 41: *Vestes suas, pecuniam et omnia preciosa sua in cuppis et doliis suis simpliciter coopertis recondunt.*

21 Ryszard Kiersnowski, "Główne momenty rozwoju środków wymiany na Pomorzu wczesnofeudalnym", *Wiadomości Archeologiczne* 23 (1956), no. 3, p. 246; his concept is cited by Jacek Adamczyk, *Płacidła*, p. 296.

22 After *Frühmittelalterliche Münzfunde*, vols 1–5.

23 Stanisław Tabaczyński, *Archeologia średniowieczna. Problemy, źródła, metody, cele badawcze* (Wrocław: Ossolineum, 1987), pp. 213–214; Jakub Łyszkowski, "Odzwierciedlenie obiegu pieniężnego we wczesnym średniowieczu przez znaleziska drobne", *Wiadomości Numizmatyczne* 50 (2006), no. 1, 15–17.

24 Marian Gumowski, *Corpus Nummorum Poloniae*, vol. 1: *Monety X i XI w.* (Kraków: Polska Akademia Umiejętności, 1939).

25 I mean deposits with youngest cross pennies in particular. At least 14 hoards can be pointed out here: Drożyna, Dolnośląskie Voivodeship (*Frühmittelalterliche Münzfunde* 4, no. 13); Ojców, Małopolskie Voivodeship (*ibid.*, no. 73); Grobla, Małopolskie Voivodeship (*ibid.*, no. 26); Naruszewo, Mazowieckie Voivodeship (*Frühmittelalterliche Münzfunde* 3, no. 89); Wodzin, Łódzkie Voivodeship (*ibid.*, no. 199); Zgłowiączka, Kujawsko-Pomorskie Voivodeship (*ibid.*, no. 208); Konin-Grójec, Wielkopolskie Voivodeship (*Frühmittelalterliche Münzfunde* 1, no. 74); Ogorzelczyn, Wielkopolskie Voivodeship (*ibid.*, no. 168); Sędzinko, Wielkopolskie Voivodeship (*ibid.*, no. 226); Kraków–Wawel, Małopolskie Voivodeship (*Frühmittelalterliche Münzfunde* 4, no. 40); Kraków, Małopolskie Voivodeship (*ibid.*, no. 45); Zawichost–Trójca, Świętokrzyskie Voivodeship (*ibid.*, no. 117); Wodzierady, Łódzkie Voivodeship (*Frühmittelalterliche Münzfunde* 3, no. 198); Rokosowo, Wielkopolskie Voivodeship (*Frühmittelalterliche Münzfunde* 1, no. 214). Some of them contained also cross pennies hypothetically attributed to Zbigniew.

26 Hoards from Karczmiska (Figure 2.2: no. 29), probably from the environs of Głogów (*Frühmittelalterliche Münzfunde* 4, no. 107), from Smolice (*ibid.*, no. 66), from Wola Skromowska (*ibid.*, no. 112) and presumably from Włodki too (*Frühmittelalterliche Münzfunde* 3, no. 197).

27 Kiersnowski, *Pieniądz kruszcowy*, pp. 432–436.

28 Tabaczyński, *Archeologia średniowieczna*, pp. 221–222; similarly, Łyszkowski, "Odzwierciedlenie obiegu," 16.

29 Helle W. Horsnæs, Jens Ch. Moesgaard, and Michael Märcher, *Denar til daler. Danmarks mønthistorie indtil 1550* (København: Danmarks Nationalbank, 2018), p. 204.

30 Jan Hunka, *Mince Arpádovcov z rokov 1000–1301. Ich podiel na vývoji hospodárstva stredovekého Slovenska* (Nitra: Archeologický ústav, Slovenská akadémia vied, 2013), p. 45 – decline in the number of finds is clear for Koloman's pennies (1095–1116).

31 Dariusz Adamczyk, *Srebro i władza. Trybuty i handel dalekosiężny a kształtowanie się państwa piastowskiego i państw sąsiednich w latach 800–1100* (Warszawa: Wydawnictwo Naukowe PWN, 2018), p. 327, Table 101: in the years 1075–1100 were registered 16 coin finds, between 1100–1130 27 hoards.

32 Bernd Kluge, *Deutsche Münzgeschichte von der späten Karolingerzeit bis zum Ende der Salier (ca. 900 bis 1125)* (Sigmaringen: Thorbecke, 1991), pp. 40–41, 60–62.

33 See for example: Mark Blackburn, "Coin circulation in Germany during the Early Middle Ages. The evidence of single-finds," in *Fernhandel und Geldwirtschaft. Beiträge zum deutschen Münzwesen in sächsischer und salischer zeit. Ergebnisse des Dannenberg-Kolloquiums 1990*, edited by Bernd Kluge (Sigmaringen: Thorbecke, 1993), p. 45; Peter Ilisch, "Les monnaies du Saint-Empire du Xe et XIe siècle: exportation ou circulation interne?" *Le Bulletin de la Société française de numismatique* 71 (2016), no. 2, p. 55.

34 Kiersnowski, *Pieniądz kruszcowy*, p. 434.

35 In Moravia in the second half of the eleventh century in relation to its first half, even fall in single finds has been recorded – Jiří Macháček and Jan Videman, "Monetisation of early medieval Moravia in the light of new archaeological discoveries in the Lower Dyje region (Czech Region)," in *Economies, Monetisation and Society in the West Slavic Lands 800–1200 AD*, edited by Mateusz Bogucki and Marian Rębkowski (Szczecin: IAE PAN, 2013), pp. 185, 194.

36 After Pavel Radoměrský, "České, moravské a slezské nálezy mincí údobí denárového," in *Nálezy mincí v Čechách, na Moravě a ve Slezsku*, vol. 2, edited by Emanuela Nohejlová-Prátová (Praha: Československá akadémia vied, 1956), pp. 7–73.

37 Śnieżko, "Znaleziska monet Bolesława," pp. 102–104.

38 After *Frühmittelalterliche Münzfunde*, volvols 1–5.

39 Hoard from Włodki of composition known vaguely (*Frühmittelalterliche Münzfunde* 3, no. 197).

40 Similar method was used by David M. Metcalf who examined the productivity of the Salian mints: David M. Metcalf, "Some further reflections on the volume of the German coinage in the Salian Period (1024–1125)," in *Fernhandel und Geldwirtschaft. Beiträge zum deutschen Münzwesen in sächsischer und salischer Zeit. Ergebnisse des Dannenberg-Kolloquiums 1990*, edited by Bernd Kluge (Sigmaringen: Thorbecke, 1993), pp. 55–72.

41 Hoarding of silver clumps unearthed in Kalisz-Dobrzec is dated to the end of the eleventh century – Adam Kędzierski, "Obieg pieniężny w Kaliszu i regionie za panowania Władysława Hermana oraz Zbigniewa," in *Kalisz na przestrzeni wieków: konferencja naukowa pod przewodnictwem prof. dr hab. Henryka Samsonowicza*, edited by Tadeusz Baranowski and Andrzej Buko (Kalisz: IAE PAN, 2013), pp. 138–140; Adam Kędzierski and Dariusz Wyczółkowski, "Skarb placków srebrnych z Kalisza-Dobrzeca. Nowe możliwości badawcze problemu srebra lanego," in *Nummi et Humanitas. Studia ofiarowane Profesorowi Stanisławowi Suchodolskiemu w 80 rocznicę urodzin*, edited by Mateusz Bogucki, Witold Garbaczewski, and Grzegorz Śnieżko (Warszawa: IAE PAN, 2017), pp. 331–351.

42 Kiersnowski, *Pieniądz kruszcowy*, p. 449, footnote 68. The salt-works functioned on the North at the turn of the eleventh and twelfth centuries in Pomerania, e.g., Budzistów near Kołobrzeg and in Kołobrzeg, Zachodniopomorskie Voivodeship–Lech Leciejewicz, "Saliny na terenie dzisiejszego miasta. Badania w 1958 r.," in *Kołobrzeg. Wczesne miasto nad Bałtykiem*, edited by Lech Leciejewicz and Marian Rębkowski, Origines Polonorum, vol. 2 (Warszawa: IAE PAN, 2007), pp. 171–176; Jerzy Wyrozumski, *Państwowa gospodarka solna w Polsce do schyłku XIV wieku* (Kraków: Uniwersytet Jagielloński, 1968), pp. 7–8. In this period salt-works existed also in Kuyavia, e.g., in Inowrocław, Kujawsko-Pomorskie Voivodeship: Aleksandra Cofta-Broniewska, "Wczesnośredniowieczna warzelnia soli w Inowrocławiu", *Ziemia Kujawska* 4 (1974), pp. 5–13; and probably in Zgłowiączka, Kujawsko-Pomorskie Voivodeship: Aldona Andrzejewska, *Średniowieczny zespół osadniczy w Zgłowiączce na Kujawach* (Włocławek: Państwowa Służba Ochrony Zabytków, 1996), p. 150.

43 Kiersnowski, *Pieniądz kruszcowy*, p. 297.

44 E.g., in the deposit from Kopacz from the beginning of the twelfth century, German penny of Otto I was recorded (*Frühmittelalterliche Münzfunde* 4, no. 29: 2).

45 Milicz, Dolnośląskie Voivodeship: Lower Saxony penny, Bardowick (*Frühmittelalterliche Münzfunde* 4, no. 43: 4); Biecz, Małopolskie Voivodeship: 40 nummi, Alexios I Komnenos, 1081–1118 (*ibid.*, no. 3: 2); Gnojno, Świętokrzyskie Voivodeship: penny, Wratislaus II, 1061–1092 (*ibid.*, no. 21: 4); Pokrzywnica Wielka, Warmińsko-Mazurskie Voivodeship: penny, emperor Henry IV, 1084–1105 (*Frühmittelalterliche Münzfunde* 3, no. 123: 1). This perspective is undoubtedly disturbed because of three reasons. The first one is still unsolved provenance of anonymous cross pennies which are the most common in single finds. Second one is a fact that reasonably is to expect that some earlier coins should be taken into account here. But we do not know which one exactly. At least the third one is a possibility that some of these four above mentioned pieces could be deposited or lost already in the twelfth century.

46 Bonin, Zachodniopomorskie Voivodeship: 2,006 entire pieces and 2,432 coin fragments (*Frühmittelalterliche Münzfunde* 2, no. 74); Mosiny, Pomorskie Voivodeship: 145 entire pieces and 142 fragments (*ibid.*, no. 143). In this period the youngest deposit with fragmented silver was hidden in the Hither Pomerania (Stolpe auf Usedom). Christoph Kilger considers it as an evidence that until the beginning of the twelfth century in Pomerania coined silver was not accepted in circulation. In his opinion, attitude of Slavs living there to coins changed, among others, because of tributes they had to pay for Saxon dukes in coins (*nomismata Bardenwiccensis* which he identifies as so called *niederelbische Agrippiner*) – Christoph Kilger, *Pfennigmärkte und Währungslandschaften. Monetarisierungen im sächsisch-slawischen Grenzland ca. 965–1120* (Royal Swedish Academy of Letters, History and Antiquities, Stockholm Numismatic Institute at the Stockholm University, 2000), pp. 143–150. This could produce effects – written sources provide information on using coined silver in Pomerania at least from twenties of the twelfth century. Herbord mentions it twice informing on the pennies that Wrymouth gave to Otto of Bamberg to the mission in Pomerania (Herbord *dialogus*, II, 9) and indicating price of cart of herring (Herbord *dialogus*, II, 41).

47 Suchodolski, "Na czym polegał system renovatio monetae?", *Biuletyn Numizmatyczny* 4 (2019), 273–285.

48 Arguably this is the reason why hoards of this period sporadically still contained uncoined silver and jewellery. They are mentioned in hoards of Sędziszowice (Figure 2.2: 19) and Wola Skromowska (Figure 2.2: 31). Kaźmirz Stronczyński, *Pieniądze Piastów od czasów najdawniejszych do roku 1300. Rozbiorem źródeł spółczesnych i wykopalisk oraz porównaniem typów menniczych objaśnione* (Warszawa, 1847), p. 65 (Sędziszowice): *były szczątki jubilerskich robót i kawałki rąbanego srebra* [there were remnants of jewellery and fragments of chopped silver] and on page 84 (Wola Skromowska): *kilka kawałeczków srebra* [contained few pieces of silver].

49 It is supposed that similar solution functioned in this period in England–Martin Allen, *Mints and Money in Medieval England* (Cambridge: University Press, 2015), p. 39.

50 After *Frühmittelalterliche Münzfunde*, vols 1–5.

51 Originally, figures of each categories were differentiated with colours. Adaptation to the publisher's requirements needed adjusting the maps to black and white printing. Proposed way to distinguish figures with additional letters may seem not very readable. However, because of the three-stage division of data on this map it was the only one.

52 Silesian penny of type I, Kraków penny of Type 3 and three Kraków pennies of Type 4 were recorded in Giecz (Figure 2.2: nos. 41–45). All of them were single finds.

53 Hoards from the environs of Głogów (Figure 2.3: no. 4), Sędziszowice (no. 19), Karczmiska (no. 29), and Wola Skromowska (no. 31) were deposited in the next decades of the twelfth century.

54 Stanisław Suchodolski, "Monety Bolesława Śmiałego w świetle skarbu znalezionego w Wiślicy," in *Studia nad Dziejami Pieniądza i Bankowości w Polsce*, vol. 4: *Pieniądz i banki w Małopolsce*, edited by Witold Garbaczewski and Roman Macyra (Poznań: Muzeum Narodowe, 2018), pp. 73–79.

55 Grzegorz Śnieżko, "Znaleziska monet Bolesława," pp. 92–93 with the addition.
56 Similarly, Dariusz Adamczyk, "Pieniądz czy strategiczny," 143–144.
57 On Figure 2.5 hoard described as *Pomorze XIII* (*Frühmittelalterliche Münzfunde* 2, no. 285) was not marked, because its precise location is undetermined.
58 This is why I cannot agree with Jakub Łyszkowski, "Odzwierciedlenie obiegu," 9, where is an observation on the period 1100–1173: *Również jedynie w Wielkopolsce rozproszenie zabytków wykracza poza znaczniejsze grody. W pozostałych dzielnicach występowanie monet zawęziło się do skupienia w głównych miejscowościach* [Also only in Greater Poland coin finds outreached the main centres. In other provinces their dispersion is limited to them]. First symptoms of change in this respect, i.e., more frequent representation of ducal coins outside the main strongholds of northern provinces, can be observed for coin finds of Władysław II.
59 Grzegorz Śnieżko, "Denary Bolesława Krzywoustego typu 1," in *Nummi et Humanitas*, p. 435 and footnote 37; Śnieżko, "Znaleziska monet Bolesława," pp. 104–105.
60 Dariusz Adamczyk, "Pieniądz czy strategiczny", 145 noticed that.
61 Gallus Anonymous mentioned that after defeating Zbigniew, *Bolesław zaś krążył po Polsce, dokądkolwiek mu się podobało* [Bolesław travelled across and within the Poland anywhere he wanted] – Anonim tzw. Gall, *Kronika polska*, translated by Roman Grodecki, introduction and elaboration by Marian Plezia (Wrocław: Ossolineum, 2008), II, 38. It was regarded as a prove of taking the reins in whole state – Rosik, *Bolesław Krzywousty*, pp. 108–109.
62 It confirms partially Dariusz Adamczyk's observations ("Pieniądz czy strategiczny," 152): *Obieg monety wydaje się przebiegać wertykalnie, to jest z góry do dołu, z grodów do podgrodzi i pobliskich wsi. Nie ma natomiast jakichkolwiek przesłanek, by odbywał się on horyzontalnie między poszczególnymi osadami* [Coin circulation seems to be vertical, i.e., from the top down, from strongholds and its environs to nearby villages. But there is no indication for horizontal circulation between the individual settlements]. Partially, because just as there is no way to confirm, there is also no way to contradict that.
63 Map of the twelfth-century markets and administrative centres – Tadeusz Lalik, "Märkte des 12. Jahrhunderts in Polen," *Kwartalnik Historii Kultury Materialnej* 10 (1962), no. 1–2, Figure 2.1.
64 Minimal volume of coinage was calculated with number of lower dies used to struck actually preserved coins. It was multiplied by 10,000 pieces, i.e., conventional output of a lower die; such score got in the experiment David Sellwood, "Medieval Minting Techniques," *British Numismatic Journal* 31 (1962), 57–65. Reconstruction of total size was accomplished with three statistical methods: Irving J. Good, "The Population Frequencies of Species and the Estimation of Population Parameters," *Biometrika* 40 (1953), no. 3–4, 237–264; Giles F. Carter, "A Simplified Method for Calculating the Original Number of Dies from Die Link Statistics," *The American Numismatic Society Museum Notes* 28 (1983), 195–206; Warren W. Esty, "The geometric model for estimating the number of dies," in *Quantifying Monetary Supplies in Greco-Roman Times*, edited by François de Callataÿ (Bari: Edipuglia, 2011), pp. 43–58. Each method has different hypothetical assumptions and their own deficiencies, but all of them allow to estimate original number of dies used in a coinage. Large discrepancies in results indicate their approximate character; similarly, also: Megan Laura Gooch, *Money and Power in the Viking Kingdom of York, c. 895–954*, doctoral thesis (Durham: Durham University, 2011), pp. 140–146, available at http://etheses.dur.ac.uk/3495/ (accessed 27 July 2020).
65 Cezary Kuklo, *Demografia Rzeczypospolitej przedrozbiorowej* (Warszawa: DiG, 2009), pp. 210–212.
66 Stanisław Suchodolski, "Polityka mennicza a wydarzenia polityczne w Polsce we wczesnym średniowieczu," in idem, *Numizmatyka średniowieczna*, 335–349.
67 Jim Bolton, *Money in the Medieval English Economy, 973–1489* (Manchester: Manchester University Press, 2012), p. 24.

68 Herbord *dialogus*, II, 41, refers to years of Bolesław's III rule in mentions that prove perception of coins with their nominal value. But it is not credible enough to consider it literally. He wrote that in 1124 in Pomerania cart of herring costed one penny. Kiersnowski, "Główne momenty," p. 244, and Kiersnowski, *Pieniądz kruszcowy*, pp. 438, 471, thought it was underpriced. In contrast, Lech Leciejewicz noticed that it could be a small two-wheeled cart but as a more likely he considered that it was hagiographer's impression of abnormally low prices of herrings in Pomerania–Leciejewicz, "Za denara otrzymasz wóz świeżych śledzi...," in *Nummus et Historia. Pieniądz Europy średniowiecznej*, edited by Stefan K. Kuczyński and Stanisław Suchodolski (Warszawa: Polskie Towarzystwo Archeologiczne i Numizmatyczne, 1985), p. 103. Anyway, nothing certain can be said.

Bibliography

Primary sources

Anonim tzw. *Gall [Anonymous so called Gallus], Kronika polska [Polish Chronicle]*, translated by Roman Grodecki, introduction and elaboration by Marian Plezia. Wrocław: Ossolineum, 2008.

Frühmittelalterliche Münzfunde aus Polen, vols 1–5, edited by Mateusz Bogucki, Peter Ilisch, and Stanisław Suchodolski. Warszawa: IAE PAN, 2013–2017.

Herbord *dialogus de vita S. Ottonis episcopi babenbergensis/Herbord: Dialog o życiu Św. Ottona biskupa bamberskiego*, translated by Jan Wikarjak, introduction and comments by Kazimierz Liman, Monumenta Poloniae Historica, 2nd series, vol. 7, part 3. Warszawa: Państwowe Wydawnictwo Naukowe, 1974.

Kętrzyński, Wojciech and Stanisław, Smolka *Kodeks dyplomatyczny klasztoru tynieckiego [The diplomatic codex of the Tyniec Cloister]*. Lwów: Zakład Narodowy im. Ossolińskich, 1875.

Kodeks Dyplomatyczny Wielkopolski [The Diplomatic Codex of Greater Poland], vol. 1. Poznań: Biblioteka Kórnicka, 1877.

Secondary literature

Adamczyk, Dariusz. "Pieniądz czy strategiczny instrument władzy? Obieg kruszcu w społeczeństwie piastowskim przełomu XI i XII wieku, załamanie w dopływie denarów z Saksonii a ekspansja Bolesława Krzywoustego na Pomorze" [Money or a strategic instrument of power? The circulation of precious metals in the Piast society at the turn of the 12th century, the collapse of the inflow of deniers from Saxony and Bolesław's Wrymouth expansion to Pomerania], *Przegląd Zachodniopomorski* 32 (2017), no. 2, 143–167.

Adamczyk, Dariusz. *Srebro i władza. Trybuty i handel dalekosiężny a kształtowanie się państwa piastowskiego i państw sąsiednich w latach 800–1100 [Silver and Power. Tributes, long-distance trade and the formation of the Piast and neighbouring states in the years 800–1100]*. Warszawa: Wydawnictwo Naukowe PWN, 2018.

Adamczyk, Jacek. *Płacidła w Europie Środkowej i Wschodniej w Średniowieczu. Formy, funkcjonowanie, ewolucja [Commodity Money in Central and Eastern Europe in the Middle Ages. Forms, Functioning, Evolution]*. Warszawa: Neriton, IH PAN, 2004.

Allen, Martin. *Mints and Money in Medieval England*. Cambridge: University Press, 2015.

Andrzejewska, Aldona. *Średniowieczny zespół osadniczy w Zgłowiączce na Kujawach [Medieval Settlement Complex in Zgłowiączka in Kuyavia]*. Włocławek: Państwowa Służba Ochrony Zabytków, 1996.

Blackburn, Mark. "Coin circulation in Germany during the Early Middle Ages. The evidence of single-finds," in *Fernhandel und Geldwirtschaft. Beiträge zum deutschen Münzwesen in sächsischer und salischer Zeit. Ergebnisse des Dannenberg-Kolloquiums 1990*, edited by Bernd Kluge, pp. 37–54. Sigmaringen: Thorbecke, 1993.

Bolton, Jim. *Money in the Medieval English Economy, 973–1489.* Manchester: Manchester University Press, 2012.

Carter, Giles F. "A Simplified Method for Calculating the Original Number of Dies from Die Link Statistics," *The American Numismatic Society Museum Notes* 28 (1983), 195–206.

Cofta-Broniewska, Aleksandra. "Wczesnośredniowieczna warzelnia soli w Inowrocławiu" [Early medieval salt-work in Inowrocław], *Ziemia Kujawska* 4 (1974), 5–13.

Dannenberg, Hermann. *Die deutschen Münzen der sächsischen und fränkischen Kaiserzeit*, vol. 2. Darmstadt: Scientia Verlag, 1967.

Dworsatschek, Mariusz. *Władysław II Wygnaniec [Władysław II the Exile].* Kraków: *Universitas*, 2009.

Esty, Warren W. "The Geometric Model for Estimating the Number of Dies," in *Quantifying Monetary Supplies in Greco-Roman Times*, edited by François de Callataÿ, pp. 43–58. Bari: Edipuglia, 2011.

Gooch, Megan Laura. Money and Power in the Viking Kingdom of York, 895–954, doctoral thesis, Durham: Durham University, 2011; available at http://etheses.dur.ac.uk/3495/ (accessed 27 July 2020).

Good, Irving J. "The Population Frequencies of Species and the Estimation of Population Parameters," *Biometrika* 40 (1953), no. 3–4, 237–264.

Gumowski, Marian. *O grzywnie i monecie piastowskiej, [On the Piast Grzywna and Coins], Rozprawy Akademii Umiejętności. Wydział Historyczno-Filozoficzny*, 2nd series, vol. 26, pp. 278–371. Kraków: Akademia Umiejętności, 1908.

Gumowski, Marian. *Corpus Nummorum Poloniae, vol. 1: Monety X i XI w. [Coins from 10th and 11th Centuries].* Kraków: Polska Akademia Umiejętności, 1939.

Horsnæs, Helle W., Jens, Ch. *Moesgaard, and Michael Märcher, Denar til daler. Danmarks mønthistorie indtil 1550 [Denar to daler. The history of Danish coins to 1550].* København: Danmarks Nationalbank, 2018.

Hunka, Jan. *Mince Arpádovcov z rokov 1000–1301. Ich podiel na vývoji hospodárstva stredovekého Slovenska [The Arpad dynasty coins from 1000–1301. Their Role in the Development of Medieval Slovakia´s Economy].* Nitra: Archeologický ústav, Slovenská akadémia vied, 2013.

Huszár, Lajos. *Münzkatalog Ungarn von 1000 bis heute.* München: Battenberg, 1979.

Ilisch, Peter. "Les Monnaies du Saint-Empire du Xe et XIe Siècle: Exportation ou Circulation Interne?," *Le Bulletin de la Société française de numismatique* 71 (2016), no. 2, 49–56.

Kędzierski, Adam. "Obieg pieniężny w Kaliszu i regionie za panowania Władysława Hermana oraz Zbigniewa" [Money circulation in Kalisz and its region under the rule of dukes: Władysław Herman and Zbigniew], in *Kalisz na przestrzeni wieków: Konferencja naukowa pod przewodnictwem prof. dr hab. Henryka Samsonowicza [Kalisz over Centuries. Scientific Conference under the Chairmanship of Prof. Henryk Samsonowicz]*, edited by Tadeusz Baranowski and Andrzej Buko, pp. 117–143. Kalisz: IAE PAN, 2013.

Kędzierski, Adam and Dariusz Wyczółkowski. "Skarb placków srebrnych z Kalisza-Dobrzeca. Nowe możliwości badawcze problemu srebra lanego" [The hoard of silver clumps of Kalisz-Dobrzec. New research possibilities for the problem of cast silver], in *Nummi et Humanitas. Studia ofiarowane Profesorowi Stanisławowi Suchodolskiemu w 80 rocznicę urodzin [Nummi et Humanitas. Studies Dedicated to Prof. Stanisław*

Suchodolski for his 80th Birthday], edited by Mateusz Bogucki, Witold Garbaczewski, and Grzegorz Śnieżko, pp. 331–351. Warszawa: IAE PAN, 2017.

Kiersnowski, Ryszard. "Główne momenty rozwoju środków wymiany na Pomorzu wczesnofeudalnym" [The development of means of exchange in early feudal Pomerania], *Wiadomości Archeologiczne* 23 (1956), no. 3, 229–251.

Kiersnowski, Ryszard. *Pieniądz kruszcowy w Polsce wczesnośredniowiecznej [Metal Money in Early Medieval Poland]*. Warszawa: Państwowe Wydawnictwo Naukowe, 1960.

Kilger, Christoph. *Pfennigmärkte und Währungslandschaften. Monetarisierungen im sächsisch-slawischen Grenzland ca. 965–1120*. Stockholm: Royal Swedish Academy of Letters, History and Antiquities, Stockholm Numismatic Institute at the Stockholm University, 2000.

Kluge, Bernd. *Deutsche Münzgeschichte von der späten Karolingerzeit bis zum Ende der Salier (ca. 900 bis 1125)*. Sigmaringen: Thorbecke, 1991.

Kuklo, Cezary. *Demografia Rzeczypospolitej przedrozbiorowej [The Demography of Pre-Partition Polish-Lithuanian Commonwealth]*. Warszawa: DiG, 2009.

Lalik, Tadeusz. "Märkte des 12. Jahrhunderts in Polen," *Kwartalnik Historii Kultury Materialnej* 10 (1962), no. 1–2, 364–367.

Leciejewicz, Lech. "Za denara otrzymasz wóz świeżych śledzi…" [You can get a cart of fresh herring for a denarius…], in *Nummus et Historia. Pieniądz Europy średniowiecznej [Nummus et Historia. Money of Medieval Europe]*, edited by Stefan K. Kuczyński and Stanisław Suchodolski, pp. 103–109. Warszawa: Polskie Towarzystwo Archeologiczne i Numizmatyczne, 1985.

Leciejewicz, Lech. "Saliny na terenie dzisiejszego miasta. Badania w 1958 r." [The saltworks within today's city. The research conducted in 1958], in *Kołobrzeg. Wczesne miasto nad Bałtykiem [Kołobrzeg. An Early Town on the Baltic Coast]*, edited by Lech Leciejewicz and Marian Rębkowski, Origines Polonorum, vol. 2, pp. 171–176. Warszawa: IAE PAN, 2007.

Łyszkowski, Jakub. "Odzwierciedlenie obiegu pieniężnego we wczesnym średniowieczu przez znaleziska drobne" [Monetary circulation in the early middle ages as reflected by small finds], *Wiadomości Numizmatyczne* 50 (2006), no. 1, 3–26.

Macháček, Jiří and Jan Videman. "Monetisation of Early Medieval Moravia in the Light of New Archaeological Discoveries in the Lower Dyje Region (Czech Region)," in *Economies, Monetisation and Society in the West Slavic Lands 800–1200 AD*, edited by Mateusz Bogucki and Marian Rębkowski, pp. 177–200. Szczecin: IAE PAN, 2013.

Metcalf, David M. "Some Further Reflections on the Volume of the German coinage in the Salian Period (1024–1125)," in *Fernhandel und Geldwirtschaft. Beiträge zum deutschen Münzwesen in sächsischer und salischer Zeit. Ergebnisse des Dannenberg-Kolloquiums 1990*, edited by Bernd Kluge, pp. 55–72. Sigmaringen: Thorbecke, 1993.

Nakielski, Witold. "Propozycja nowej atrybucji monet śląskich przełomu XI i XII w. w świetle depozytu z miejscowości Kopacz gm. Złotoryja" [A proposed new attribution of Silesian coins from the late 11th and early 12th centuries in light of the deposit from Kopacz, Złotoryja Municipality], in *Studia nad Dziejami Pieniądza i Bankowości w Polsce [Studies on the History of Money and Banking in Poland], vol. 2: Pieniądz i banki na Śląsku [Money and Banks in Silesia]*, edited by Witold Garbaczewski and Roman Macyra, pp. 147–184. Poznań: Muzeum Narodowe, 2012.

Radoměrský, Pavel. "České, moravské a slezské nálezy mincí údobí denárového" [Finds of coins of the denar period in Bohemia, Moravia and Silesia], in *Nálezy mincí v Čechách, na Moravě a ve Slezsku [Finds of coins in Bohemia, Moravia and Silesia]*, vol. 2, edited by Emanuela Nohejlová-Prátová, pp. 7–73. Praha: Československá akadémia vied, 1956.

Rosik, Stanisław. *Bolesław Krzywousty [Bolesław Wrymouth]*. Wrocław: Chronicon, 2013.

Sellwood, David. "Medieval Minting Techniques," *British Numismatic Journal* 31 (1962), 57–65.

Sobietzky, Gerd. "Der Denarfund von Stolpe II/Usedom," *Bodendenkmalpflege im Mecklenburg-Vorpommern* 59 (2012), 89–106.

Stronczyński, Kaźmirz. *Pieniądze Piastów od czasów najdawniejszych do roku 1300. Rozbiorem źródeł spółczesnych i wykopalisk oraz porównaniem typów menniczych objaśnione [Piast's Money from the Oldest Times to the 1300. Explained with the Contemporary Sources and Finds Analyses and Comparison of Coin Types]*. Warszawa: 1847.

Suchodolski, Stanisław. *Mennictwo polskie w XI i XII wieku [Mintage in Poland in the 11th and 12th Centuries]*. Wrocław: Ossolineum, 1973.

Suchodolski, Stanisław. "Kult św. Wacława i św. Wojciecha przez pryzmat polskich monet z wczesnego średniowiecza" [The cult of St Wenceslas and St Adalbert of Prague through the prism of Polish early medieval coins], in idem, *Numizmatyka średniowieczna. Moneta źródłem archeologicznym, historycznym i ikonograficznym [Medieval Numismatics. Coin as an Archaeological, Historical and Iconographical Source]*, pp. 397–402. Warszawa: Trio, 2012a.

Suchodolski, Stanisław. "Polityka mennicza a wydarzenia polityczne w Polsce we wczesnym średniowieczu" [Coinage Policy and Political Events in Early Medieval Poland], in idem, *Numizmatyka średniowieczna. Moneta źródłem archeologicznym, historycznym i ikonograficznym [Medieval Numismatics. Coin as an Archaeological, Historical and Iconographical Source]*, pp. 335–349. Warszawa: Trio, 2012b.

Suchodolski, Stanisław. "Monety Bolesława Śmiałego w świetle skarbu znalezionego w Wiślicy" [Coins of Bolesław II Śmiały (the Bold) in light of the Wiślica Hoard], in *Studia nad Dziejami Pieniądza i Bankowości w Polsce [Studies on the History of Money and Banking in Poland]*, vol. 4: Pieniądz i banki w Małopolsce [Money and Banks in Lesser Poland], edited by Witold Garbaczewski and Roman Macyra, *pp. 51–80*. Poznań: Muzeum Narodowe, 2018.

Stanisław, Suchodolski. "Na czym polegał system renovatio monetae?" [What was the idea of renovatio monetae system?], *Biuletyn Numizmatyczny* 4 (2019), 273–285.

Śnieżko, Grzegorz. "Denary Bolesława Krzywoustego typu 1" [Denarii of Bolesław III the Wrymouth, Type 1], in *Nummi et Humanitas. Studia ofiarowane Profesorowi Stanisławowi Suchodolskiemu w 80 rocznicę urodzin [Nummi et Humanitas. Studies Dedicated to Prof. Stanisław Suchodolski for his 80th Birthday]*, edited by Mateusz Bogucki, Witold Garbaczewski, and Grzegorz Śnieżko, pp. 417–449. Warszawa: IAE PAN, 2017.

Śnieżko, Grzegorz. "Znaleziska monet Bolesława Krzywoustego na tle porównawczym" [Finds of Bolesław III Wrymouth's Coins: A Comparative Study], in *Studia nad Dziejami Pieniądza i Bankowości w Polsce [Studies on the History of Money and Banking in Poland]*, vol. 4: Pieniądz i banki w Małopolsce [Money and Banks in Lesser Poland], edited by Witold Garbaczewski and Roman Macyra, *pp. 81–112*. Poznań: Muzeum Narodowe, 2018.

Šmerda, Jan. *Denáry české a moravské. Katalog mincí českého státu od X. do počátku XIII. století [Bohemian and Moravian pennies. Catalogue of coins of the Czech state from 10th to the beginning of 13th century]*. Brno: Datel, 1996.

Tabaczyński, Stanisław. *Archeologia średniowieczna. Problemy, źródła, metody, cele badawcze [Medieval Archaeology. Problems, Sources, Methods, Research Objectives]*. Wrocław: Ossolineum, 1987.

Videman, Jan and Josef Paukert, *Moravské denáry 11. a 12. století [Moravian pennies of the 11th and 12th centuries]*. Kroměříž: Česká numismatická společnost, 2009.

Wyrozumski, Jerzy. *Państwowa gospodarka solna w Polsce do schyłku XIV wieku [State Salt Economy to the End of 14th Century]*. Kraków: Uniwersytet Jagielloński, 1968.

3 Two stages of monetisation
Periodic recoinages and coin debasement in the Czech lands

Roman Zaoral

The establishment of an independent church organisation and coin minting belong to the main attributes of European Christian realms. Both goals were reached in Bohemia in the early 970s. The Prague bishopric was founded in 973 and local coins began to be minted just a few years earlier. It is not possible to separate these, because coin minting required not only technical experience and skills, but also, first of all, the literacy of those who provided an ideological basis for the iconography of deniers. In fact, there was placed on the obverse and reverse of the oldest Bohemian coins not only the name and titles of the ruler, but also symbols of the Christian faith. The coin design demonstrated both political and economic power of its issuer, and his favour with the Christian faith. Nevertheless, looking from the perspective of the economic and social history, monetisation as a long-term process was not completed until the coin became available to the weakest segment of society.

Monetisation is a many-sided process. The aim of this paper is to shed light on two main methods (besides reminting of foreign coins and bullion) of using coinage as a monetary tax: the *renovatio monetae* system of periodic recoinages and coin debasement. In the Czech lands, the former evolved gradually during the reign of prince Vratislaus II (1061–1092), since 1085 the first king of Bohemia, and was replaced by the latter in 1300, perhaps because it was no longer regarded as an essential element of the kingdom's fiscal system. Suitable conditions for periodic recoinages existed in those countries where few types of coin were in circulation, and it was easy to distinguish between them. This monetary policy was particularly widespread in the less-developed economic systems of Central and Northern Europe. The short lifetime of coins (*deniers, bracteates, pfennigs*) was the main condition and purpose of coin renewal as an effective form of trade and inhabitants' taxation,[1] while coin debasement was primarily related to those regions of Europe (Figure 3.1) in which long-lived coins (*grossi*) circulated and where, owing to this, the mintage profit of coin issuers (*gross seigniorage*) was small.

New impulses making monetisation more intense appeared in the twelfth and thirteenth centuries when mineral resources were counted among the rulers' "regalian rights" that were supposed to generate revenues.[2] Mining was entrusted to organisations called *gewerken,* which sold a fixed percentage of the bullion they produced at a fixed price to the ruler, whose mint then had to buy it at a similarly

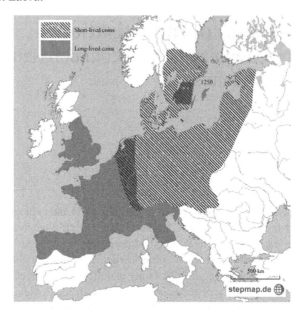

Figure 3.1 Short-lived and long-lived coinage systems in Europe, 1140–1300. Source: Roger Svensson, Periodic Recoinage as a Monetary Tax: Conditions for the Rise and Fall of the Bracteate Economy, *Economic History Review*, Vol. 69 (4) (2016), p. 1113.

fixed but higher price.[3] The interests of both manorial lords and the Papal Curia to collect rents, taxes and other fees in form of coins went hand in hand with the discovery of new deposits of precious metals and with the use of emphyteusis, "ground rent", that allowed the holder, against payment of a certain financial amount, the perpetual right to the enjoyment of his property. It was no accident that the Fourth Lateran Council (1215) banned Jews from lending money upon usury and that the Papal Curia started to collect tithes just at that time.

The process of monetisation proved to be of different intensity in different European regions. While the *grosso* as a new higher denomination was introduced in Venice in 1193 and spread rapidly in the most developed regions of southern and Western Europe, in Central Europe deniers in the form of two-sided pfennigs or one-sided bracteates circulated within the country's borders controlled by local rulers (the period of a regional pfennig).[4] In the Czech lands in the period 1222–1300, one-sided bracteates and two-sided deniers of the pfennig type were minted simultaneously.[5] Until the 1250s bracteates were mostly spread in central and northern Bohemia, while in south-western Bohemia deniers and pfennigs circulated; due to the first coin reform of Přemysl II Ottokar, duke of Austria (1251–1276) and king of Bohemia (1253–1278), dated back to the early 1250s, bracteates were minted across all regions of Bohemia and Moravia and in 1300 were replaced by Prague *groschen*.[6]

A whole range of internal and external factors conditioned the economic growth. Mining, coinage and the metal trade had a multiplying effect on the economy of East-Central Europe. New settlers became increasingly interested in Bohemia and Hungary, not only because they were seeking free arable land, but also due to the opening of new silver and gold mines. Foreign prospectors, mining entrepreneurs and financiers took technical innovations in various fields of life with them, including the Law of Emphyteusis (adopted from Roman law), which made it possible to convert agricultural products into money through paying rent. The general dissemination of fixed money rent helped to transform payment-in-kind into a monetary system. Monetary payments of peasants to manorial lords in Bohemia are documented in the first half of the twelfth century. As is evident from the deed of the Únětice church, peasants were obliged to pay 12 deniers per year, which they had to gain at the market. The value of 12 deniers was a bearable amount for peasants; it corresponded to about 14 kg of live weight, which represented one sheep or 20 hens at that time.[7]

The growing importance of coins in Bohemia in the course of the thirteenth century is evident from the maps of coin hoards (Figures 3.2–3.4) based on the published data.[8] Although hoards cannot be considered a fully reliable source because of their random character, their depositing, preservation and processing places them in the position of the selective sample. The larger number of coins, mostly of the Meissen origin, is documented from the 1230s and 1240s, while Bohemian coins markedly increased in number in the second half of the thirteenth century. Rapid money supply growth was connected with the structural changes of the society, including the funding of towns, villages, castles and monasteries, as well as with the interest of foreign miners in Bohemian silver. The maps show that coins were most often hoarded alongside major rivers (the Elbe, the Eger, the Vltava, the Berounka, the Sázava) and at the border areas with Saxony and Bavaria, from where coins penetrated.

Symbols signify different types of coins:

■ old deniers, ● bracteates, ▲ deniers of the pfennig type

Maps indicate how the territory of Bohemia was thickened with coin hoards during the thirteenth century. Colours mark the origin of particular coins and roughly distinguish, as far as it is possible, particular decades during which coins were hoarded. Red colour (Figure 3.2) indicates the oldest hoards with old deniers, mostly of Bohemian origin, concealed at the very beginning of the thirteenth century; black symbols cover all hoards closer, unspecified in terms

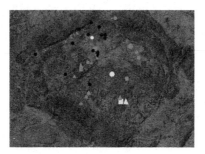

Figure 3.2 Coin hoards in Bohemia, 1200–1250. Drawn by Roman Zaoral.

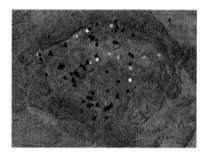

Figure 3.3 Coin hoards in Bohemia, 1250–1300. Drawn by Roman Zaoral.

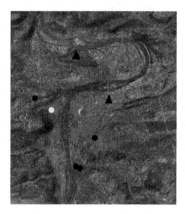

Figure 3.4 Coin hoards in Prague, 1250–1300. Drawn by Roman Zaoral.

of time, and often of foreign origin. From the placement of hoards, it is evident that the penetration of coins followed main watercourses. The size of symbols roughly reflects the size of hoards.

The circulation of short-lived coins was conditioned by several factors: exchange monopoly, geographical constraint (the invalidity of foreign coins), market right necessity, profit of the coin issuer (*gross seigniorage*) resulting from the minting of bullion, and reminting of foreign coins, frequent recoinages connected with exchange fee and the small volume of coins circulating in the less-developed economy characterised by incomplete monetisation.[9] Periodic recoinages were especially frequent in areas where one-sided bracteates were minted. In Bohemia they were carried out twice a year: on St Peter's Day (29 June) and Candlemas (2 February).[10] Bracteates had several favourable characteristics for such a policy. First, only one die was needed, which reduced production costs and time. Second, a far larger number of coins could be minted with a specific die. Third, the relatively large diameter (up to 50 mm) made it easy to distinguish between valid and invalid types. Fourth, old bracteates were easy to hammer out and overstrike. Fifth, the fragility of the bracteates was not a significant problem since these coin types were not in circulation for a long time due to frequent renewals.[11]

Recoinages always occur in a short-lived coinage system, but never in a long-lived system. On the contrary, debasement can occur in both systems. Thus, recoinages and debasement are not inherently mutually exclusive and can be applied simultaneously. Owing to large silver supply, debasement was not frequent in thirteenth-century Bohemia, as is evident from the fineness analysis of bracteates hoarded in Levínská Olešnice (Eastern Bohemia).[12] Both types of monetary taxes could have caused old coins to be driven out of circulation, either through administrative reminting (periodic recoinages) or due to Gresham's Law (debasement). The monetary standard (denomination, weight, fineness, diameter, and shape of the flan) largely remained the same at periodic recoinages, only the image of the coin was changed. An exchange fee was charged within the time of the recoinage as a way to tax trade and inhabitants. For example, in the case that the fee was four old coins for three new ones, a *gross seigniorage* reached 25%.

Periodic recoinages had positive as well as negative sides: it secured steady currency in term of weight and fineness and prevented a long-term inflation because a number of coins before and after the exchange was the same. Negative consequences can be expressed using the Fisher equation of exchange in its simplest form $MV = PT$, where M is the total amount of money in circulation, V is the average number of times each coin changes hands or its velocity of circulation, P is the average level of prices of all goods traded for money and T is the total volume of monetary transactions taking place, which was later replaced by the quantity of real output (Q). It is evident that periodical recoinages were unsuitable for the development of long-distance trade: they caused short-term fluctuations of the price level and impeded trade growth.[13] It is not known so far if and how market prices were changing, depending on the fluctuation in fineness of coins. In any case, a free price system set by the interchange of supply and demand is expected.

Attempts for comparison of prices in Bohemia, Saxony and England, which prove similar figures in the thirteenth century, show that around 1280 prices considerably increased. The thirteenth-century annals known as the Second Continuation of Cosmas mention that in the 1270s (before the price increase), it was possible to buy 50 eggs for one denier.[14] A similar price for 50 eggs can be found also in England, where the unbroken records of prices have been kept already since 1259.[15] After prices increased in 1280, the purchasing power of one denier fell to 30 eggs. Referring to Mirror of the Saxons[16] compiled in the 1220s or 1230s, according to which foreign settlers spread the Law of Emphyteusis in Central Europe, and the so-called St Paul's formulary book,[17] it is possible to show how big the differences were between town and countryside in thirteenth-century Bohemia, conditioned by the different degrees of monetisation. The mentioned hoard of Levínská Olešnice consisting of 836 bracteates (2.6 Prague marks of silver) represented a big value for peasants, because it was possible to buy three to four horses or about ten cows for it, but it was not enough for 35 ells (21 metres) of Flemish cloth, which sold at the Prague market for 6 marks.[18]

As a result of three king Ottokar II's monetary reforms, realised in the 1250s and 1260s as a follow-up to the discovery of large silver supplies in the area of the Bohemian–Moravian Highlands, coin production was decentralised into 17 Bohemian and Moravian mints, which the king leased for rent to private entrepreneurs, as he was not able to keep control over the growing quantities of precious metal.[19] After all, one of the most effective bases for the expansive development of monetisation in the Czech lands is necessary to search for an uncontrolled mass production of coins that had an inflationary character. Just in this way it was possible to multiply incomes and create conditions for enforcement of a royal domain in mining and coinage. Nevertheless, Ottokar II's attempt for broader monetary integration in the Czech and Alpine lands was only partly successful.

The process of monetisation was not linear in the thirteenth and early-fourteenth century; it developed parallel to demonetisation, manifesting itself at the market in the use of unminted metal and damaged bracteates. The profit on unminted metal seems to have been greater than has been judged until now.[20] Owing to mintage, coins brought a temporary increase in the price of silver. This seems to have been the reason why cheaper unminted metal became widespread as a means of payment at the market.[21] To merchants it represented an advantageous counter-value for imported goods. It could often be carried without high customs duties; transporting it was less expensive than coins and also provided a guarantee of greater independence from weather conditions. Jiří Majer calculated that about 90% of the silver mined in the thirteenth-century Czech lands was sold in unminted form,[22] and a similar situation has been demonstrated for Hungary as well.[23]

The use of unminted metal was established primarily by larger payments and taxes.[24] The Venice Mint allowed silver ingots to be purchased in 1273 and thus assisted in their spread. At the end of the thirteenth century, unminted silver of Central European origin was also accepted as a means of payment in Bruges and Florence. This practice was still common at the beginning of the fourteenth century. South German and Italian merchants took precious metals in various forms with them: silver ore, silver and gold jewellery, valid and devalued coins as well as silver ingots.[25] Such a variety of metal objects contained, for example, the hoard of Fuchsenhof (Upper Austria), which might be interpreted as one of many silver and gold supplies for the German trading house in Venice (*Fondaco dei Tedeschi*).[26] Its value seems to have been calculated on the basis of the weight of precious metal. Silver ingots, concealed together with whole and broken bracteates, occur in a number of hoards from Bohemia (Tetín, Lhůta, Lukovna, Kolín II, Zrnětín, Černožice), Moravia (Olomouc–Povel, Stará Říše, Uhřice, Střelice) and Silesia (Opava).[27] The hoard from Olomouc–Povel contained silver ingots solely. Gold and silver jewels in the coin hoards are also known from Stihnov and Libčany (both Eastern Bohemia) and Mnichovice near Prague.[28]

On the other hand, bracteates sometimes represented too high value for their use in small trade. The thin flan made it easy to cut them into halves (Hälblinge) or quarters (Vierlinge) when the need arose. Halved bracteates are quite common in German and Bohemian coin hoards.[29] Another economic motive might have been the minting authority hoped the fragile coins would be damaged when circulating. In that circumstance they could then be exchanged at a discount, giving the issuer an extra profit. Presumably, it was easier for people to accept fragile bracteates in areas where weakly struck half-bracteates had circulated rather than stable two-sided coins.[30] Moreover, the fact that coins did not have to circulate in the firmly established nominal exchange rate should be taken into account; supply and demand was rather determined by the exchange rate of different coins.

Payments in unminted metal are also documented in the written sources. The last will of Bruno of Schauenburg, bishop of Olomouc (1245–1281), dating to 1267 refers to unminted denier flans as a specific medium of payment. Bruno's efforts to avoid loss in the incomes of clerics caused by the mintage of light coins lay behind these measures. It is evident from the rule that wages for two hundred priests in the amount of 12 deniers each were to be paid not in a common devalued coin but in unminted metal.[31]

The weight reduction of coins was another typical feature of the Bohemian coinage. In the undated formulary book, originated presumably under the reign of Wenceslas II, king of Bohemia (1278/83–1305), there is a regulation which sets down to coin 316 deniers from a Prague mark of 253 g *(viginti sex solidos breves, et quatuor denarios de marcha argenti)* until St Peter's Day (29 June) and 364 deniers *(XXX solidos breves et quatuor denarios)* after that.[32] Using these data, it is possible to calculate that the prescribed weight of a medium-sized bracteate should have been 0.70–0.80 g, but in fact, a number of Bohemian bracteates minted in the 1260s–1280s weigh 0.60 g only, as is evident from the metrological analysis of bracteates deposited in the hoard of Levínská Olešnice.[33] Similar data are known from the hoard of Fuchsenhof (Upper Austria).[34] In that circumstance, light specimens remained in circulation for a longer time than heavy pieces, which were withdrawn from circulation and hidden. Supposing the volume of mint production was high, this barely perceptible weight difference yielded a considerable sum, making the income from mintage very profitable, despite the fact that the high fineness of coins (around 950/1000) remained unreduced.

Not only silver ingots, but also bracteate rolls served as means of payment. It seems to have been more advantageous to conceal coins as a "raw material", which bears witness to the fact that coin values were valued by the weight of their precious metal, rather than by face value. Bracteate rolls usually helped to even up required amounts paid in silver ingots. A number of bracteate rolls, mostly of Bohemian origin, form parts of the hoards from Dresden (Saxony),[35] Fuchsenhof (Upper Austria), Králice (Moravia)[36] and Černožice (Eastern Bohemia).[37] Both silver ingots and bracteates rolls did not disappear from circulation all at once. As is evident from the hoard of Černožice concealed between 1305 and 1308, they were used still in the early fourteenth century, together with Prague *groschen*.

Monetisation was closely connected with commercialisation. Failure to control supply during the initial upswing in golden and silver mining led to local money markets in East-Central Europe being flooded with coin. Overpricing of domestic products caused most of the silver and gold to pass into the hands of merchants who exported it, receiving manufactured goods from Western and southern Europe in exchange.[38] A manuscript compiled in the last third of the thirteenth century provides a detailed picture of the nature of this trade, listing the most important goods transported to Bruges. The references to Hungary, Bohemia, and Poland contain special information about the wares traded in this period: *Dou royaume de Hongrie Vient cire, or et argent plate. Dou royaume de Behaingne Vient cire, or et argent et estain. Dou royaunte de Polane Vient or et argent en plate, cire, vairs etgris et coivre.*[39]

The kings Ottokar II and Wenceslas II supported not only long-distance trade, particularly with Venice as the largest market with precious and non-ferrous metals in Europe,[40] but also foreign experts in mining and finance. An important step towards the more intense monetisation was taken with the establishment of the private Florentine trading and financial company in Bohemia in 1299 formed by Rinieri, Apardo, and Cyno called Lombardian. These partners acted as a bank and rented the office of Mint Master and a mine from the King, including royal income from smelted precious metals (the so-called *urbura*) with the aim of carrying out a complete monetary reform.[41] These Florentine financiers were able to improve their knowledge and experience thanks to the good quality of Bohemian and Moravian coins that had resulted from previous reforms.[42] They acquired the exclusive status in the framework of the Prague long-distance trade because they were exempt from the ordinance that goods of foreign provenience could only be sold with a written authentication of their origin. Thus, they could deal in luxury goods without restraints. Up to 1305, they carried on business in real estate and for a short time were charged with important powers related to economic administration. Nevertheless, the anticipation of fabulous gains from conducting business in the lands of the "silver" king clearly did not prove true, because Apardo travelled to Bohemia in 1311 to recover his claims. Many owed him money. In 1316, King John the Blind (1310–1346) acknowledged the debt of his predecessors on the Bohemian throne in the amount of 28,000 silver marks. Such a high sum was in fact unenforceable.[43]

Trade expansion in the 1290s made Prague "a city with extraordinary consumption conditions within the scope of a local market," in which a relatively populous Italian colony was settled.[44] Like in other countries, they were the Italian experts who introduced new higher denominations into circulation in the Czech lands – silver Prague *groschen* (1300) and gold Bohemian florins (1325). Thanks to their quality, both these coin types were in demand throughout late medieval Europe, as is evident from the diaries of Italian and South German merchants.[45] The problem, however, was that the large quantities of mined silver did not put pressure on local makers to produce high-quality goods which would be competitive at foreign markets. All goods of the highest quality were, in fact, possible to buy "cheap" in terms of silver. In spite of that, it is no doubt that trade accompanied with cultural exchange helped to connect different regions of Europe and to reduce differences among them, which I take as one of the most important processes of late medieval history.

New impulses for an increasing monetisation came not only from the sovereign, but also from the church. The clergy in Bohemia had paid a regular tithe to Rome since 1229.[46] Master Simon, scribe of Pope Gregory IX (1227–1241), the first known papal money collector for Bohemia, Moravia, Poland, and Pomerania, is named in a papal letter dating to 29 May 1230.[47] Collecting money was made possible thanks to the more favourable conditions which had recently been established in Bohemia. In 1222, Ottokar I, king of Bohemia (1198–1230), concluded a concordat with the church and, roughly at the same time, began to coin bracteates as a new form of quality denier.[48]

In the early 1260s, the Czech lands seem to have played an important role in the management of papal collections.[49] On 26 September 1261, Pope Urban IV (1261–1264) appointed his nuncio Peter of Pontecorvo, *clericus capellae*, archdeacon of Hradisko Monastery, to deposit money collected from Poland, Hungary, Bohemia, and Moravia at the court of Bruno of Schauenburg, bishop of Olomouc (1245–1281), and to secure its transfer to the treasury in St Mark's Basilica in Venice.[50] At the same time, the pope issued an order with the aim of providing security for money transfer from Olomouc to Venice.[51] There is no doubt that the concentration of papal collections in Olomouc stimulated long-distance trade. Precious metals became an instrument for a more effective connection of East-Central Europe with the advanced hub of the European economy. Not only mining and coinage, but also collecting money for the Papal Curia assisted the penetration of Italian financiers and merchants into East-Central Europe.

The high earnings of patricians, which had their origin in colonisation, mining business and silver trade, enabled members of the upper class, settled in Bohemia and Moravia, to purchase foreign luxury goods on a large scale. Demand was considerable. They could purchase from foreign merchants cheap (in terms of silver) cottons and linens woven in Syria and Egypt, silk,[52] painted or enamel glass manufactured in Italy and Syria,[53] as well as a whole range of spices from India and Arabia that passed through the Levant. It was possible to buy these articles in Prague and Brno so that they seem to have become available even to persons outside the royal and bishop's courts. The finds of Venetian *grossi*[54] and Venetian glass from the space of the Olomouc cathedral hillock, dated back to the 1250s and 1260s, and the privilege of building the merchant's house in Olomouc and issued in 1261 by King Ottokar,[55] support this idea of interconnection between papal collectors and merchants. The first known evidence of the use of credit in the Czech lands comes from the same time. Ottokar II's court was in 1262 in contact with the papal banker Dulcis de Burgo, merchant of Florence, who settled the debt to the Papal Curia, which originated from King Ottokar II. After he had divorced his first wife, Margaret of Austria, it was necessary to secure the legalisation of his three natural children.[56]

The process of monetisation in the Czech lands was largely completed during the fourteenth century. Its advanced degree was characterised by the growing volume of trade, the growing number of peasants paying feudal rent in money, the growth of towns, the interconnection of local and superregional market and by the development of society from Gemeinschaft to Gesellschaft. The short-lived coin of regional type became unpractical. With the growing wealth of townsmen, it was more advantageous to use *groschen* and gold coins.

*

This paper was supported by the Czech Ministry of Education, Youth and Sports – Institutional Support for Long-term Development of Research Organizations – Charles University, Faculty of Humanities, 2018.

Notes

1 Peter Spufford, "Monetary practice and monetary theory in Europe (12th–15th centuries)," in *Moneda y Monedas en la Europa Medieval (siglos XII–XV)*, edited by Esteban Hernández Esteve (Pamplona: Gobierno de Navarra, 2000), pp. 54–58. See also Roger Svensson, *Renovatio Monetae. Bracteates and Coinage Policies in Medieval Europe* (London: Spink, 2013), pp. 55–61, 244–247.

2 Hans Thieme, "Die Funktion der Regalien im Mittelalter," *Zeitschrift der Savigny-Stiftung für Rechtsgeschichte. Germanistische Abteilung* 62 (1942), pp. 57–88.

3 Oliver Volckart, *Technologies of Money in the Middle Ages: The 'Principles of Minting.'* Economic History Working Papers, No. 275 (London: London School of Economics and Political Science, 2018), p. 15.

4 Kurt Leipner, *Die Münzfunde in Sachsen aus der Zeit der regionalen Pfennigmünze (12. und 13. Jahrhundert)* (Hamburg: Museum für Hamburgische Geschichte, 1969).

5 The idea of the mintage of two-sided deniers of the Regensburg type in the Pilsen mint during the 1220s and 1230s has been recently supported by the hoard of Tetín (Central Bohemia), concealed in about 1240. See Roman Zaoral and Jiří Militký, "The hoard of Tetín (Czech Republic) in the light of currency conditions in thirteenth-century Bohemia," in *Proceedings of the XIVth International Numismatic Congress–Glasgow 2009*, vol. 2 (Glasgow: International Numismatic Commission, 2011), pp. 1664–1670; Roman Zaoral, "Der Bayerische und der Böhmische Pfennig. Grenzüberschreitende Währungsräume im Hochmittelalter," in *Tschechien und Bayern. Gegenüberstellungen und Vergleiche vom Mittelalter bis zur Gegenwart*, edited by Milan Hlavačka, Robert Luft, and Ulrike Lunow (München: Collegium Carolinum, 2016), pp. 29–50.

6 Petr Schneider, Marek Fikrle, Jiří Militký, and Roman Zaoral, *Levínská Olešnice. Nález mincí ze 13. století,* (Prague: Národní museum, 2018), pp. 23–28.

7 Zdeněk Smetánka, *Legenda o Ostojovi. Archeologie obyčejného života* (Prague: Nakladatelství Lidové noviny, 2004), pp. 74, 179–182.

8 *Nálezy mincí v Čechách, na Moravě a ve Slezsku* (henceforth *Nálezy*), vol. 2, edited by Emanuela Nohejlová-Prátová (Prague: Nakladatelství Československé akademie věd, 1956); *Numismatický sborník* 1 (1953) – 32 (2018). The lists of thirteenth-century coin hoards containing Bohemian bracteates have been recently published in Schneider et al., *Levínská Olešnice*, pp. 23–61.

9 Roger Svensson, "Periodic recoinage as a monetary tax: conditions for the rise and fall of the bracteate economy," *The Economic History Review* 69 (2016), no. 4, pp. 1108–1131, here p. 1115.

10 *Regesta diplomatica nec non epistolaria Bohemiae et Moraviae* (henceforth *RBM*), vol. 2: 1253–1310, edited by Josef Emler (Prague: Typis Grégerianis, 1882), pp. 1014–1015 (no. 2334).

11 Svensson, "Periodic recoinage," p. 1123.

12 Schneider et al., *Levínská Olešnice*, pp. 63–84.

13 Jim L. Bolton, *Money in the Medieval English Economy, 973–1489* (Manchester: Manchester University Press, 2012), pp. 3–17.

14 *Fontes rerum Bohemicarum*, vol. 2, edited by Josef Emler and Václav Vladivoj Tomek (Prague: Nákladem Musea Království českého, 1874), p. 340.

15 James E. Thorold Rogers, *A History of Agriculture and Prices in England*, vol. 1 (Oxford: Clarendon, 1866).

16 See the Czech edition of the Meissen copy of the Mirror of the Saxons used in medieval Bohemia: *Das Meißner Rechtsbuch. Historischer Kontext, linguistische Analyse, Edition*, edited by Vladimír Spáčil and Libuše Spáčilová (Olomouc: Nakladatelství Olomouc, 2010).

17 *Das St. Pauler Formular. Briefe und Urkunden aus der Zeit König Wenzel II.*, edited by Johann Loserth (Prag: Selbstverlag des Vereines und in Commission bei H. Dominicus, 1896).

18 Roman Zaoral, "Ceny a mzdy ve středověku", in *Příběhy starých mincí*, edited by Michal Mašek, Zdeněk Petráň, and Michal Lutovský (Prague: Nakladatelství Lidové noviny, 2019), pp. 146–147.

19 Ottokar II's monetary reforms are in detail discussed by Roman Zaoral, "Silver and glass in medieval trade and cultural exchange between Venice and the Kingdom of Bohemia," *The Czech Historical Review/Český časopis historický* 109 (2011), no. 2, pp. 235–261.

20 This fact was pointed out by Frederic C. Lane and Reinhold C. Mueller, *Money and Banking in Medieval and Renaissance Venice*, vol. 1: *Coins and Moneys of Account* (Baltimore–London: Johns Hopkins University Press, 1985), pp. 134–142.

21 Supply of Venice by unminted metal is in more detail analysed by Louise B. Robbert, "Il sistema monetario," in *Storia di Venezia. Dalle origini alla caduta della Serenissima*, vol 2: *L'età del comune*, edited by Giorgio Cracco and Gherardo Ortalli (Roma: Istituto della Enciclopedia Italiana Treccani, 1995), pp. 409–436. See also Ian Blanchard, *Mining, Metallurgy and Minting in the Middle Ages*, vol. 3: *Continuing Afro-European Supremacy, 1250–1450* (Stuttgart: Franz Steiner Verlag, 2005), pp. 936–970, and Alan M. Stahl, *Zecca: The Mint of Venice in the Middle Ages* (Baltimore: The Johns Hopkins University Press, 2000).

22 Jiří Majer, "Development of Quality Control in Mining, Metallurgy, and Coinage in the Czech Lands (up to the 19th Century)," in *A History of Managing for Quality: The Evolution, Trends, and Future Directions of Managing for Quality*, edited by Joseph M. Juran (Milwaukee, Wisconsin: ASQC Quality Press, 1995), pp. 264–266; Jiří Majer, *Rudné hornictví v Čechách, na Moravě a ve Slezsku* [The Ore Mining in Bohemia, Moravia and Silesia] (Prague: Libri, 2004), p. 60.

23 See, for example, Márton Gyöngyösi, "Magyar pénztörténet: 1000–1526" [Hungarian Coinage: 1000–1526], in *Magyar középkori gazdaság- és pénztörténet. Jegyzet- ésforrásgyijtemény* [Sources on the Medieval Economy and Coinage in Hungary], edited by idem (Budapest: Bölcsész Konzorcium, 2006), pp. 227–286; idem and Heinz Winter, *Münzen und Medaillen des ungarischen Mittelalters: 1000–1526* (Vienna: Kunsthistorisches Museum and Milano: Skira, 2007).

24 The unpunished use of unminted metal is documented, for example, in the report of the so-called Saar memorials from 1250, according to which a magnate weighed out 10 marks of gold and 104 marks of silver to his son-in-law. *Fontes rerum Bohemicarum*, vol. 2, p. 528.

25 Klaus Fischer, *Regensburger Hochfinanz. Die Krise einer europäischen Metropole* (Regensburg: Universitätsverlag Regensburg, 2003), p. 185. Fine silver and gold ingots were changed into Venetian *grossi* and ducats even later, as is evident from the accounting book of the Runtinger family of Regensburg, dated back to 1383–1407. Cf. Franz Bastian, *Das Runtingerbuch 1383–1407 und verwandtes Material zum Regensburger-südostdeutschen Handel und Münzwesen*, vols 1–3 (Regensburg: Bosse, 1935–1944).

26 Roman Zaoral, "Die böhmischen und mährischen Münzen des Schatzfundes von Fuchsenhof," in *Der Schatzfund von Fuchsenhof*, edited by Bernhard Prokisch and Thomas Kühtreiber (Linz: Bibliothek der Provinz, 2004), pp. 130–132.

27 Josef Petrtyl, "Funkce slitkového stříbra v našich zemích ve 13. století", in *Sborník II. numismatického symposia 1969* (Brno: Moravské museum, 1976), pp. 85–105. See also *Der Schatzfund von Fuchsenhof*, pp. 83–88, 289–291, 666–689.

28 *Nálezy*, vol. 2, p. 80 (no. 1753), p. 81 (no. 1762), p. 88 (no. 1804). See also František Šebek, "K libčanskému nálezu brakteátů", *Numismatické listy* 27 (1972), pp. 105–108; František Cach, *Nejstarší české mince*, vol. 3 (Prague: Česká numismatická společnost, 1974), p. 69.

29 See, for example, the hoard of České Budějovice II. *Nálezy*, vol. 2, pp. 84–85 (no. 1784); Pavel Radoměrský, "Studie k českému mincovnictví 13. století. Nález brakteátů v Českých Budějovicích z r. 1936 a otázka českobudějovické mincovny ve 13. století" [A study of the mintage in 13th-century Bohemia and the question of the mint in České Budějovice], *Časopis Národního muzea* 135 (1966), pp. 5–24.

30 Svensson, "Periodic recoinage," pp. 1123–1124.

31 *Závěť olomouckého biskupa Bruna z roku 1267*, edited by Jindřich Šebánek (Ostrava: Městský archiv, 1967), pp. 17, 25. See also Jiří Sejbal, "Příspěvek k metrologickým základům moravského mincovnictví 13. století", *Numismatický sborník* 11 (1970), pp. 5–11.

32 *RBM*, vol. 2, pp. 1014–1015 (no. 2334); Libor Jan, *Václav II. a struktury panovnické moci* (Brno: Matice moravská, 2006), p. 93; Libor Jan, *Václav II. Král na stříbrném trůnu, 1283–1305* (Prague: Argo, 2015), pp. 485–486.

33 Schneider et al., *Levínská Olešnice*, p. 28.

34 For example, 46% of 164 examined specimens of one coin type Cach 820 minted in the 1260s ranged within the weight span 0.50–0.69 g, 36% reached the prescribed parameters (0.70–0.80 g) and only 18% surpassed this regulation (0.81–0.95 g). See Roman Zaoral, "Die böhmischen und mährischen Münzen," pp. 95–132; idem, "Das böhmische und mährische Münzwesen des 13. Jahrhunderts im Licht des Schatzfundes von Fuchsenhof (Österreich)," in *XIII Congreso Internacional de Numismática, Madrid 2003. Actas–Proceedings–Actes*, vol. 2 (Madrid: Ministerio de Cultura, 2005), pp. 1418–1419.

35 Günther Kurt, "Der Brakteatenfund von Dresden," *Arbeits- und Forschungsberichte zur Sächsischen Bodendenkmalspflege* 1 (1951), pp. 201–241.

36 Cach, *Nejstarší české mince*, p. 78.

37 Věra Němečková and Jiří Sejbal, *Nález mincí a slitkového stříbra z Černožic* (Hradec Králové: Univerzita Hradec Králové a Muzeum východních Čech, 2006).

38 Bálint Hóman, "La Circolazione delle monete d'oro in Ungheria dal X al XIV secolo e la crisi europea dell' oro nel secolo XIV," *Rivista italiana di numismatica*, 2nd Series 5 (1922), pp. 109–156, here pp. 134 and 140.

39 *Hansische Urkundenbuch*, vol. 3, edited by Konstantin Höhlbaum (Halle: Verlag der Buchhandlung des Waisenhauses, 1882–1886), p. 419.

40 On trade between Bohemia and Italy see Zaoral, "Silver and glass," pp. 235–261.

41 Jan, *Václav II. a struktury*, pp. 144–146. See also Winfried Reichert, "Oberitalienische Kaufleute und Montanunternehmer in Ostmitteleuropa während des 14. Jahrhunderts," in *Hochfinanz. Wirtschaftsräume. Innovationen. Festschrift für Wolfgang von Stromer*, vol. 1, edited by Uwe Bestmann, Franz Irsigler, and Jürgen Schneider (Trier: Auenthal, 1987), pp. 269–356; Winfried Reichert, "Mercanti e monetieri italiani nel regno di Boemia nella prima metà del XIV secolo," in *Sistema di rapporti ed élites economiche in Europa (secoli XII–XVII)*, edited by Mario Del Treppo (Napoli: Liguori, 1994), pp. 337–348.

42 Ivo Pánek, "Das Münzvermächtnis des 13. Jahrhunderts in Böhmen," *Numismatický sborník* 12 (1973), pp. 65–74.

43 Jan, *Václav II. a struktury*, pp. 147–148.

44 Peter Spufford, *Power and Profit: The Merchant in Medieval Europe* (London: Thames & Hudson, 2002), p. 134.

45 For example, Francesco Balducci Pegolotti, *La pratica della mercatura*, edited by Allan Evans (Cambridge, Mass.: The Mediaeval Academy of America, 1936), pp. 60, 81. See also Lucia Travaini, *Monete, mercanti e matematica. Le monete medievali nei trattati di aritmetica e nei libri di mercatura* (Roma: Jouvence, 2003).

46 The fundamental work on the Papal Curia and the church administration of the pre-Hussite Czech lands has been published by Kamil Krofta, "Kurie a církevní správa zemí českých v době předhusitské", *Český časopis historický* 10 (1904), pp. 15–36, 125–132, 249–275; 12 (1906), pp. 7–34, 178–191; 14 (1908), pp. 18–34.

47 *RBM*, vol. 1, edited by Karel Jaromír Erben (Prague: Haase, 1855), p. 356 (no. 759).

48 The conditions under which the first Bohemian bracteates began to be coined within the Meissen-Bohemian monetary union have been analyzed by Roman Zaoral, "Die Anfänge der Brakteatenwährung in Böhmen," in *XII. Internationaler Numismatischer Kongress – Berlin 1997. Akten – Proceedings – Actes*, vol. 2, edited by Bernd Kluge and Bernhard Weisser (Berlin: Staatliche Museen zu Berlin, 2000), pp. 993–999.

49 Roman Zaoral, "The Management of Papal Collections and Long-Distance Trade in the Thirteenth-Century Czech Lands," *Mélanges de l'École française de Rome: Moyen Âge* 127 (2015), no. 2, http://mefrm.revues.org/2732 (accessed 27 April 2020).
50 *RBM*, vol. 2, pp. 125–126 (no. 328).
51 *RBM*, vol. 2, p. 141 (no. 368).
52 Helena Březinová, *Textilní výroba v českých zemích ve 13.–15. století* (Praha: Ústav pro pravěk a ranou dobu dějinnou, Filozofická fakulta UK, 2007), pp. 96–98.
53 The written evidence of the Venetian glass trade in Prague at the end of the thirteenth century is traced by František Graus, "Die Handelsbeziehungen Böhmens zu Deutschland und Österreich im 14. und zu Beginn des 15. Jahrhunderts," *Historica* 2 (1960), pp. 77–110, here p. 94 note 119. The finds of Venetian and Islamic glass in Bohemia and Moravia have been published by Hedvika Sedláčková, "Ninth- to Mid-16th-Century Glass Finds in Moravia," *Journal of Glass Studies* 48 (2006), pp. 191–224; Eva Černá and Jaroslav Podliska, "Sklo – indikátor kulturních a obchodních kontaktů středověkých Čech", in *Odorik z Pordenone: Z Benátek do Pekingu a zpět – Odoric of Pordenone: From Venice to Peking and Back*, edited by Petr Sommer and Vladimír Liščák (Prague: Filosofia, 2008), pp. 237–256.
54 Vít Dohnal, "Gotická studna u svatováclavské katedrály v Olomouci", *Zprávy Krajského vlastivědného muzea v Olomouci* 260 (1989), pp. 3–4; Vít Dohnal, *Olomoucký hrad v raném středověku*, vol. 1 (Olomouc: Esmedia DTP, 2001), p. 291, fig. 72.
55 *RBM*, vol. 2, p. 126 (no. 330).
56 *RBM*, vol. 2, p. 146 (no. 374).

Bibliography

Primary sources

Vladimír Spáčil and Libuše Spáčilová (ed.)*Das Meißner Rechtsbuch. Historischer Kontext, linguistische Analyse*. Nakladatelství Olomouc: Olomouc, 2010.

Das St. Pauler Formular. *Briefe und Urkunden aus der Zeit König Wenzel II.*, edited by Johann Loserth. Prag: Selbstverlag des Vereines und in Commission bei H. Dominicus, 1896.

Josef Emler and Václav Vladivoj Tomek *Fontes rerum Bohemicarum*, vol. 2. Prague: Nákladem Musea Království českého, 1874.

Konstantin Höhlbaum (ed.). *Hansische Urkundenbuch*, vol. 3. Halle: Verlag der Buchhandlung des Waisenhauses, 1882–1886.

Emanuela Nohejlová-Prátová (ed.) *Nálezy mincí v Čechách, na Moravě a ve Slezsku [The coin hoards in Bohemia, Moravia and Silesia]*, vol. 2. Prague: Nakladatelství Československé akademie věd, 1956.

Francesco Balducci Pegolotti. *La pratica della mercatura*, edited by Allan Evans. Cambridge, MA: The Mediaeval Academy of America, 1936.

Josef Emler (ed.). *Regesta diplomatica nec non epistolaria Bohemiae et Moraviae*, vol. 2: 1253–1310. Prague: Typis Grégerianis, 1882.

James E. Rogers. *A History of Agriculture and Prices in England*, vol. 1. Oxford: Clarendon, 1866.

Šebánek Jindřich (ed.). *Závěť olomouckého biskupa Bruna z roku 1267 [The Testimony of Bruno, Bishop of Olomouc, 1267]*. Ostrava: Městský archiv, 1967.

Secondary literature

Bastian, Franz. *Das Runtingerbuch 1383–sw1407 und verwandtes Material zum Regensburger-südostdeutschen Handel und Münzwesen*, vols 1–3. Regensburg: Bosse, 1935–1944.

Blanchard, Ian. *Mining, Metallurgy and Minting in the Middle Ages, vol. 3: Continuing Afro-European Supremacy, 1250–1450.* Stuttgart: Franz Steiner Verlag, 2005.

Bolton, Jim L. *Money in the Medieval English Economy, 973–1489.* Manchester: Manchester University Press, 2012.

Březinová, Helena. *Textilní výroba v českých zemích ve 13.–15. století [Textile Manufacture in the Czech Lands in 13th–15th Centuries].* Praha: Ústav pro pravěk a ranou dobu dějinnou, Filozofická fakulta UK, 2007.

Cach, František. *Nejstarší české mince [The Oldest Bohemian Coins],* vol. 3. Prague: Česká numismatická společnost, 1974.

Černá, Eva, and Jaroslav Podliska, "Sklo – indikátor kulturních a obchodních kontaktů středověkých Čech" [Glass – the indicator of cultural and trade contacts of medieval Bohemia], in *Odorik z Pordenone: Z Benátek do Pekingu a zpět – Odoric of Pordenone: From Venice to Peking and Back,* edited by Petr Sommer and Vladimír Liščák (Prague: Filosofia, 2008), pp. 237–256.

Bernhard, Prokisch and Thomas, Kühtreiber. (eds.). *Der Schatzfund von Fuchsenhof.* Linz: Bibliothek der Provinz, 2004.

Dohnal, Vít. *Olomoucký hrad v raném středověku [The Olomouc Castle in the Early Middle Ages],* vol. 1. Olomouc: Esmedia DTP, 2001.

Dohnal, Vít., "Gotická studna u svatováclavské katedrály v Olomouci" [A Gothic well at the site of St Wenceslas Cathedral in Olomouc]. *Zprávy Krajského vlastivědného muzea v Olomouci* 260 (1989), pp. 1–7.

Fischer, Klaus. *Regensburger Hochfinanz. Die Krise einer europäischen Metropole.* Regensburg: Universitätsverlag Regensburg, 2003.

Graus, František. "Die Handelsbeziehungen Böhmens zu Deutschland und Österreich im 14. und zu Beginn des 15. Jahrhunderts", *Historica* 2 (1960), pp. 77–110.

Günther, Kurt. "Der Brakteatenfund von Dresden", *Arbeits- und Forschungsberichte zur Sächsischen Bodendenkmalspflege* 1 (1951), pp. 201–241.

Gyöngyösi, Márton, "Magyar pénztörténet: 1000–1526" [Hungarian Coinage: 1000–1526], in *Magyar középkori gazdaság- és pénztörténet. Jegyzet- ésforrásgyijtemény [Sources on the Medieval Economy and Coinage in Hungary],* edited by Márton Gyöngyösi (Budapest: Bölcsész Konzorcium, 2006), pp. 227–286.

Gyöngyösi, Márton, and Heinz Winter. *Münzen und Medaillen des ungarischen Mittelalters: 1000–1526.* Vienna: Kunsthistorisches Museum and Milano: Skira, 2007.

Hóman, Bálint. "La Circolazione delle monete d'oro in Ungheria dal X al XIV secolo e la crisi europea dell'oro nel secolo XIV," *Rivisita italiana di numismatica,* 5 (1922), pp. 109–156.

Jan, Libor. *Václav II. Král na stříbrném trůnu, 1283–1305 [Wenceslas II: The King on the Silver Throne, 1283–1305].* Prague: Argo, 2015.

Jan, Libor. *Václav II. a struktury panovnické moci [Wenceslas II and the Structures of Sovereign Power].* Brno: Matice moravská, 2006.

Krofta, Kamil. "Kurie a církevní správa zemí českých v době předhusitské" [Curia and church administration of the Czech Lands in the pre–Hussite period], *Český časopis historický* 10 (1904), pp. 15–36, 125–132, 249–275; 12 (1906), pp. 7–34, 178–191; 14 (1908), pp. 18–34.

Lane, Frederic C., and Mueller, Reinhold C. *Money and Banking in Medieval and Renaissance Venice, vol. 1: Coins and Moneys of Account.* Baltimore–London: Johns Hopkins University Press, 1985.

Leipner, Kurt. *Die Münzfunde in Sachsen aus der Zeit der regionalen Pfennigmünze (12. und 13. Jahrhundert).* Hamburg: Museum für Hamburgische Geschichte, 1969.

Majer, Jiří. *Rudné hornictví v Čechách, na Moravě a ve Slezsku [The Ore Mining in Bohemia, Moravia and Silesia]*. Prague: Libri, 2004.

Majer, Jiří. "Development of Quality Control in Mining, Metallurgy, and Coinage in the Czech Lands (up to the 19th Century)," in *History of Managing for Quality*, edited by Joseph M. Juran, chapter 8. Milwaukee, Wisconsin: ASQC Quality Press, 1995.

Numismatický sborník 1 (1953)–32 (2018).

Pánek, Ivo. "Das Münzvermächtnis des 13. Jahrhunderts in Böhmen," *Numismatický sborník* 12 (1973), pp. 65–74.

Josef Petrtyl. "Funkce slitkového stříbra v našich zemích ve 13. století" [The function of silver ingots in our countries in the 13th century], in *Sborník II. numismatického sympo-sia* 1969 (Brno: Moravské museum, 1976), pp. 85–105.

Radoměrský, Pavel. "Studie k českému mincovnictví 13. století. Nález brakteátů v Českých Budějovicích z r. 1936 a otázka českobudějovické mincovny ve 13. století" [A study of the mintage in 13th-century Bohemia and the question of the mint in České Budějovice], *Časopis Národního muzea* 135 (1966), pp. 5–24.

Reichert, Winfried. "Mercanti e monetieri italiani nel regno di Boemia nella prima metà del XIV secolo," in *Sistema di rapporti ed elites economiche in Europa (secoli XII–XVII)*, edited by Mario Del Treppo (Napoli: Liguori, 1994), pp. 337–348.

Reichert, Winfried. "Oberitalienische Kaufleute und Montanunternehmer in Ostmitteleuropa während des 14. Jahrhunderts," in *Hochfinanz. Wirtschaftsräume. Innovationen. Festschrift für Wolfgang von Stromer*, vol. 1, edited by Uwe Bestmann, Franz Irsigler, and Jürgen Schneider (Trier: Auenthal, 1987), pp. 269–356.

Robbert, Louise B. "Il sistema monetario," in *Storia di Venezia. Dalle origini alla caduta della Serenissima, vol 2: L'età del comune*, edited by Giorgio Cracco and Gherardo Ortalli (Roma: Istituto della Enciclopedia Italiana Treccani, 1995), pp. 409–436.

Schneider, Petr, Marek Fikrle, Jiří Militký, and Roman Zaoral. *Levínská Olešnice. Nález mincí ze 13. století [Levínská Olešnice. The 13th-Century Coin Hoard]*. Prague: Národní museum, 2018.

Šebek, František. "K libčanskému nálezu brakteátů" [The bracteates hoard of Libčany], *Numismatické Listy* 27 (1972), pp. 105–108.

Sejbal, Jiří. "Příspěvek k metrologickým základům moravského mincovnictví 13. století" [The metrological basis of the mintage in 13th-century Moravia], *Numismatický sborník* 11 (1970), pp. 5–11.

Smetánka, Zdeněk. *Legenda o Ostojovi. Archeologie obyčejného života [The Legend of Ostoja. The Archeology of Ordinary Life]*. Prague: Nakladatelství Lidové noviny, 2004.

Spufford, Peter. *Power and Profit: The Merchant in Medieval Europe*. London: Thames & Hudson, 2002.

Spufford, Peter. "Monetary practice and monetary theory in Europe (12th–15th centuries)," in *Moneda y Monedas en la Europa Medieval (siglos XII–XV)*, edited by Esteban Hernández (Pamplona: Gobierno de Navarra, 2000), pp. 53–86.

Stahl, Alan M. *Zecca. The Mint of Venice in the Middle Ages*. Baltimore: The Johns Hopkins University Press, 2000.

Svensson, Roger. "Periodic recoinage as a monetary tax: conditions for the rise and fall of the bracteate economy," *The Economic History Review* 69 (2016), no. 4, pp. 1108–1131.

Svensson, Roger. The Bracteate as Economic Idea and Monetary Instrument, *IFN Working Paper, No. 973*. Stockholm: Research Institute of Industrial Economics (IFN), 2013a.

Svensson, Roger. *Renovatio Monetae. Bracteates and Coinage Policies in Medieval Europe*. London: Spink, 2013b.

Thieme, Hans. "Die Funktion der Regalien im Mittelalter," *Zeitschrift der Savigny-Stiftung für Rechtsgeschichte. Germanistische Abteilung* 62 (1942), pp. 57–88.

Travaini, Lucia. *Monete, mercanti e matematica. Le monete medievali nei trattari di aritmetica e nei libri di mercatura*. Roma: Jouvence, 2003.

Volckart, Oliver. Technologies of Money in the Middle Ages: The 'Principles of Minting', *Economic History Working Papers, No. 275*. London: London School of Economics and Political Science, 2018.

Zaoral, Roman. "Ceny a mzdy ve středověku [Prices and Wages in the Middle Ages]," in *Příběhy starých mincí [The Stories of Old Coins]*, edited by Michal Mašek, Zdeněk Petráň, and Michal Lutovský, pp. 146–151. Prague: Nakladatelství Lidové noviny, 2019.

Zaoral, Roman. "Der Bayerische und der Böhmische Pfennig. Grenzüberschreitende Währungsräume im Hochmittelalter," in *Tschechien und Bayern. Gegenüberstellungen und Vergleiche vom Mittelalter bis zur Gegenwart*, edited by Milan Hlavačka, Robert Luft and Ulrike Lunow (München: Collegium Carolinum, 2016), pp. 29–50.

Zaoral, Roman. "Silver and glass in medieval trade and cultural exchange between Venice and the Kingdom of Bohemia," *The Czech Historical Review/Český časopis historický* 109 (2011), no. 2, pp. 235–261.

Zaoral, Roman. "Das böhmische und mährische Münzwesen des 13. Jahrhunderts im Licht des Schatzfundes von Fuchsenhof (Österreich)," in *XIII Congreso Internacional de Numismática, Madrid 2003. Actas–Proceedings–Actes*, vol. 2, edited by Carmen Alfaro Asíns, Carmen Marcos and Paloma Otero (Madrid: Ministerio de Cultura 2005), pp. 1417–1425.

Zaoral, Roman. "Die böhmischen und mährischen Münzen des Schatzfundes von Fuchsenhof," in *Der Schatzfund von Fuchsenhof*, edited by Bernhard Prokisch and Thomas Kühtreiber (Linz: Bibliothek der Provinz, 2004), pp. 95–132.

Zaoral, Roman. "Die Anfänge der Brakteatenwährung in Böhmen," in *XII. Internationaler Numismatischer Kongress–Berlin 1997. Akten–Proceedings–Actes*, vol. 2, edited by Bernd Kluge and Bernhard Weisser (Berlin: Staatliche Museen zu Berlin, 2000), pp. 993–999.

Zaoral, Roman, and Jiří Militký. "The hoard of Tetín (Czech Republic) in the light of currency conditions in thirteenth-century Bohemia," in *Proceedings of the XIVth International Numismatic Congress – Glasgow 2009*, vol. 2 (Glasgow: International Numismatic Commission, 2011), pp. 1664–1670.

4   The trade between Slesvig/Lübeck and Novgorod c. 1050 until c. 1450

Carsten Jahnke

It is good form to start an article with a *captatio benevolentiae*. Especially so in this case, with Dariusz Adamczyk and Christoph Kilger,[1] two of the most proven experts in the field of monetarisation, contributing to this volume. What can I add, when the battles of research were battled on battlegrounds which are not my own?

I have to confess that I thought long about what an historian of economic connections can contribute to the lively discussion about the monetarisation of the Baltic Sea area. What I can do is a *tour d'horizon* about the practicalities of economical contacts between the east and the west. The main focus will be directed to the question: To what extent did abstract units play a role in trade between the east and the west? And in answering, address how this may have been in pre-monetary, proto-monetary or monetary forms. In doing so, "money" will be defined as "all quantifiable objects which could be used in certain circumstances as means of payment, whether as medium of exchange (Tauschmittel), as scale of value (Wertmaßstab) or in storage means (Aufbewahrungsmittel)" following Raphaela Czech-Schneider and Karl Polanyi.[2]

But before the concrete examples can be analysed, three preconditions have to be stated:

- The trade in northern Europe from the eighth century onwards developed not, if you will follow Neil Middleton,[3] out of the black hole of a tribal society. Instead, it was shaped by developments in Arabia and Byzantium as successors of the Roman Empire. By this it is the question under what kind of presumptions the archaeological and historical finds in the Baltic Sea Areas can be interpreted.
- The basics of the transaction–cost theory[4] are also valid for the Scandinavian "Viking Age"; i.e., the Early and High Middle Ages. If you will not see the inhabitants of this area as wild and illogical barbarians, they would certainly have tried to raise the profits of their economical transactions and – in the framework of their possibilities – to minimise the transaction costs. Economical transactions and the reduction of transaction costs can withal be imbedded in different institutions like kin-relations, politics or religion[5] – and even in the field of gift-giving,[6] economical thinking, in the widest form, may have played a role.

- Out of this, the development of the important trading-emporia of the ninth and tenth centuries, and later the urban settlements in the Baltic Sea area, can be interpreted anew. Within the trade over the borders of kin-groups some hurdles have to be minimised to start interregional trade and to reduce transaction costs. Beside the search-costs (such as the knowledge of where to find vendors and goods), you will need to reduce the securing costs of trade and try to standardise the transactions (e.g., the goods, the measurements of the quantity of goods, the scale of value and the medium of exchange).

Under these points, the question of your personal security as well as that of the trade is of utmost importance for choosing trading partners, because it is relatively impractical to kill your partner in trade each time a problem occurs (and it will also hinder future possibilities). Certain principles of legal certainty and of market peace had to be found.[7] In an optimal case the market peace included ways to and from the market too.[8] This led to a concentration of trade at certain places: harbours, as places of legal certainty and peace, and markets.[9] At these markets the goods turnover will raise, which led to the possibility of multiple trade. That again would create problems for the direct barter trade. To use a classical picture: If I will barter my cow at the market for glass beads for my wife, I come into trouble when the vendor will only have a sheep instead, or when the value of the cow is higher than the value of the beads. In this case, pre- or proto-monetary developments occur. The term "proto-monetary" is defined as the standardisation of items of value in regard to weight and size whereas "pre-monetary" is defined as forms of items made in metal, whose value and scale of value is defined situational.[10]

For this development, the "wiks" of England[11] (i.e., the legally secured harbours and market-places) can be used as an example. In 935 King Æthelstan ordered that all trade-transactions over the value of 20 pennies could be conducted only in harbours or ports, under the control of the market-reeve.[12] Not only can the centralisation described above be seen in this case, but also that the King described the boundaries for the transactions in pre-monetary terms: *nene ceap … buton porte ofer XX penega*. That means that in the world of king Æthelstan in the tenth century, transactions were thought and done in a defined equivalent.

This is of interest, as a new metal-detector discovery in the city of Ribe has shown the (until now) biggest single quantity of minted scatteas in Northern Europe.[13] Initial asessment has given reason to assume that at this market scatteas were minted and given out regularly. This can, with all due caution, be interpreted that all transactions at the market of Ribe had to be undertaken using a pre-monetary equivalent. In terms of the transaction–cost theory this would have been for the trader's advantage because the "costs for searching an equivalent value" would have been low. At the same time the owner of the market would have had a regularly income, by minting and changing. In contrast the situation in the Baltic Sea area in an overall view is far from being as clear as in Ribe. But it can *cum grano salis* be stated, that the trade in the upcoming emporia in this area had been performed with pre-monetary equivalents whether it had been

Arabic dirhems, Saxon coins, scatteas or whether it has been with hacksilver, as archaeological finds indicate.[14] But these finds show only one side of the coin. If we are looking at the few, indirect sources from this time there are definitely signs of barter trade respectively proto-monetary equivalents too.

A first point to acknowledge is the basis of the trading expeditions in general, the creation of a hansa or a félag. In the Scandinavian sources an association of "merchants", willing to trade overseas, was conducted in two steps. In the first step a merchant who wanted to sail abroad (and who didn't own a ship) could ask the captain of the ship (skipper), skipdróttin, to be taken into it.[15] By this he became a farþegi, a fellow traveller, a member of the ship's society, the skipssogn.[16] But more important for the personal security of the "merchant" was his integration in the food community of his ward in the ship. By putting his supply into the stockpile of his ward the merchant became a mǫtunautre.[17] To be a mǫtunautre meant not only to share supplies, but to become a member of a legally defined social group which guaranteed personal security, defence and recovery. Important in this connection is the fact that all these traditions functioned without any value equivalent. This can be interpreted that the making of trading groups was not based on monetary processes, but on other values, like honour, or military or nautical capabilities. Similar exchange relationships can also be adumbrated in the pre-emption rights in the city of Slesvig.[18] Pre-emption rights are, as such, a bribe of the merchants to the ruler of the market for their protection. This fee descended from the earliest times of north-European trade, when the trade was conducted in the halls of the rulers and under his eyes. It was during the Middle Ages that these fees first became monetarised and impersonal.[19]

In the case of the city of Slesvig[20] the bylaw from around 1200 stated[21] that the lord of the town owned the pre-emption right and the *laudaticum* (a market fee)[22] for *marten-fur*, which was converted into a onetime fee of the furriers.[23] Marten furs were (and are) a symbol of status and an important trading good in the Baltic Sea area, especially in the trade with Novgorod. This fee could have been intended for the supply of the court. But marten furs are also, perhaps remarkably, the basis for and name of the first Novgorodian proto-monetary (and later pre-monetary) value system.[24] Before the time of the Roubel, the Novgorodians counted in *grivna*, a silver unit, of 25 respectively 100 kuna or 100 up to 400 veverica respectively belka. *Grivna* originally meant "necklace", kuna "marten-fur", and veverica and belka "squirrel fur" (petit gris).[25] In the course of the eleventh century these terms became the name of silver equivalents, whose weight was geared to German and Arabic examples. The pre-emption right of the Slesvig town lord can by this be interpreted in two ways: in the west, this would have been a fee for the supply of the court, and in the east, a scale of value. The latter interpretation is not totally irrelevant, because Slesvig was the final destination of the Novgorodian trading system.

The trade between the Jutian peninsula and Novgorod alone illustrates the problems and developments of monetisation in the Baltic Sea area, because here merchants from different systems and development stages met. It is *communis opinio* that the Baltic Sea area in the Viking age passed through an up-and-down-movement from Arabic dirhem to weighted money (Gewichtsgeld) with hacksilver to a coin-economy (Münzgeldwirtschaft),[26] whereas Novgorod for a long time stood still in the proto-monetary form of the *grivna* of 150 g silver.[27]

Of more interest for our *tour d'horizon* are the developments in Westfalia, Saxony and later in the Elbslavonian areas east of the river Elbe. Here, landscapes of pennies (Pfenniglandschaften), as Christoph Kilger has called them, developed.[28] In this area the importance of minted coins as means of payments and abstract monetary systems as units of account increased. In the course of the eleventh century a system developed in the Holy Roman Empire in which local lords forced the use of minted silver at their marketplaces, whereas weighted silver dominated the interregional trade, as Heiko Steuer[29] and Christoph Kilger have shown.

It can be noted, however, that counting in abstract units of money began its triumphant success in commercial circles from that time onwards. The prerequisite for this new kind of trade was the securing and control of the standard of minted silver coins. It is therefore no wonder that the burghers of Slesvig in the time between 1050 and 1150[30] worked hard to the intendancy of the urban mint:

> *Secunda est, ut argentum ciuitatis in Sleswicensium sit potestate et arbitrio, quale debeat esse, hoc tamen pacto, ut plus solido cupri de una marca nequeat comburi.*
>
> *Tercia est, cum rex nouam monetam iusserit fieri, ciues tantum debent regi offere, quantum confert monetarius; postea ipsi fieri faciant monetam secundum uelle regis, et sint prouidi inspectores, ne aliqua falsitas in nummis fiat.*
>
> [It should furthermore be known, that secondly the silver of the city is under the power and arbitrariness of the citizens of Slesvig, but under the condition that pro Mark silver not more than one shilling (solidus) copper, is to be melted. Thirdly, that when the citizens, by the order of the king, issue a new coin they discharge the same amount to the king as to the master of the mint, only then they are allowed to carry this coin and they are bound to summon overseers, so that no forgeries are amongst the coins.][31]

These words of paragraph 31 of the Slesvig bylaw indicate clearly that the king and the burghers attempted to keep the standard of the mint. This standard was of particular importance because the interregional trade since the twelfth century was also based on monetary units. So defines the bylaw of the city of Medebach from c. 1144 that:

> *Qui pecuniam suam dat alcui concivi suo, ut inde negocietur in Datia vel Rucia vel in alia regione ad utilitatem utriusque, assumere debet concives suos fideles, ut videant et sint testes huius rei.*
>
> [If someone gives his money (*pecuniam suam*) to a fellow citizen who takes it with him to Denmark or Russia or other regions for trade of reciprocal benefit, so this burgher is obligated to consult reliably fellow citizens who will see and can attest to this transaction.][32]

It is the monetary equivalent that dominates the reasoning of trade to Russia via Slesvig (Denmark), but until the sixteenth century it was common practice to pay the deposit in firms, in kind or goods only, to be accounted for in monetary units.[33] So formulated e.c. the bylaw of the city of Soest in the same chapter as in Medebach, the wording is in terms of goods (*bona*) instead of money (*pecunia*).[34] But only the conversion of the value of goods into scales of values made the new form of trading companies of the twelfth and thirteenth centuries, the commission business,[35] possible. In these companies the trade was no longer conducted by the merchant himself, but instead by third parties. By this, the merchants were able to widen their trading radius and to spin a network of trade over the whole of Europe.

With the increasing influx of merchants into the Baltic Sea area accounting in abstract units, and with the increasing development of urban settlements with Saxon bylaw, abstract accounting using monetary units became increasingly common. The mark became, at least in the western part of the area, the predominant unit of account. In the Lübeck chronicle of Arnold of Lübeck, the mark pennies (mark denarium) appear for the first time at the end of the twelfth century.[36] When Duke Henry the Lion founded the Abbey of St John in the city of Lübeck in the 1170s, he gave 100 M den. annually as an income.[37] From then on, the use of the mark denariorum can be taken for granted in the Lübeck written sources, just as the use of the pound in Hamburg. It looks like the monetary penetration of this area started in the cities. This corresponds to the tendencies in other areas of the Holy Roman Empire. There the use of monetary units was accepted as normal since no later than twelfth century.[38]

An inspection of the Wismar register of debts from 1272 to 1297 shows, however, that settlements in mark denariorum were only used within the city or between burghers of different cities. Not one settlement in mark denariorum was made between burghers and people of the countryside.[39] But the slow transition from inter-urban accounting in mark to a regional phenomenon can be shown in the oldest Lübeck merchant ledger from 1333.[40] The Lübeck burghers Widekin and Johannes Klingenberg owned manors in the countryside of Mecklenburg, which had to pay duties in grain. Those who were liable for duties counted and paid in grain, but when they bought goods in the town, they accounted for them in mark denariorum. So Tale Wilteres and her sons in 1333 bought one piece of cloth and other goods from the Klingenberg's in a value of 3 M minus 5 shilling.[41] They paid for these things in goods which were accounted for in cash; *solvi in parata pecunia*. This is one of the first steps of the coalescence of the city and its region.

Even in Denmark the mark pennies or the pound pennies occurred in some sources in the middle of the twelfth century.[42] Michael Kræmmer showed in his analysis of the use of the mark that mark pennies were commonly exchanged in Denmark since the second half of that century.[43] By using written sources he states that the monetarisation of Denmark happened between 1150 and 1250 – parallel with the extended wave of new urban foundations.[44] So registered *exempli causa* the Danish Census Book from the beginning of the thirteenth century on the one side mentions royal revenues from the mints in Slesvig and Roskilde.[45]

But on the other side were the accounts used for taxes in goods, as they were accounted for in mark denariorum. This corresponds to the appearance of the first army of mercenaries in Denmark in 1134, which also can be seen as a driving factor of monetarisation of the nobility.[46]

This result, however, is in total contrast to the findings of archaeologists and numismatics. Their findings of regulated coins went back as far as the 1060s. This discrepancy has not yet been solved. It is the same discrepancy we can see in the interpretation of paragraph 31 of the Slesvig bylaw, mentioned above. If this privilege can be dated to the 1050s,[47] it would be parallel to the results of the archaeologists. If we are dating this chapter to the middle of the twelfth century it would be parallel to the first mentions of the mark penny in the written Danish material.

In regard to this development attention should be paid to the fact that even when the new cities with Saxon law around the coast of the Baltic Sea[48] were the driving forces, they pushed the old centres – and they adapted the new possibilities eagerly and successfully. So, can we, for example, see an assimilation of old Danish merchant-elites into the Saxon and Westfalian groups of merchants in the new towns.[49] By this they also adapted the new forms of accounting and use of money, Helmich and Johannes Grove took a loan of 200 M den. (mark pennies) from Christian of N. and Henning Holdensen, burgher in Næstved, which was registered in the Hamburg book of debts. In the case of refunds, a written order from the city of Næstved, *litteras civitatis Nestwede ex parte eorum*, could also be used.[50] This shows that many of the instruments of money transfer and accounting were already established in these areas at the end of the thirteenth century.

With the first handed-down books of debts in the Western Baltic Sea area from the 1250s onwards, a fully developed system of debts basing on the mark denariorum can be seen. It was likewise used by Saxon, Westfalian and Danish merchants, shippers and elites. By 1250 the world of international trade in this area was totally monetarised, even if though the council of Wismar was still using weighted sterlings, *sterlingos ponderatas* as late as 1290.[51] Around the same time, however, it was common practise when in 1262 the Rostock citizen John of Næstved registered that he had paid the English merchants Wilhelm Prest and Adam Scheth 6 last grain and at two dates £ 11 sterling, whereat the pound sterling was explicitly called *istius pecunie*.[52]

It follows an economical logic that the regional trade is orientated at the bigger port towns and follows the rules of transaction–cost theory. Following this logic it is clear that commercial hurdles were reduced. In the case of the Western Baltic Sea area, it is the city of Lübeck which took over the role of a port town from Slesvig.[53] Not only did the city at the River Trave become the centre for the new city-laws,[54] the Lübeck law, but also the mark Lübeck became the key currency of this region. Already in the 1250s the town book of Wismar stated, without any comment, that Nonno von Krukow had a pawn of 60-mark Lübeck pennies in the house of Theoderich von Pattenhusen in Wismar,[55] even though the city itself had its own coin and mint. But at the same time, the city considered beside this also *pondus Lubicensis monete*.[56]

In regard of the dominance of the city of Lübeck, it is no wonder that the cities tried to standardise the currency of the western Baltic area. In 1255 the cities of Hamburg and Lübeck agreed to a standardisation of the coinage.[57] Both cities tried to accomplish the same mint price and a mutual circulation of their coins. This standardisation movement was extended until the fourteenth century. The precondition for this was that many cities of the Lower Saxony area came into the possession of their own mint until 1325 at the latest.[58] For economic reasons alone, they tried to standardise the coinage.[59] In Wismar, for example,. the old mark slavorum was replaced by a new mark, minted after the Lübeck standard,[60] and in 1379 the so called Wendian coinage union (Wendischer Münzverein) was established, which created one standard in the whole area.[61]

As in the western parts of the Baltic Sea area, the eastern parts also saw the establishment of key currencies, in this case by the coinage of Danzig and Riga, whereas the coinage of Denmark fell into decay. If we follow the written urban and economical sources, we can state that the monetarisation of the Baltic Sea area was mostly completed by the beginning of the fourteenth century. Money and coins are the common scales of value und units of accounting. But the coinage of nominals – and here I am carrying coals to Newcastle – dragged behind the theoretical recognition, only think of the minting of the mark Lübeck as late as in 1509.

But to return to the main theme of this paper, the monetarisation on the way between Slesvig/Lübeck and Novgorod, it has to be noted that the monetarisation by western examples only covered the Latin Christian areas. The system of the mark denariorum reached its borders in the Hanseatic kontor in Novgorod and the other commercial offices of the Hanse in the east. Outside of the walls of the kontor, the world was different. So envisaged the privileges of the western merchants in Novgorod beside a trade per acquisition by money (*emere pro pecunia*) mostly a barter trade (*equum pro equo dare*).[62] In regard to the monetary developments in the Baltic Sea area the *equum pro equo dare* was outdated at the end of the thirteenth century at the latest, and replaced by a monetarised commission trade; but not in Novgorod. The regulations of the kontor, the Schraen, mention *dat he vorcope unde weder cope* (that he was selling and buying), but the same chapter calls this transaction *wandelinge*; barter trade.[63] As late as in 1466 it was ordered that nobody shall sell cloth to Russians, but that it shall be *dan in bute, so dat van aldinges hefft gewest*, (done in barter trade, as it has been all the time).[64] This regulation was repeated until 1514.[65]

At the same time, some Hanseatic merchants defied this – in their view, outdated – idea of barter trade. So the merchants in Flandres raised the question: if this will *prophijtlyk syn to dogende ofte nycht* (give profit or not).[66] From the point of the transaction–cost theory this behaviour promised on the first glance a minor profit. But the trade between the west and Novgorod suffered from severe linguistic problems, regarding trust and security. The mutual distrust meant that a total monetarisation of the trade was impossible.

If we are now looking at the regulations of the Hanseatic kontor in Novgorod we can find very mixed results. On the one hand, the regulations are constantly counting in Novgorodian coinage (i.e., the mark kuna), even for barter trade inside the kontor. As an example, "those who will brew with the kindlings of the kontor are to pay half a mark kuna, and those, who will bake with these kindlings, 5 kunas."[67] Even bribes were counted in kuna[68] as the salary of the carriers, unloading the ships.[69] On the other hand, there were punishments inside the kontor, and these were expressed in mark silver[70] as the salary of the (Latin) priest of the kontor.[71] The tax of the kontor, the Schot, was accounted in mark[72] as the so called hand-penny (the penny of the Holy-Ghost).[73] Taking this into account, it can be said that the monetarisation of the kontor was not complete in the sense of the transaction–cost theory. Beside the barter trade, silver was weighted,[74] and different transactions were performed in different systems. Because of this, Novgorod and the other Hanseatic offices in the east became special zones inside a mostly monetarised society.

In summary, it can be noted, that – if we follow the written sources – the monetarisation of the Baltic Sea area was driven by the needs of the merchants from the south. From the perspective of economical reasoning alone, they were interested in standardised equivalents of value. This led to the development of first pre- and later proto-monetary systems. In the end, the whole area was monetarised, starting from the cities and from there to the countryside. But whether or not this was the one and only means of distribution is questionable. The interests of the Holy Roman Church, as that of the elites, had also to be taken into account.

But striking is the fact that the extension of monetarisation in the Baltic ended at the borders of the Latin Christianity. In Novgorod – one of the most important trading centres of north-European trade – a strange ritardando can be seen: the penny reigned the world,[75] however, not everywhere.

Notes

1 Unfortunately, Christoph Kilger could not deliver his paper (editors).
2 Raphaela Czech-Schneider, *Anathemata. Weihgaben und Weihgabenpraxis und ihre Bedeutung für die Gesellschaft und Wirtschaft der frühen Griechen*, postdoctoral thesis, Westfälische Wilhelms-Universität Münster (Münster/North Rhine Westphalia, 1998), p. 211, https://repositorium.uni-muenster.de/document/miami/7a5e4944-2167-4ffb-a56b-90746b87eb1b/habilschr_czech-schneider.pdf (accessed 20 September 2019); Karl Polanyi, *Ökonomie und Gesellschaft* (Frankfurt am Main: Suhrkamp, 1979), p. 333: "Die Definition des primitiven Geldes ist von dessen Verwendung abgeleitet. Die Formen der Geldverwendung sind Bezahlung, Hortung und Tausch. Geld wird als quantifizierbare Objekte definiert, die für einen der oben genannten Verwendungsformen benützt werden."
3 Neil Middleton, "Early medieval port customs, tolls and controls on foreign trade," *Early Medieval Europe* 13 (2005), 313–358.
4 Douglass C. North, "Transaction Costs in History," *Journal of European Economic History* 14 (Winter 1985), no. 3, 557–576.
5 Polanyi, *Ökonomie und Gesellschaft*, pp. 119–236. See, in general, Andrea Maurer, "Die Institutionen des modernen Kapitalismus: Karl Polanyi contra Max Weber," in *Kapitalismus, Globalisierung, Demokratie*, edited by Katharina Hirschbrunn, Gisela Kubon-Gilke, and Richard Sturn (Marburg: Metropolis, 2017), pp. 105–133.
6 Polanyi, *Ökonomie und Gesellschaft*, p. 234.

7 Stephen E. Sachs, "Conflict Resolutions at the Medieval English Fair," in *Eine Grenze in Bewegung: private und öffentliche Konfliktlösung im Handels- und Seerecht. Une frontière mouvante: justice privée et justice publique en matières commerciales et maritimes*, edited by Albrecht Cordes and Serge Dauchy, Schriften des Historischen Kollegs. Kolloquien 81 (München: de Gruyter Oldenbourg, 2013), pp. 19–38.

8 Carsten Jahnke, "Hafen", in *Handwörterbuch zur deutschen Rechtsgeschichte*, 2nd ed., edited by Albrecht Cordes, Heiner Lück, Dieter Werkmüller, and Ruth Schmidt-Wiegand (Berlin: Erich Schmidt, 2010), cols 649–652.

9 Carsten Jahnke, "Customs and toll in the Nordic Area c. 800–1300," in *Nordic Elites in Transformation c. 1050–1250*, vol. 1: *Material Resources*, edited by Helle Vogt, Bjørn Poulsen, and Jón Viðar Sigurdsson (Oxon–New York: Routledge, 2019), pp. 183–211, here 196.

10 Czech-Schneider, *Anathemata*, p. 218, note 978.

11 Middleton, "Early medieval."

12 "Die Gesetze der Könige Eadweard I, Aethelstan, Eadmund I, Eadgar und Aethelred II.," in *Die Gesetze der Angelsachsen, herausgegeben im Auftrage der Savigny-Stiftung*, edited by Felix Lieberman, vol. 1 (Halle: Max Niemeyer, 1903), p. 156, §§ 12–13 (Æt Greatanleage).

13 Claus Feveile and Jens Christian Moesgaard, "Damhus-skatten – et fantastisk indspark til den tidlige mønthistorie," *By, Marsk og Geest* 30 (2018), 28–30.

14 Hendrik Mäkeler, "Wikingerzeitlicher Geldumlauf im Ostseeraum – Neue Perspektiven," *Quaestiones Medii Aevi Novae* 10 (2005), 121–149.

15 Hjalmar Falk, "Altnordisches Seewesen," *Wörter und Sachen. Kulturhistorische Zeitschrift* IV (1912), 1–117, here 5.

16 Max Pappenheim, "Stýrimenn und Hásetar im älteren westnordischen Seeschiffahrtsrecht," in *Deutsche Islandsforschung 1930*, vol. 1, edited by Walther Heinrich Vogt (Breslau: Ferdinand Hirt, 1930), pp. 246–282, here 257, 261 ff.

17 Max Pappenheim, "Die Speisegemeinschaft (motuneyti) im älteren westnordischen Recht," in *Ehrengabe dem deutschen Juristentage überreicht vom Verein für Lübeckische Geschichte und Altertumskunde* (Lübeck: Verlag des Vereins, 1931), pp. 1–20.

18 Jahnke, "Customs and toll," pp. 185, 192 f.

19 Jahnke, "Customs and toll," pp. 184–187.

20 "Slesvig stadsret," in *Danmarks gamle Købstadslovgivning*, vol. I: *Sønderjylland*, edited by Erik Kroman (København: Rosenkilde og Bagger, 1951), Text I, pp. 3–17.

21 Michael Gelting, "Kong Svend, Slesvig Stadsret og arvekøbet i de jyske købsteder: Spor af Danmarks ældste købstadprivilegier," in *Svend Estridsen*, edited by Lasse C. A. Sonne and Sarah Croix (Odense: Syddansk Universitetsforlag, 2016), pp. 195–216; Jahnke, Carsten. "Nyt og gammelt om Svend Estridsen," *Historisk Tidsskrift* 117 (2017), no. 1, 222–228.

22 Hildegard Adam, *Das Zollwesen im Fränkischen Reich und das spätkarolingische Wirtschaftsleben. Ein Überblick über Zoll, Handel und Verkehr im 9. Jahrhundert*, Vierteljahrschrift für Sozial- und Wirtschaftsgeschichte. Beihefte 126 (Stuttgart: Franz Steiner Verlag, 1996), pp. 62–63; Carsten Jahnke, "Customs and toll," p. 193.

23 "Slesvig stadsret," Text I, § 31, p. 9.

24 Denise Eeckaute, "Les systèmes monétaires Russes du Xe au XVIIe siècle et les influences étrangères," *Revue de études slaves* 65 (1993), no. 1, 21–39, here 21.

25 Eeckaute, "Les systèmes monétaires," pp. 21 f.

26 See as overview Mäkeler, "Wikingerzeitlicher Geldumlauf."

27 Heiko Steuer, "Die Ostsee als Kernraum des 10. Jahrhunderts und ihre Peripherien," *Siedlungsforschung* 22 (2004), 59–88, here 69 ff.; Eeckaute, "Les systèmes monétaires," p. 27.

28 Christoph Kilger, *Pfennigmärkte und Währungslandschaften, Monetarisierungen im sächsisch-slawischen Grenzland ca. 965–1220* (Stockholm: The Royal Swedish Academy of Letters, History and Antiquities, 2000).

29 Steuer, "Die Ostsee," pp. 69–78.

30 The dating of this paragraph is contested. See Gelting, "Kong Svend."

31 "Slesvig stadsret," Text I, § 31, p. 9.

32 *Diplomatarium Danicum*, edited by Lauritz Weibull, vol. I.2 (København: Ejnar Munksgaards Forlag, 1963), no. 166, pp. 312 ff.

33 Carsten Jahnke, *Netzwerke in Handel und Kommunikation an der Wende vom 15. zum 16. Jahrhundert am Beispiel zweier Revaler Kaufleute*, postdoctoral thesis, Christian-Albrechts-Universität zu Kiel (Kiel, 2004), https://www.hansischergeschichtsverein.de/vereinsfremde-literatur (accessed 20 July 2020).

34 *Diplomatarium Danicum*, vol. I.2., no. 166, p. 313, note for line 22–1: *Item si quis conciui suo bona sua ad negociandum commiserit.*

35 Albrecht Cordes, *Spätmittelalterlicher Gesellschaftshandel im Hanseraum*, Quellen und Darstellungen zur Hansischen Geschichte, Neue Folge 45 (Köln–Weimar–Wien: Böhlau Verlag, 1998).

36 Arnold von Lübeck, *Arnoldi Chronica Slavorum*, Ex recensione I. M. Lappenbergii, edited by Georgius Heinricus Pertz, MGH, SS rer. germ. in usum scholarum XIV (Hannover: Hahn, 1868), pp. 35, 41, 84, 149; Michael Kræmmer, *Højmiddelalderens jordmål og betalingsmål*, doctoral thesis, Århus University (Århus 2015), http://www.tancredi.dk/pdf/phd.pdf (accessed 28 July 2020), p. 120.

37 Arnold von Lübeck, *Arnoldi Chronica Slavorum*, p. 35.

38 Dieter Kartschoke, "Regina pecunia, dominus nummus, her phennic. Geld und Satire oder die Macht der Tradition," in *Geld im Mittelalter, Wahrnehmung – Bewertung – Symbolik*, edited by Klaus Grubmüller and Markus Stock (Darmstadt: Wissenschaftliche Buchgesellschaft, 2005), pp. 182–203, here 182.

39 *Das zweite Wismarsche Stadtbuch 1272–1297*, edited by Lotte Knabe, Quellen und Darstellungen zur Hansischen Geschichte, Nova Series XIV (Weimar: Hermann Böhlaus Nachfolger, 1966), nos 29, 78, 113, 119, 129, 187 etc.

40 Fritz Rörig, "Das älteste erhaltene deutsche Kaufmannsbüchlein," in Fritz Rörig, *Wirtschaftskräfte im Mittelalter, Abhandlungen zur Stadt- und Hansegeschichte*, edited by Paul Kaegbein (Weimar: Hermann Böhlaus Nachfolger, 1959), pp. 167–215.

41 Rörig, "Das älteste erhaltene," p. 204.

42 Kræmmer, *Højmiddelalderens jordmål*, p. 120.

43 Kræmmer, *Højmiddelalderens jordmål*, pp. 120 f.

44 Kræmmer, *Højmiddelalderens jordmål*, pp. 121 f.

45 *Kong Valdemars Jordebog*, vol. 1: *Text*, edited by Svend Aakjær (København, Samfund til Udgivelse af gammel Nordisk Litteratur, 1926–1943), pp. 9, 54, foll. 15r. & 39v.

46 Hermann Kamp, "Gutes Geld und böses Geld. Die Anfänge der Geldwirtschaft und der 'Gabentausch' im hohen Mittelalter," in *Geld im Mittelalter. Wahrnehmung – Bewertung – Symbolik*, edited by Klaus Grubmüller and Markus Stock (Darmstadt: Wissenschaftliche Buchgesellschaft, 2005), pp. 91–112, here 92 ff.

47 Gelting, "Kong Svend," pp. 198–205.

48 See, in general, Carsten Jahnke, "Der Aufstieg Lübecks und die Neuordnung des südlichen Ostseeraumes im 13. Jahrhundert," in *Städtelandschaften im Ostseeraum im Mittelalter und in der Frühen Neuzeit*, edited by Roman Czaja and Carsten Jahnke (Toruń: Towarzystwo Naukowe w Toruniu, 2009), pp. 29–72.

49 Jahnke, *The City of Næstved*, in preparation.

50 *Das hamburgische Schuldbuch von 1288*, edited by Erich von der Lehe, Veröffentlichungen aus dem Staatsarchiv der Freien und Hansestadt Hamburg IV (Hamburg: Hans Christians Verlag, 1956), no. 908, p. 117.

51 *Das zweite Wismarsche Stadtbuch*, no. 1814, p. 245.

52 *Das älteste Rostocker Stadtbuch (Etwa 1254–1273)*, edited by Hildegard Thierfelder (Göttingen: Vandenhoeck & Ruprecht 1967), no. I.50, p. 107.

53 Carsten Jahnke, "'…und er verwandelte die blühende Handelsstadt in ein unbedeutendes Dorf.' Die Rolle Schleswigs im internationalen Handel des 13. Jahrhunderts," in *Von Menschen, Ländern Meeren. Festschrift für Thomas Riis zum 65. Geburtstag*, edited by Gerhard Fouquet, Mareike Hansen, Carsten Jahnke, and Jan Schlürmann (Tönning: Der andere Verlag, 2006), pp. 251–268.

54 Jahnke, "Der Aufstieg Lübecks," pp. 58–69.

55 *Das älteste Wismarsche Stadtbuch von etwa 1250 bis 1272. Festschrift für die Jahresversammlung des hansischen Geschichtsvereins und des Vereins für Niederdeutsche Sprachforschung Pfingsten 1912*, edited by Friedrich Techen (Wismar: Hinstorf, 1912), no. 225, p. 13.

56 *Das älteste Wismarsche Stadtbuch*, no. 371, p. 21.

57 *Codex diplomaticus Lubecensis, Urkundenbuch der Stadt Lübeck*, Abt. 1, vol. I, edited by Friedrich Techen (Lübeck: Friedrich Aschenfeldt, 1843), no. CCXVIII, pp. 198 f.

58 Wilhelm Jesse, *Der wendische Münzverein* (Lübeck: Hansischer Geschichtsverein, 1928), pp. 67 ff.

59 Jesse, *Der wendische Münzverein*, pp. 69–71.

60 Jesse, *Der wendische Münzverein*, p. 71.

61 Jesse, *Der wendische Münzverein*, pp. 78–91.

62 Leopold Karl Goetz, *Deutsch-russische Handelsgeschichte des Mittelalters* (Lübeck: Waelde, 1922), p. 355.

63 *Die Nowgoroder Schra in sieben Fassungen vom XIII. bis XVII. Jahrhundert*, edited by Wolfgang Schlüter (Dorpat: Mattiesen, 1911), no. IIIa, § 4, p. 117.

64 *Die Nowgoroder Schra*, no. V, § 141, p. 174.

65 Goetz, *Deutsch-russische Handelsgeschichte*, p. 356.

66 See i.a. *Hansisches Urkundenbuch*, vol. 5: *1392–1414*, edited by Konstantin Höhlbaum and Karl Kunze (Leipzig: Duncker & Humblodt, 1899), no. 1140, p. 592.

67 *Die Nowgoroder Schra*, no. I–IIR, pp. 66f.

68 *Die Nowgoroder Schra*, no. II.L–II.R, 44, p. 96.

69 *Die Nowgoroder Schra*, no. IV.26, p. 135.

70 *Die Nowgoroder Schra*, no. II.L–II.R, 14, p. 72, no. IIIa, L, 17, p. 121, no. V, 8, p. 129.

71 *Die Nowgoroder Schra*, no. IIIa, R–L, 6, p. 118.

72 *Die Nowgoroder Schra*, no. IV–V, 76 & 86, p. 146.

73 *Die Nowgoroder Schra*, no. II.L–II.R, 35, p. 90.

74 *Die Nowgoroder Schra*, no. IV–V, 13 & 21, p. 132.

75 Kartschoke, "Regina pecunia."

Bibliography

Primary sources

Arnold von Lübeck. *Arnoldi Chronica Slavorum, Ex recensione I. M. Lappenbergii*, edited by Georgius Heinricus Pertz, MGH, SS rer. germ. in usum scholarum XIV. Hannover: Hahn, 1868.

Friedrich Techen *Codex diplomaticus Lubecensis, Urkundenbuch der Stadt Lübeck*, Abt. 1, vol. I. Lübeck: Friedrich Aschenfeldt, 1843.

Hildegard Thierfelder (ed.). *Das älteste Rostocker Stadtbuch (Etwa 1254–1273)*,. Göttingen: Vandenhoeck & Ruprecht 1967.

Friedrich Techen (ed.), *Das älteste Wismarsche Stadtbuch von etwa 1250 bis 1272. Festschrift für die Jahresversammlung des hansischen Geschichtsvereins und des Vereins für Niederdeutsche Sprachforschung Pfingsten 1912* . Wismar: Hinstorf, 1912.

Erich von der Lehe (ed.). *Das hamburgische Schuldbuch von 1288*, Veröffentlichungen aus dem Staatsarchiv der Freien und Hansestadt Hamburg IV. Hamburg: Hans Christians Verlag, 1956.

Lotte Knabe (ed.). *Das zweite Wismarsche Stadtbuch 1272–1297*,Quellen und Darstellungen zur Hansischen Geschichte, Nova Series XIV. Weimar: Hermann Böhlaus Nachfolger, 1966.

Felix Lieberman (ed.)."Die Gesetze der Könige Eadweard I, Aethelstan, Eadmund I, Eadgar und Aethelred II," in *Die Gesetze der Angelsachsen, herausgegeben im Auftrage der Savigny-Stiftung*, vol. 1. Halle: Max Niemeyer, 1903.

Wolfgang Schlüter *Die Nowgoroder Schra in sieben Fassungen vom XIII. bis XVII. Jahrhundert*, . Dorpat: Mattiesen, 1911.

Lauritz Weibull (ed.). *Diplomatarium Danicum*, , vol. I.2. København: Ejnar Munksgaards Forlag, 1963.

Konstantin Höhlbaum and Karl Kunze (eds.), *Hansisches Urkundenbuch*, vol. 5: 1392–1414, . Leipzig: Duncker & Humblodt, 1899.

Svend Aakjær (ed.). *Kong Valdemars Jordebog*, vol. 1: Text. København: Samfund til Udgivelse af gammel Nordisk Litteratur, 1926–1943.

Rörig, Fritz. "Das älteste erhaltene deutsche Kaufmannsbüchlein," in Fritz Rörig, Wirtschaftskräfte im Mittelalter, Abhandlungen zur Stadt- und Hansegeschichte, edited by *Paul Kaegbein*, pp. 167–215. Weimar: Hermann Böhlaus Nachfolger, 1959.

Erik Kroman (ed.) "Slesvig stadsret," in *Danmarks gamle Købstadslovgivning*, vol. I: Sønderjylland, pp. 3–17. København: Rosenkilde og Bagger, 1951.

Secondary literature

Adam, Hildegard. *Das Zollwesen im Fränkischen Reich und das spätkarolingische Wirtschaftsleben. Ein Überblick über Zoll, Handel und Verkehr im 9. Jahrhundert, Vierteljahrschrift für Sozial- und Wirtschaftsgeschichte. Beihefte 126.* Stuttgart: Franz Steiner Verlag, 1996.

Cordes, Albrecht. *Spätmittelalterlicher Gesellschaftshandel im Hanseraum, Quellen und Darstellungen zur Hansischen Geschichte, Neue Folge 45.* Köln–Weimar–Wien: Böhlau Verlag, 1998.

Czech-Schneider, Raphaela. Anathemata. *Weihgaben und Weihgabenpraxis und ihre Bedeutung für die Gesellschaft und Wirtschaft der frühen Griechen, postdoctoral thesis*, Westfälische Wilhelms-Universität Münster, North Rhine-Westphalia, 1998, https://repositorium.uni-muenster.de/document/miami/7a5e4944-2167-4ffb-a56b-90746b87eb1b/habilschr_czech-schneider.pdf (accessed September 20 2019).

Eeckaute, Denise. "Les systèmes monétaires Russes du Xe au XVIIe siècle et les influences étrangères," *Revue de études slaves* 65 (1993), no. 1, 21–39.

Falk, Hjalmar. "Altnordisches Seewesen," *Wörter und Sachen. Kulturhistorische Zeitschrift IV* (1912), 1–117.

Feveile, Claus, and Jens Christian Moesgaard. "Damhus-skatten – et fantastisk indspark til den tidlige mønthistorie," *By, Marsk og Geest* 30 (2018), 28–30.

Gelting, Michael. "Kong Svend, Slesvig Stadsret og arvekøbet i de jyske købsteder: Spor af Danmarks ældste købstadprivilegier," in *Svend Estridsen*, edited by Lasse C. A. Sonne and Sarah Croix, pp. 195–216. Odense: Syddansk Universitetsforlag, 2016.

Goetz, Leopold Karl. *Deutsch-russische Handelsgeschichte des Mittelalters.* Lübeck: Waelde, 1922.

Jahnke, Carsten. "Customs and toll in the Nordic Area c. 800–1300," in *Nordic Elites in Transformation c. 1050–1250, vol. 1: Material Resources*, edited by Helle Vogt, Bjørn Poulsen, and Jón Viðar Sigurdsson, pp. 183–211. Oxon–New York: Routledge, 2019.

Jahnke, Carsten. "Nyt og gammelt om Svend Estridsen," *Historisk Tidsskrift* 117 (2017), no. 1, 222–228.

Jahnke, Carsten. "Hafen", in *Handwörterbuch zur deutschen Rechtsgeschichte*, 2nd ed., edited by Albrecht Cordes, Heiner Lück, Dieter Werkmüller, and Ruth Schmidt-Wiegand, cols 649–652. Berlin: Erich Schmidt, 2010.

Jahnke, Carsten. "Der Aufstieg Lübecks und die Neuordnung des südlichen Ostseeraumes im 13. Jahrhundert," in *Städtelandschaften im Ostseeraum im Mittelalter und in der Frühen Neuzeit*, edited by Roman Czaja and Carsten Jahnke, pp. 29–72. Toruń: Towarzystwo Naukowe w Toruniu, 2009.

Jahnke, Carsten. "'… und er verwandelte die blühende Handelsstadt in ein unbedeutendes Dorf.' Die Rolle Schleswigs im internationalen Handel des 13. Jahrhunderts," in *Von Menschen, Ländern Meeren. Festschrift für Thomas Riis zum 65. Geburtstag*, edited by Gerhard Fouquet, Mareike Hansen, Carsten Jahnke, and Jan Schlürmann, pp. 251–268. Tönning: Der andere Verlag, 2006.

Jahnke, Carsten. Netzwerke in Handel und Kommunikation an der Wende vom 15. zum 16. *Jahrhundert am Beispiel zweier Revaler Kaufleute*, postdoctoral thesis, Christian-Albrechts-Universität zu Kiel, 2004, https://www.hansischergeschichtsverein.de/vereinsfremde-literatur (accessed 20 July 2020).

Jahnke, Carsten. *The City of Næstved. A Port in Different Roles*, in preparation (n.d.).

Jesse, Wilhelm. *Der wendische Münzverein*. Lübeck: Hansischer Geschichtsverein, 1928.

Kamp, Hermann. "Gutes Geld und böses Geld. Die Anfänge der Geldwirtschaft und der 'Gabentausch' im hohen Mittelalter," in *Geld im Mittelalter. Wahrnehmung – Bewertung – Symbolik*, edited by Klaus Grubmüller and Markus Stock, pp. 91–112. Darmstadt: Wissenschaftliche Buchgesellschaft, 2005.

Kartschoke, Dieter. "Regina pecunia, dominus nummus, her phennic. Geld und Satire oder die Macht der Tradition," in *Geld im Mittelalter, Wahrnehmung – Bewertung – Symbolik*, edited by Klaus Grubmüller and Markus Stock, pp. 182–203. Darmstadt: Wissenschaftliche Buchgesellschaft, 2005.

Kilger, Christoph. *Pfennigmärkte und Währungslandschaften, Monetarisierungen im sächsisch-slawischen Grenzland ca. 965–1220*, Stockholm: The Royal Swedish Academy of Letters, History and Antiquities, 2000.

Kræmmer, Michael. *Højmiddelalderens jordmål og betalingsmål, doctoral thesis*, Århus University, 2015, http://www.tancredi.dk/pdf/phd.pdf (accessed 28 July 2020).

Mäkeler, Hendrik. "Wikingerzeitlicher Geldumlauf im Ostseeraum – Neue Perspektiven," *Quaestiones Medii Aevi Novae 10* (2005), 121–149.

Maurer, Andrea. "Die Institutionen des modernen Kapitalismus: Karl Polanyi contra Max Weber," in *Kapitalismus, Globalisierung, Demokratie*, edited by Katharina Hirschbrunn, Gisela Kubon-Gilke, and Richard Sturn, pp. 105–133. Marburg: Metropolis, 2017.

Middleton, Neil, "Early medieval port customs, tolls and controls on foreign trade," *Early Medieval Europe* 13 (2005), 313–358.

North, Douglass C. "Transaction Costs in History," *Journal of European Economic History* 14 (Winter 1985), no. 3, 557–576.

Pappenheim, Max. "Die Speisegemeinschaft (motuneyti) im älteren westnordischen Recht," in *Ehrengabe dem deutschen Juristentage überreicht vom Verein für Lübeckische Geschichte und Altertumskunde*, pp. 1–20. Lübeck: Verlag des Vereins, 1931.

Pappenheim, Max. "Stýrimenn und Hásetar im älteren westnordischen Seeschiffahrtsrecht," in *Deutsche Islandsforschung 1930, vol. 1*, edited by Walther Heinrich Vogt, pp. 246–282. Breslau: Ferdinand Hirt, 1930.

Polanyi, Karl. *Ökonomie und Gesellschaft*. Frankfurt am Main: Suhrkamp, 1979.

Sachs, Stephen E., Conflict Resolutions at the Medieval English Fair", in *Eine Grenze in Bewegung: private und öffentliche Konfliktlösung im Handels- und Seerecht. Une frontière mouvante: justice privée et justice publique en matières commerciales et maritimes*, edited by Albrecht Cordes and Serge Dauchy, *pp. 19–38, Schriften des Historischen Kollegs. Kolloquien 81*. München: de Gruyter Oldenbourg, 2013.

Steuer, Heiko. "Die Ostsee als Kernraum des 10. Jahrhunderts und ihre Peripherien," *Siedlungsforschung* 22 (2004), 59–88.

5   Limited use of money in late-medieval commerce

Economic considerations on the viability of Hanseatic "reciprocal trade"

Ulf Christian Ewert

This article is about the correlation of late-medieval mercantile practice – in particular the merchants' use of money in a broader sense – with the institutional arrangement of the respective trading system. Taking the case of the Hansards' trade in the Baltic Sea, my aim is to explain why the Hansards' use of money and other financial instruments was – to some degree, at least – limited, and therefore different from other merchant groups of the time; and why the Hansards, in holding on to "reciprocal trade", not only avoided the transfer of money – in either cash or payable formal debt – for much of their internal commercial exchange, but also ran into an institutional "lock-in" by which economic development in the Baltic Sea region was restrained. So, the argument I would like to bring forward in this article contributes to a long-standing debate in economic history about the impacts of institutional design in medieval trade on economic development and economic growth,[1] and I am following ideas about the path-dependent development of the institutional arrangement of Hanseatic trade which Stephan Selzer and I published previously.[2]

Late-medieval Baltic Sea trade and the Hansards' limited use of money

It is widely accepted among economic historians that both monetisation and commercialisation can very well serve as indicators of economic development across epochs. Measured against these two indicators, the Baltic Sea in the late Middle Ages presented itself as an economically rather highly developed region. During the European boom period of the high Middle Ages, immigration of western settlers into the Baltic Sea region was enormous. A dense network of towns had sprung up along the southern Baltic shore, and the colonisation of the hinterland brought about a huge expansion of arable land and sustained agricultural development.[3] Trade in medieval Northern Europe can basically be described as the commercial exchange between crafted goods such as linen and cloth from the West for raw materials like ore, wax, timber and furs, as well as foodstuffs like grain, herrings or dried cod, from the East and North.[4] Such an east–west transfer of goods, especially of luxuries, existed, although much less intensive, even before the turn of the millennium. Numerous trading centres of the Viking Age, which in recent decades have been excavated mainly in the western Baltic Sea region, are proof of this.[5] Then, as a result of agricultural development and population growth, Baltic Sea trade was given a significant quantitative boost throughout the thirteenth century. Even before, it had already been relocated from the early trading centres to the towns newly founded along the southern Baltic coast. Being permanent and legally protected markets, these new urban communities represented the very model of the European medieval town. Urban dwellers, some of which were quite wealthy, consumed far more than what was necessary for subsistence. Their increasing demand for necessities and luxuries could be satisfied by an ever-intensifying commerce.[6] The new and somewhat closed trading system emerging in this period was based on privileges that were granted by local rulers to groups of Low German merchants at some important markets at the periphery of the North Sea and the Baltic Sea, that were in London, Bruges, Novgorod, and later also in Bergen. After having ousted former competitors from long-distance trade in this region, the Low German traders – better known as merchants of the Hanse or Hansards – operated most of the Baltic Sea trade in the late Middle Ages. They predominantly traded within kinship and friendship networks, and in economic terms the dominance of Baltic Sea trade they could secure for themselves until the late fifteenth century can be addressed as a cartel.[7]

Of course, the transfer of commodities between the Hanse's outposts – the Kontore – in Novgorod, Bruges, London and Bergen on the one hand, and the many cities and towns in the Baltic Sea region on the other hand, is barely conceivable without the existence of money. Hence, various gold and silver currencies existed that could be used for commercial exchange.[8] Each season Hansards brought silver and coins to the Saint Peter's court in Novgorod as well as to the Bruges fairs.[9] Thus, the Hansards used money as a medium of exchange and as a means of storing value, and different currencies served as a computing unit – in order to address only the three essential functions of money.[10] The computing function of money is all too obvious when looking into some of the merchants' account books and ledgers that have survived from the fourteenth and fifteenth centuries.[11] In wills, too, a merchant's material wealth was usually stated in a certain currency or even in several different currencies – in book money as well as in real money. A prominent example is certainly the will of Sivert Veckinchusen, written down and sealed in Lübeck on the 9th of May 1406, where numerous benefits in kind Sivert wanted to be given to his heirs are enlisted, each marked with its proper value in *marc lübisch* (Mark of Lübeck).[12]

So, why speak of a Hansards' limited use of money, or even of non-use? To answer this question, it would not be sufficient to assess only the degrees of commercialisation and monetisation in the Baltic Sea region in the late Middle Ages. Undisputedly, the Baltic economy already was highly developed, as proved by a widespread and intense commercial exchange all across the region, mainly of Hansards. Moreover, as noted above, since money was available in different currencies and a lot of people also used book money for their computing and accounting purposes, also monetisation must have reached a quite advanced degree. Hence, is non-use of money therefore not a good indication of an even more commercialised economy, an economy where commercial agents can substitute cash with other financial instruments?[13] In addition, appears though that in the late Middle Ages even high degrees of commercialisation and monetisation not automatically produced some kind of standard or universal trading practice, and quite obviously merchants from a different regional and cultural background developed rather different trading techniques.[14] Therefore it would be necessary to analyse how merchants as key agents in commercial exchange made use of the money available or substituted alternative financial instruments for money.

Limits to the Hansards' use of money for trade in this broader sense are very obvious when compared to the standards that were firmly established among Italian traders at the same time. Late-medieval Italian merchants, for instance, were able to use the bill of exchange a lot more virtuously than their contemporaries in Northern Europe. For Italian traders this financial instrument was not only a common means of a sedentary merchant to change money in different currencies, or to make cashless payments abroad; the bill of exchange was also used even to take out a loan, and more importantly, around 1400 they began to primarily take advantage of the arbitrage resulting from fluctuations of the exchange rate in various markets in Europe. This was a lucrative business, indeed, and some merchants now traded mainly with bills of exchange, becoming merchant bankers in the process.[15] There existed, however, barely anything comparable to it in the Baltic Sea region.

Why was that? Reasons that are recurrently mentioned in literature are an alleged lack of credit, or even a sort of anti-credit stance of the Hansards as well as their supposed allegedly innovative backlog in all organisational, legal and financial matters of long-distance trade.[16] These arguments can easily be disproved, and scholars have done so in the past. For example, in an article published in 1982 Stuart Jenks convincingly shows that merchants of the Hanse who traded in England and Flanders quite often bought on loan and used bills of exchange as a means of payment and also as a means of borrowing. To achieve the liquidity required for their business in Bruges, it was a standard procedure for Hansards to draw on bills of exchange of their trading partners in Cologne or Gdańsk, for example. The debt was redeemed by the proceeds of the sale of goods that then were sent to these partners.[17] Although this can primarily be shown for commercial activities of Hansards in the economically already highly developed western regions, there are no signs of either ignorance or hostility in general of Hansards *vis-à-vis* a use of bills of exchange or related financial instruments.[18] Quite the opposite, the Hansards were able to act extremely flexible in financial matters, as is proved by a famous case where three Prussian merchants – Gerhard von Allen, Matthias Wyse and Heinrich Schönhals – handled a debt of a group of English crusaders in Prussia to the Teutonic Order. To settle the debt that was acknowledged by Humphrey de Bohun, the leader of the group, in January 1363, the three merchants issued two obligatory bonds. Both letters of payment belonging to these bonds at first were brought to England by Thomas Albon, a London wool monger, who then repaid one of them in Bruges at Easter the same year. The other letter of payment was repaid, again in Bruges, to Reynold Papen, a Hansard who was closely connected to Gerhard von Allen, the original issuer of one of the bonds obligatory.[19] Resuming this latter case, it seems though that Hansards in principle were well-able to employ rather advanced techniques of trade whenever required. This notwithstanding, they did not systematically trade with either letters of payment or bills of exchange, so their use of financial instruments was limited in comparison to what Italian merchants commonly did.

There may have been other boundaries to a full exploitation of available financial instruments as well – lacking capital or institutional deficiencies, for instance. Around 1400, for example, merchants from Venice, Genoa, Pisa, Siena, Florence and other Italian cities were able to easily draw on capital from third parties for their trading activities. Italians used various forms of contract for either trade or raising capital where profits and risks were shared between partners, and which were guaranteed by municipal notaries. Such contractual schemes, for example, are the *rogadia, foenus nauticum, societas maris, commenda* or *collegantia*, all of them being more or less sophisticated developments of a basic form of contract of Greco-Roman origin. Thus, in Italian cities something similar to a venture capital market already existed, through which traders were provided with enough capital for their sometimes risky commercial endeavours.[20] Hansards employed several formal contractual schemes, too, which had an incentive structure very similar to those used by Italian traders, the only difference being that such contracts were not certified by notaries, as was customary in Italian cities, but were legally protected by the respective town council. One of these types, much simpler of course than some of the more sophisticated Italian contracts, was the so-called *vera societas* (real partnership), by which trading capital could be raised from inactive partners. Here, the partners commonly agreed upon how they would distribute profits of trade amongst themselves, and who of them had to bear the risk of a potential loss of capital.[21] On 1st November 1358, for example, the merchants Arnold Lowe and Rudolf Wittenborch from Lübeck wrote a contract, saying that they had entered into a formal partnership where Arnold Lowe as inactive partner paid 800 *marc lübisch* to Rudolf Wittenborch, who was to trade using this money for the benefit of both. Profits as well as losses were to be divided equally, and in case the active partner Rudolf Wittenborch should die, Arnold Lowe should be paid off with the whole sum of his deposit.[22] This *vera societas* contract was registered in the Niederstadtbuch, one of the town books in the city of Lübeck.[23] However, even though formal contractual schemes for spreading commercial risk and sharing profits existed, a venture capital market as is observed in Italian cities, however, never really developed in the towns of the Hanse,[24] and trade that relied on such *vera societas* contracts made up for only a smaller portion of Hanseatic trade.

Just like the Hansards' limited use of some at the time well advanced financial instruments, also their use of venture capital was thus not principally restricted by the institutional setting. These episodes might be a hint for the fact that Hansards, in principle, could employ both financial instruments and contractual schemes in a multitude of ways, but for some reason they were not always doing it. Also, the Hansards' obvious renunciation of exploiting the full power of financial instruments and contractual schemes available to them did not mean that in return they were restricted to primarily use cash. Interestingly enough, they found something different to operate the commercial exchange between them with a minimum of cash possible, a pattern of exchange that probably can be best labelled "reciprocal trade".

How this pattern worked, and why it remained in wide use even in fourteenth and fifteenth centuries, will be discussed in the following sections of this article.

Avoidance of money use – Hanseatic "reciprocal trade"

At first, the focus of my considerations on why the late-medieval Hansards, all in all, have been quite reluctant in using money or other financial instruments, is therefore on this very specific Hanseatic form of bilateral exchange between merchants, the so-called reciprocal trade. Since the majority of Hanseatic businesses were self-employed merchants, commercial exchange of Hansards in general had to be handled on a partnership basis.[25] Business transactions between Hansards that were operated as reciprocal trade were of great importance in quantitative terms. Estimations published in the literature say that such transactions may have accounted for a majority of all transactions between Hansards in fourteenth and fifteenth centuries, very likely in the order of between more than a half and two thirds (Stark 1984). And even in the sixteenth century this pattern of trade was still prevalent among the merchants of the Hanse.[26] This is why it seems crucially important to analyse this trading pattern in particular.

What is Hanseatic reciprocal trade? Business partners who worked at distant locations in the Baltic Sea region sent goods to each other, which were then sold on by the respective recipients on their own responsibility. The commercial risks related to the transportation and sale of goods were divided between the two partners. The sender of goods had to take the risk of transportation, whereas the recipient had to care about the risk of sale. The sender of goods also pocketed the profits of sale. All this was done without a fixed written contract between the two partners involved.[27] It is a very important feature of this trading pattern that partners often were relatives or considered themselves as friends.[28] For example, the probably most prominent late-medieval merchant of the Hanse, Hildebrand Veckinchusen, who for most of his life was a trader at the Bruges market, maintained such informal trading relationships with various relatives living in Lübeck, Riga, Reval (Talinn) and Dorpat (Tartu).[29] All these relatives themselves traded as legally independent merchants. Thus, trade of single members of the broader Veckinchusen family was not the trade of a family business at all. A second important feature of reciprocal trade is the usually long endurance of informal partnerships. Some of the partners involved in reciprocal trade exchanged goods with each other for over more than 20 years. Finally, an individual merchant usually entered into several such informal partnerships at the time, as there was no formal ban of competition among Hansards.[30] In the account book of Johan Pyre from Gdańsk that covers a period of 32 years, for instance, more than 40 trading partners are enlisted.[31]

Concerning the contractual basis as well as the spread of risk, reciprocal trade differed significantly from another sort of business transaction that also was commonly employed by the Hansards, which was called *sendeve* (sent away good). The *sendeve* was more a typical commission business of the kind that is even nowadays still widespread. Here, a particular merchant – the commission agent – transported the goods of another merchant and sold them by order and on behalf of this merchant. The owner of goods formally instructed the sale, he had to bear all potential risks, and similar to reciprocal trade he also received all the profits of sale, but he had to pay for the commission agent's service.[32]

Hence, reciprocal trade was a means by which the Hansards were able to avoid, by and large, the transfer of cash, because usually the profits of a sale could be paid to the sender by sending back own goods to him. He then could sell these return goods at a profit at his hometown market. This notwithstanding, the cleverer design of the institution of reciprocal trade is obvious, because no formal contract or formal order was required in this trading pattern, and therefore the proceeds of a sale did not have to be returned to the sender immediately. Since reciprocal trade by definition had an enduring element in it, mutual debts could be redeemed within a longer period of time. Furthermore, as long as the recipient of the goods had not yet returned the sale's profits to the sender, it was possible for him within this period to use the sale's proceeds to buy new goods. Thus, reciprocal trade was also a financial instrument providing credit to merchants without letting them pay an interest.

However, it is the informal character of this trading pattern that makes the analysis of reciprocal trade so difficult. The lack of written contracts is why it is almost impossible for legal history to classify this specific form of partnership.[33] This notwithstanding, by taking into account that reciprocal trade is nonetheless an informal and implicit contract, principal–agents theory and game theory can be used to derive the incentive structure and the performance of this institutional design, at least from a theoretical perspective.[34] What makes the empirical analysis even more difficult is that reciprocal trade can neither systematically nor clearly be detected in the account books that have survived from merchants of the Hanse of the fourteenth and fifteenth centuries. Exactly because of lacking formal agreements between merchants, it is simply impossible for many of the entries to show that they definitely were noted in connection with an informal partnership.

Why was "reciprocal trade" a viable institution?

Compared to the sophistication of means of financing used by other groups of merchants in the fourteenth and fifteenth centuries, the Hansards' reciprocal trade appears simple and outdated, of course. Since this pattern of exchanging goods between trading partners worked without a significant transfer of cash, one might also think that very likely it was inefficient. Money or equivalents of money are usually viewed as being essential to make exchange more efficient. Nevertheless, the Hansards employed this trading pattern very intensively for their business with each other, and they held on to this practice for quite a long time. Therefore, there must have been good economic reasons why the merchants of the Hanse did this, if one does not want to assume Hansards were not "clever" businessmen in general. To explain this, three points are briefly outlined below, which made the institution of reciprocal trade advantageous for both the individual merchant and for the group of all Hansards.

Firstly, the key to understanding the considerable efficiency of reciprocal trade as a means of exchange and financing is that it was embedded in the broad social network of the merchants of the Hanse. This network had emerged since the late twelfth century when merchants were still travelling and accompanying their goods themselves, and it became more and more dense later on, when many merchants had already settled down.[35] The key terms to focus on here are trust and reputation. Trust played a crucial role in bilateral trade relationships without a contractual basis. However, trust itself was based on reputation. Every merchant within the trade network was keen to maintain a good reputation. Once reputation had been lost, due to, for example, inadequate care for goods, or even fraudulent behaviour, it was not only a single partnership that was destroyed for the merchant. Because of his bad reputation also other merchants would no longer want to do business with him. Hence, betrayal within a single partnership would result in a multilateral ban.[36] In a game-theory approach, this central importance of reputation can be demonstrated within a game of trust, which Avner Greif has proposed for the analysis of the incentive structure of institutions used in medieval trade.[37] This simple one-shot game can be extended to an infinite game and, in accordance with the structure of reciprocal trade, it can be modified insofar as the recipient of the goods who operates the sale on its own responsibility only achieves a positive reputation in each round if he proves able, careful and honest – that is, selling the partner's goods at a profit and sending back own goods to him which the partner could sell in the next round to realise his profits. With such an incentive structure, betrayal is not a real option for rationally behaving merchants, because fraudulent behaviour would very soon result in a loss of all trading partnerships and thus in the economic "death" of the betrayer.[38] News of a merchant's bad reputation spread through the network – not necessarily very quickly, but nevertheless reliably – and thus ensured a properly working multilateral reputation mechanism.[39] Being embedded in the social network of the merchants of Hanse, reciprocal trade proved then to be a self-enforcing and therefore viable institution.[40]

Secondly, because of this self-enforcing character reciprocal trade produced manifest economic benefits for the individual merchant. In this trading practice essential components of the transaction costs remained relatively low, in particular information costs, cost of contract enforcement and financing costs.[41] In the trusted relationships of Hansards it was not necessary for merchants to procure their own information if they wanted to send goods to a partner for sale. Commonly, the trading partner had enough information about what was going on in his home town market. Merchants could also trust that a trading partner would sell the goods at a profit in his own interest, because he wanted to send his own goods back. There were no costs for the enforcement of contracts because with reciprocal trade there was no contract in a legal sense. Mutual fairness, however, resulted from embedding reciprocal trade into a network structure through which reputation was communicated. Financing costs were also low because little capital was needed to be able to trade at all, and because the proceeds from the sale of the goods received from the trading partner were used as a loan to buy new goods. In terms of transportation costs only, there was likely no particular saving in reciprocal trade compared to other conceivable forms of trade, because the goods had to be transported in any case. All in all, reciprocal trade made the merchants extremely flexible, because easily-established contacts with many other merchants in the network enabled everyone to offer a wide range of products without having to spend a lot of capital or transfer cash. In addition, little start-up capital was required to start trading, and young merchants typically started trading small quantities within the network until they had gained enough reputation to do bigger business.[42]

Thirdly, reciprocal trade had noticeable positive effects at the group level, as well, and was thus of economic benefit for the entire Hanse's trading system. The system was extremely effective in distributing the goods across space. The network, consisting of many bilateral relationships, made it possible to distribute goods all across the Baltic Sea region. Like in a relay, goods could be sent on from town to town.[43] In addition, by using this trading pattern, the Hansards as a group were able to compensate for the lack of a single currency in the Baltic Sea region and the difficulties that resulted from an only local or regional validity of the existing currencies. From an economic point of view, money or currency has to be understood as a public good. Because of potential "free-riding" the incentive structure is quite unfavourable for any individual engagement, typically communities or states become responsible for both the provision and maintenance of public goods.[44] However, a central administrative structure of the Hanse was not yet well-developed in the fifteenth century. Therefore, the Hanseatic League, in being only a loose and by no means permanent association of towns, had repeatedly great problems in reacting unanimously to all sorts of external threats[45], and also was more or less unable to credibly guarantee a universal and Northern-Europe-wide currency. However, shortcomings of the monetary system in the Baltic Sea region were only of secondary importance for the viability of reciprocal trade. In their bookkeeping, the Hansards used the existing currencies to determine the value of the goods they sent away, but these were mostly paid for with the goods sent in return by the trading partner.

Yet, around 1400 there was no economic reasons for giving up reciprocal trade and replacing it with newer trading and financing techniques, even more so because the estimated average margin of around 15% that could be earned in Hanseatic trade was not small, compared with the profit rates of Italian traders at the time.[46] As the institution of reciprocal trade proved to be efficient and viable, also the Hansards' limited use of money and other financial instruments seems to have been simply a rational choice.

Path dependence and "lock-in" – long-term effects of not using money

So far, we have seen that the pattern of reciprocal trade which the Hansards frequently employed for commercial exchange within long-lasting informal partnerships had several desirable properties, indeed. It was efficacious, as distant markets could be supplied through bilateral exchange, and a variety of goods could be distributed all across the Baltic Sea region quite easily. It was also efficient inasmuch as transaction costs could be minimised. In particular, neither the transfer of money between distant markets was necessary to keep the business alive, nor that of financial instruments by which merchants could draw on credit. And finally, reciprocal trade was viable, because it was self-enforcing and because due to relatively low transaction costs it provided individual merchants with an economic benefit. So, why the Hansards should have given up such an advantageous institution?

Maybe this is simply the wrong question to ask. In the fifteenth century, there are increasing signs that the merchants of the Hanse are beginning to lose some of their economic potential compared to other merchants in Europe. Only three points are mentioned here as examples: firstly, around 1400, the Hansards' did not enter the Italians' newly evolving trade with letters of exchange. Whether or not the Hansards in principle were unable to exploit this new business is not quite clear. Stuart Jenks is able to convincingly show that special circumstances in the Bruges market in late 1399 and early 1400 – a regulation of the city's magistrate with the clear aim at coping with the shortage of coins, saying that bills of exchange shall be redeemed by paying in cash only – helped the Italian merchants considerably in promoting this new business, while at the same time the diet of the Hanseatic League had forbidden that Hansards in Bruges bought on loan.[47] However, in the further course of the fifteenth century there were no attempts by the Hansards to organise anything comparable within the internal trade of the Hanse. Secondly, the famous *Venedische selscop* (Venetian society), which some members of the Veckinchusen family had founded to trade furs from Russia and Finland in Venice, soon developed into a financial disaster and went bankrupt within a short period of time.[48] There were, of course, many reasons for this, but it was certainly decisive that the Hansards in Venice were outside their usual trading network, and so their own financing techniques were not really compatible with the techniques established on the Venetian market. Finally, when the centre of Western European trade moved from Bruges to Antwerp around 1500, the merchants of the Hanse were unable to assert themselves against the emerging strong Upper German competitors, who had much more capital at hand. As a result, the Hansards could neither maintain their cartel regarding long-distance trade in the Baltic Sea region furthermore, nor gain a foothold in the new and capital-intensive transatlantic trade.[49]

Yet, it is likely more adequate to ask: why did the merchants of the Hanse not basically adopt the more modern techniques of trade and finance which their Italian contemporaries already employed? Both groups of merchants came regularly into contact with each other in Bruges and in London, and due to these contacts, the Hansards knew about the Italian techniques of trade and finance. Nevertheless, apart from a few single cases that were discussed above, such an adoption cannot be observed in general, but especially not for the Hanse's internal trade.

At this point, path dependence comes into play. In economics, this concept was formulated in connection with the aim at explaining why technical standards prevail and still dominate even when they are no longer efficient. The starting conditions play a decisive role here, as they structure the further development.[50] Institutions and institutional arrangements develop path-dependent as well.[51] Applied to medieval trading systems, this means that initial conditions of these systems are reflected in the design of institutions, and their further development often remains tied to the path that was taken at the time they were created. Therefore, path dependence is a theoretical concept that argues also with the past, which is why it seems suitable to explain institutional developments in medieval long-distance trade. The dominance of a particular institutional solution is typically promoted early in the development process by a large number of users. This creates a network effect by which the costs of switching to any other competing institution are increased significantly. Exactly this in turn often makes switching to alternative solutions unattractive, since the additional benefits expected from the use of competing institutions are usually lower than the costs of switching. As a consequence, and contrary to any simple economic logic, inefficient institutions cannot simply be modified or replaced. Moreover, often either modification or replacement of individual institutions within an institutional arrangement are difficult or even impossible because of their inter-dependence which had evolved in the process. A typical consequence of such a quasi-irreversibility is the so-called "lock-in" of the institutional arrangement.[52]

That is exactly what happened in the Hanse's trading system. As a result of a path-dependent institutional development, in the fifteenth century this system seems to have been trapped in such a "lock-in". The Hansards' preference to still trade mainly within kinship and friendship networks in the fourteenth and fifteenth centuries was path-dependent, of course. And so was the lasting dom-inance of reciprocal trade. This specific pattern of trade thus reflected in many ways the initial conditions that once in the thirteenth century had promoted the emergence of the Hanse's reputation-based network organisation of trade, namely the huge regional differences in economic development that existed across the Baltic Sea region, a traditional shortage of precious metals and coins, the com-mon practice of privileging entire merchant groups according to their region of origin, and a weak legal system.[53] Furthermore, since the information and coor-dination problems typical of cartels could be solved rather easily via contacts based on relatives and friends, the trade network remained stable even after many of the merchants of the Hanse had settled in the late Middle Ages. For Hansards the network organisation was a powerful vehicle to organise and to maintain their trading cartel in the Baltic Sea region.[54] However, both network organisation and reciprocal trade not only developed path-dependent, they also were mutu-ally dependent, in particular so because reciprocal trade was embedded in the Hanse's network organisation of trade. To operate commerce through kinship and friendship networks promoted the pattern of reciprocal trade insofar as the network enabled merchants to get easily in contact with a lot of other merchants from the same Low German-speaking background. In this respect, the Hanse can very well be understood as a "small world", a large, but fragmented network, where nonetheless distant subgroups are loosely connected through "bridging persons".[55] The network also enhanced fairness among its members, thus mem-bers were protected by the multilateral reputation mechanism, which was pivotal for reciprocal trade to work properly.[56] In turn, through reciprocal trade trusted relationships were created which increased the number of possible connections and further intensified the cohesion of the whole network.[57] As a consequence of the mutual interdependence of Hanseatic institutions of trade, a single Hansard could not simply quit the Hanse's system of trade and adopt instead trading habits and financing techniques of other European merchants at the time, namely those of Italian merchant bankers. This would have meant losing all connections within the Hanse network, renouncing from all benefits coming from it, and giving up business after all. It should be clear though, why the Hansards did not switch to alternative techniques of finance.

That the merchants of the Hanse were not able to substantially change the institutional arrangement of their internal trade in the fifteenth century is also a result of the fact that the practice of reciprocal trade had a pronounced negative impact on economic development, especially on the development of capital markets and a sophisticated finance of trade. As seen above, for reciprocal trade usually not much capital was required, which is why, in the short term, newcomers could start a trading business quite easily. In the long run, however, such a common low-capital trading among Hansards inhibited both the development and growth of a venture capital market in the towns of the Hanse.[58] It's no surprise, of course, that even in the fifteenth century most of the Hanseatic trading businesses were self-employed merchants or small firms, and that because merchants were used to operate with only little capital larger companies did not emerge.[59] The same was true for the development of more complex financial instruments, because such instruments were simply not necessary for the exchange of goods in trusted relationships.[60] Hence, the majority of Hansards – those who did not trade at either the market of Bruges or London – simply had no opportunity within their own business to exploit the manifold financial possibilities that bills of exchange can provide. These serious deficits in the commercial development of the Baltic Sea region in the late Middle Ages therefore neither reduced reciprocal trade, nor did this specific trading pattern become redundant. Quite the reverse, the practice of reciprocal trade was even more supported by this. Thus, commercial exchange with merchants from outside the Hanse – the so-called *butenhansen* – in general remained difficult, as in such cases the multilateral reputation mechanism was ineffective and financing techniques were often not compatible to each other. This lock-in further stabilised, because to keep the network of the Hansards closed, many towns of the Hanse prohibited formal trading companies with partners from outside the Hanse.[61] In addition, to protect the Hanse's privilege, the Bruges Kontore repeatedly banned purchases on loan, which to some extent exacerbated the notorious lack of credit and financing there.[62] It seems reasonable, therefore, that many Hansards held on to reciprocal trade in the late fifteenth century and even beyond, and did not make any attempt to employ sophisticated techniques of finance. In the early sixteenth century, the Hansards finally had too little venture capital available and their financing techniques were too simple for really being able to enter into the then emerging capital-intensive transatlantic trade.[63]

Concluding remarks

With the rapidly progressing commercialisation and monetisation of the economy in various European regions during the high and late Middle Ages also the use of money within trade changed accordingly. Merchants all across Europe developed techniques to circumvent the notorious shortage of precious metals and the ever-rising diversity of local currencies, and within long-distance trade they began to use book money, minimised the number of risky coin transfers, and finally, tried to avoid payments in cash. Similar to other European regions, trade in Northern Europe had also reached this new level of monetisation – that is, merchants were substituting financial instruments for cash wherever and whenever possible.

As well as other merchant groups, the Hansards used book money, and reduced the number of cash transfers to a minimum possible. However, the Hansards did not employ sophisticated financial instruments like the Italian merchants did. And even though they knew about these more modern financing techniques, they were barely an attempt to copy these techniques. Within much of their internal trade, the Hansards held on to the practice of reciprocal trade which allowed them to avoid the transfer of real money. Interestingly enough, this informal pattern of trade was so simple that sophisticated financial instruments, by which merchants can draw on credit or transfer payable debts, were not necessary either. Thus, the Hansards' use of money within long-distance trade was extremely limited, indeed, but as reciprocal trade was embedded in a reputation-based kinship and friendship network, this practice proved for long to be efficient and viable.

For the period around 1500, there is no question that reciprocal trade had actually become inefficient and seriously inhibited both the development of trade and economic growth in the Baltic Sea region. For this reason, it should, of course, have been replaced by more efficient institutions of trade. However, due to the mutual interdependence of the trading network and the practice of reciprocal trade the merchants of the Hanse were hardly able to change their trading habits and adopt more modern techniques of finance. Thus, the Hansards' use of financial instruments remained limited. This lock-in was the result of individual rational decisions made by the merchants in the short term, but it meant that in the long run the Hansards could neither expand their business nor even maintain their long-standing trade cartel. For them, taking a step further to reach an even higher level of monetisation where finance would have become an important element of economic development and growth was simply impossible.

Notes

1 Douglass C. North, *Institutions, Institutional Change and Economic Performance* (Cambridge and New York: Cambridge University Press, 1990); Paul R. Milgrom, Douglass C. North and Barry R. Weingast, "The Role of Institutions in the Revival of Trade: The Law Merchant, Private Judges, and the Champagne Fairs," *Economics and Politics* 2 (1990), 1–23; Avner Greif, "The Fundamental Problem of Exchange. A Research Agenda in Historical Institutional Analysis," *European Review of Economic History* 4 (2000), 251–284; idem, "Institutions and Impersonal Exchange. From Communal to Individual Responsibility," *Journal of Institutional and Theoretical Economics* 158 (2002), 168–204; idem, *Institutions and the Path to the Modern Economy: Lessons from Medieval Trade* (New York: Cambridge University Press, 2006); idem, Paul Milgrom, and Barry R. Weingast, "Coordination, Commitment, and Enforcement: The Case of the Merchant Guild," *Journal of Political Economy* 41

(1994), 745–776; Sheilagh C. Ogilvie, "'Whatever Is, Is right'? Economic Institutions in Pre-industrial Europe," *Economic History Review* 60 (2007), 649–684; Yadira González de Lara, "The Secret of Venetian Success: A Public-order, Reputation-based Institution," *European Review of Economic History* 12 (2008), 247–285; Jeremy Edwards and Sheilagh C. Ogilvie, "What Lessons for Economic Development Can We Draw from the Champagne Fairs?," *Explorations in Economic History* 49 (2012), 131–148; Sheilagh C. Ogilvie and André W. Carus, "Chapter 8: Institutions and Economic Growth in Historical Perspective," in *Handbook of Economic Growth*, vol. 2A, edited by Philippe Aghion and Steven Durlauf (Amsterdam: North Holland, 2014), pp. 403–513.

2 Ulf Christian Ewert and Stephan Selzer, "Wirtschaftliche Stärke durch Vernetzung. Zu den Erfolgsfaktoren des hansischen Handels," in *Praktiken des Handels. Geschäfte und soziale Beziehungen europäischer Kaufleute in Mittelalter und früher Neuzeit*, edited by Mark Häberlein and Christof Jeggle (Konstanz: UVK Verlagsgesellschaft, 2010), pp. 39–69; Ulf Christian Ewert and Stephan Selzer, *Institutions of Hanseatic Trade: Studies on the Political Economy of a Medieval Network Organisation* (Frankfurt/Main: Peter Lang Edition, 2016).

3 Carsten Jahnke, "Lübeck: Early Economic Development and the Urban Hinterland," in *A Companion to Medieval Lübeck*, edited by idem, (Leiden and Boston: Brill 2019), pp. 226–252.

4 Rolf Hammel-Kiesow, *Die Hanse* (München: C.H. Beck, 2000); Stephan Selzer, *Die mittelalterliche Hanse* (Darmstadt: Wissenschaftliche Buchgesellschaft, 2010); Carsten Jahnke, *Die Hanse* (Stuttgart: Reclam, 2014).

5 Dariusz Adamczyk, "Fernhandelsemporien, Herrschaftszentren, Regional- und Lokalmärkte: Die ökonomischen Funktionen von Silber, oder wie lässt sich der Grad der Monetarisierung in den frühmittelalterlichen Gesellschaften des Ostseeraumes 'messen'?," in *Economies, Monetisation and Society in the West Slavic Lands AD 800–1200*, edited by Tateusz Bogucki and Marian Rębkowski (Szczecin: Wydawnictwo IAE PAN, 2013), pp. 115–136; Dariusz Adamczyk, "Wollin und sein Hinterland im kontinentalen und transkontinentalen Beziehungsgeflecht um das Jahr 1000," in *Geschichte, um zu verstehen. Traditionen, Wahrnehmungsmuster, Gestaltungsperspektiven Carl-Hans Hauptmeyer zum 65. Geburtstag*, edited by Heike Düselder, Detlef Schmiechen-Ackermann, Thomas Schwark, Martin Stöber and Christiane Schröder (Bielefeld: Verlag für Regionalgeschichte, 2013), pp. 299–317; Sunhild Kleingärtner, *Die frühe Phase der Urbanisierung an der südlichen Ostseeküste im Frühmittelalter* (Neumünster: Wachholtz, 2013); Stephan Selzer and Ulf Christian Ewert, "Nord- und Ostsee, 500–1600," in *Globale Handelsräume und Handelsrouten von der Antike bis zur Gegenwart*, edited by Markus A. Denzel and Mark Häberlein (Berlin: De Gruyter, 2021), [forthcoming].

6 Franz Irsigler, "Der hansische Handel im Spätmittelalter," in *Die Hanse. Lebenswirklichkeit und Mythos. Eine Ausstellung im Museum für Hamburgische Geschichte in Verbindung mit der Vereins- und Westbank*, edited by Jörgen Bracker (Lübeck: Museum für Hamburgische Geschichte; Vereins- und Westbank, 1989), pp. 518–532; Hammel-Kiesow, *Die Hanse*.

7 Ewert and Selzer, "Wirtschaftliche Stärke"; iidem, *Institutions of Hanseatic Trade*.

8 Dariusz Adamczyk, "How and why did Dirhams flow to Scandinavia during the Ninth Century?," *Quaestiones Medii Aevi Novae* 23 (2018), 139-151; idem, "The Use of Silver by the Norsemen of Truso and Wolin: The Logic of the Market or Social Prestige?," in *Social Norms in Medieval Scandinavia*, edited by Jakub Morawiec, Aleksandra Jochymek and Grzegorz Bartusik (Leeds: Arc Humanities Press, 2019), pp. 19–34.

9 Stuart Jenks, "War die Hanse kreditfeindlich?," *Vierteljahrschrift für Sozial- und Wirtschaftsgeschichte* 69 (1982), 305–337.

10 Rolf Sprandel, *Das mittelalterliche Zahlungssystem nach hansisch-nordischen Quellen des 13.–15. Jahrhunderts* (Stuttgart: Anton Hiersemann, 1975); Sebastian Steinbach, "What is Money?," in *Methods in Premodern Economic History: Case Studies from the Holy Roman Empire, c. 1300 – c. 1600*, edited by Ulla Kypta, Julia Bruch, and Tanja Skambraks, (London: Palgrave Macmillan, 2019), pp. 132–145.

11 *Das Handlungsbuch des Vicko von Geldersen*, edited by Hans Nirrnheim (Hamburg: Voss, 1895); *Das Handlungsbuch von Hermann und Johann Wittenborg*, edited by Carl Mollwo (Leipzig: Dyk, 1901); Witold von Slaski, *Danziger Handel im 15. Jahrhundert auf Grund eines im Danziger Stadtarchiv befindlichen Handlungsbuches geschildert* (Heidelberg: Beisel, 1905); Anna Paulina Orłowska, "Handel in einem Kaufmannsnetz: Der Danziger Johann Pyre," in *Vertraute Ferne. Kommunikation und Mobilität im Hanseraum*, edited by Joachim Mähnert and Stephan Selzer (Husum: Husum Druck- und Verlagsgesellschaft, 2012), pp. 32–39; eadem, *Johan Pyre. Ein Kaufmann und sein Handelsbuch im spätmittelalterlichen Danzig. Darstellung und Edition* (Cologne: Böhlau, 2020); *Die Handelsbücher des Hildebrand Veckinchusen: Kontobücher und übrige Manuale*, edited by Michail P. Lesnikov and Walter Stark (Cologne: Böhlau, 2013); Gert Koppe, "Hans Wynekes Revaler Handlungsbuch (1490–1497). Ein Beitrag zur Ausbildung hansischer Kaufleute," in *Menschen – Märkte – Meere. Bausteine zur spätmittelalterlichen Wirtschafts- und Sozialgeschichte zwischen Hamburg, Lübeck und Reval*, edited by Stephan Selzer, pp. 123–179 (Münster: Verlag für Wissenschaft, 2018).

12 Hildebrand Veckinchusen, *Briefwechsel eines deutschen Kaufmanns im 15. Jahrhundert*, edited by Wilhelm Stieda (Leipzig: S. Hirzel, 1921).

13 Adrian R. Bell, Chris Brooks, and Tony K. Moore, "The Non-Use of Money in the Middle Ages," in *Money and its Use in Medieval Europe. Three Decades on Essays in Honour of Professor Peter Spufford*, edited by Martin Allen and Nicolas J. Mayhew (London: Royal Numismatic Society, 2017), pp. 137–151.

14 Ulf Christian Ewert, "Pfadabhängigkeit und 'Lock-in' – Fernhandelspraxis im Hanseraum jenseits italienischer Vertragsstandards," in *Italien als Vorbild? Ökonomische und kulturelle Verflechtungen europäischer Metropolen am Vorabend der „ersten Globalisierung" (1300–1600)*, edited by Jörg Oberste and Susanne Ehrich (Regensburg: Schnell & Steiner GmbH, 2019), pp. 151–166.

15 Jenks, "War die Hanse kreditfeindlich?"; Francesco Guidi-Bruscoli, "The Florentines and European 'Capitals' at the Dawn of the 'First Globalisation'," in *Italien als Vorbild? Ökonomische und kulturelle Verflechtungen europäischer Metropolen am Vorabend der „ersten Globalisierung"(1300–1600)*, edited by Jörg Oberste and Susanne Ehrich (Regensburg: Schnell & Steiner GmbH, 2019), pp. 137–150.

16 Wolfgang von Stromer, "Der innovatorische Rückstand der hansischen Wirtschaft," in *Beiträge zur Wirtschafts- und Sozialgeschichte des Mittelalters. Festschrift für Herbert Helbig zum 65. Geburtstag*, edited by Knut Schulz (Cologne and Vienna: Böhlau 1976), pp. 204–217.

17 Jenks, "War die Hanse kreditfeindlich?".

18 Michael North, Kreditinstrumente in Westeuropa und im Hanseraum," in *"kopet uns werk by tyden." Beiträge zur hansischen und preußischen Geschichte. Festschrift für Walter Stark zum 75. Geburtstag*, edited by Nils Jörn, Detlef Kattinger and Horst Wernicke (Schwerin: Thomas Helms Verlag, 1999), pp. 43–46.

19 Werner Paravicini, *Die Preussenreisen des europäischen Adels*, Part 2 (Sigmaringen: Thorbecke, 1995); Bell, Brooks and Moore, "The Non-Use of Money".

20 Avner Greif, "On the Political Foundations of the Late Medieval Commercial Revolution: Genoa during the Twelfth and Thirteenth Centuries," *Journal of Economic History* 94 (1994), 271–287.

21 Albrecht Cordes, *Spätmittelalterlicher Gesellschaftshandel im Hanseraum* (Cologne: Böhlau, 1998); idem, "Einheimische und gemeinrechtliche Elemente im hansischen Gesellschaftsrecht des 15.–17. Jahrhunderts. Eine Projektskizze," in *"kopet uns werk by tyden." Beiträge zur hansischen und preußischen Geschichte. Festschrift für Walter Stark zum 75. Geburtstag*, edited by Nils Jörn, Detlef Kattinger, and Horst Wernicke (Schwerin: Thomas Helms Verlag, 1999), pp. 67–71; idem, *Wie verdiente der Kaufmann sein Geld? Hansische Handelsgesellschaften im Spätmittelalter* (Lübeck: Schmidt-Römhild, 2000).

22 Philippe Dollinger, *Die Hanse*, 4 edn. (Stuttgart: Kröner, 1989).

23 Harm von Seggern, "The 'Niederstadtbuch'. A Source of History of Private Life of Lübeckers around 1500," in *A Companion to Medieval Lübeck*, edited by Carsten Jahnke (Leiden–Boston: Brill, 2019), pp. 352–371.

24 Angela Huang and Alexandra Sapoznik, "Fremdes Geld. Auswärtige Kapitalbeziehungen des Braunschweiger Rentenmarktes im 15. und 16. Jahrhundert," *Vierteljahrschrift für Sozial- und Wirtschaftsgeschichte* 106 (2019), no. 1, 29–66.

25 Ewert and Selzer, *Institutions of Hanseatic Trade*.

26 Hildegard Thierfelder. *Rostock-Osloer Handelsbeziehungen im 16. Jahrhundert. Die Geschäftspapiere der Kaufleute Kron in Rostock und Bene in Oslo* (Weimar: H. Böhlaus Nachfolger, 1958), pp. 194–207.

27 Gunnar Mickwitz. "Neues zur Funktion hansischer Handelsgesellschaften," Hansische Geschichtsblätter 62 (1937), 191–201; idem, *Aus Revaler Handelsbüchern. Zur Technik des Ostseehandels in der ersten Hälfte des 16. Jahrhunderts* (Helsingfors: Akademische Buchhandlung, 1938); Walter Stark, "Über Platz- und Kommissionshändlergewinne im Handel des 15. Jahrhunderts," in *Autonomie, Wirtschaft und Kultur der Hansestädte*, edited by Konrad Fritze, Eckehard Müller-Mertens and idem, (Weimar: Böhlau, 1984), pp. 130–146; idem, "Über Handelstechniken auf dem Brügger Markt um die Wende vom 14. zum 15. Jahrhundert," in *Hansekaufleute in Brügge*, Part 4: *Beiträge der Internationalen Tagung in Brügge April 1996*, edited by Nils Jörn, Werner Paravicini and Horst Wernicke (Frankfurt/Main: Peter Lang, 2000), pp. 97–107; Cordes, *Spätmittelalterlicher Gesellschaftshandel*; idem, *Wie verdiente der Kaufmann sein Geld?*.

28 Ulf Christian Ewert and Stephan Selzer. "Chapter 5: Social Networks," in *A Companion to the Hanseatic League*, edited by Donald J. Harreld (Leiden and Boston: Brill, 2015), pp. 162–193.

29 Franz Irsigler, "Der Alltag einer hansischen Kaufmannsfamilie im Spiegel der Veckinchusen-Briefe," *Hansische Geschichtsblätter* 103 (1985), pp. 75–99; Walter Stark, "Über Techniken und Organisationsformen des hansischen Handels im Spätmittelalter," in *Der hansische Sonderweg? Beiträge zur Sozial- und Wirtschaftsgeschichte der Hanse*, edited by Stuart Jenks and Michael North, (Cologne, Weimar and Vienna: Böhlau, 1993), pp. 191–201; Cordes, *Spätmittelalterlicher Gesellschaftshandel*; Mathias Franc Kluge, "Zwischen Metropole, Fürst und König: Die Venedische Handelsgesellschaft der Kaufleute Veckinchusen und ihr Niedergang," *Hansische Geschichtsblätter* 131 (2013), 33–76.

30 Rolf Sprandel, "Die Konkurrenzfähigkeit der Hanse im Spätmittelalter," *Hansische Geschichtsblätter* 102 (1984), 21–38.

31 Sprandel, "Konkurrenzfähigkeit"; Orłowska, "Handel in einem Kaufmannsnetz"; eadem, *Johan Pyre*.

32 Cordes, *Spätmittelalterlicher Gesellschaftshandel*; idem, "Einheimische und gemein-rechtliche Elemente", pp. 67–71; idem, *Wie verdiente der Kaufmann sein Geld?*.

33 Stephan Selzer and Ulf Christian Ewert, "Verhandeln und Verkaufen, Vernetzen und Vertrauen. Über die Netzwerkstruktur des hansischen Handels," *Hansische Geschichtsblätter* 119 (2001), 135–161.

34 Avner Greif, "Chapter 52: Economic History and Game Theory," in *Handbook of Game Theory with Economic Explanations*, vol. 3, edited by Robert Aumann and Sergiu Hart (Amsterdam: North Holland, 2002), pp. 1989–2004; Ewert and Selzer, "Wirtschaftliche Stärke"; iidem, *Institutions of Hanseatic Trade*.

35 Ulf Christian Ewert and Marco Sunder, "Trading Networks, Monopoly, and Economic Development in Medieval Northern Europe: An Agent-based Simulation of Early Hanseatic Trade," in *Raumbildung durch Netzwerke? Der Ostseeraum zwischen Wikingerzeit und Spätmittelalter aus archäologischer und geschichtswissenschaftlicher Perspektive*, edited by Sunhild Kleingärtner and Gabriel Zeilinger (Bonn: Rudolf Habelt), pp. 131–153; iidem, "Modelling Maritime Trade Systems: Agent-based Simulation and Medieval History," Historical Social Research 43 (2018), no. 1, 110–143.

36 Selzer and Ewert, "Verhandeln und Verkaufen"; Ulf Christian Ewert and Stephan Selzer, "Netzwerkorganisation im Fernhandel des Mittelalters: Wettbewerbsvorteil oder Wachstumshemmnis?," in *Unternehmerische Netzwerke. Eine historische Organisationsform mit Zukunft?*, edited by Hartmut Berghoff and Jörg Sydow (Stuttgart: Kohlhammer, 2007), pp. 45–70.
37 Greif, "The Fundamental Problem".
38 Ewert and Selzer, "Wirtschaftliche Stärke"; iidem, *Institutions of Hanseatic Trade*.
39 Selzer and Ewert. "Verhandeln und Verkaufen"; Ewert and Selzer, "Wirtschaftliche Stärke".
40 Ewert and Selzer, *Institutions of Hanseatic Trade*.
41 Selzer and Ewert. "Verhandeln und Verkaufen"; iidem, "Die Neue Institutionenökonomik als Herausforderung an die Hanseforschung," *Hansische Geschichtsblätter* 123 (2005), 7–29; Stuart Jenks, "Transaktionskostentheorie und die mittelalterliche Hanse," *Hansische Geschichtsblätter* 123 (2005), 31–42; Ewert and Selzer, "Wirtschaftliche Stärke"; iidem, *Institutions of Hanseatic Trade*.
42 Ewert and Selzer, "Wirtschaftliche Stärke"; iidem, *Institutions of Hanseatic Trade*.
43 Selzer and Ewert. "Verhandeln und Verkaufen"; Ewert and Selzer, "Wirtschaftliche Stärke"; iidem, *Institutions of Hanseatic Trade*.
44 Ulf Christian Ewert, "Collective Goods in the Middle Ages," in *Methods in Premodern Economic History: Case Studies from the Holy Roman Empire, c. 1300 – c. 1600*, edited by Ulla Kypta, Julia Bruch and Tanja Skambraks (London: Palgrave Macmillan, 2019), pp. 64–67.
45 Ewert and Selzer, *Institutions of Hanseatic Trade*.
46 Walter Stark, *Untersuchungen zum Profit beim hansischen Handelskapital in der ersten Hälfte des 15. Jahrhunderts* (Weimar: H. Böhlaus Nachfolger, 1985).
47 Jenks, "War die Hanse kreditfeindlich?".
48 Wilhelm Stieda, *Hansisch-Venetianische Handelsbeziehungen im 15. Jahrhundert. Festschrift der Landes-Universität Rostock zur zweiten Säcularfeier der Universität Halle a. S.* (Rostock: Dr. v. Adler's Erben, 1894); Mathias Franc Kluge, "Zwischen Metropole, Fürst und König", 33–76.
49 Ewert and Selzer, "Wirtschaftliche Stärke"; iidem, *Institutions of Hanseatic Trade*; Ulla Kypta, "Die Hanse und die Krise des Spätmittelalters. Überlegungen zum Zusammenspiel von wirtschaftlichem und institutionellem Wandel," in *Wirtschaftskrisen als Wendepunkte*, edited by Dariusz Adamczyk and Stephan Lehnstaedt (Osnabrück: fibre, 2015), pp. 159–184; *Hansischer Handel im Strukturwandel vom 15. zum 16. Jahrhundert*, edited by Rolf Hammel-Kiesow and Stephan Selzer (Trier: Porta Alba Verlag, 2016).
50 Paul A. David, "Clio and the Economics of QWERTY," *American Economic Review* 75 (1985), no. 2, 332–337; W. Brian Arthur, "Competing Technologies, Increasing Returns, and Lock-in by Historical Events," *The Economic Journal* 99 (1989), 116–131.
51 Paul A. David, "Why are Institutions the 'Carriers of History'? Path Dependence and the Evolution of Conventions, Organizations and Institutions," *Structural Change and Economic Dynamics* 5 (1994), 205–220; Jörg Sydow, Georg Schreyögg and Jochen Koch. "Organizational Path Dependence: Opening the Black Box," *Academy of Management Review* 34 (2009), 689–709.
52 Ulf Christian Ewert, "Pfadabhängigkeit und 'Lock-in'".
53 Ewert and Selzer, "Wirtschaftliche Stärke"; iidem, *Institutions of Hanseatic Trade*.
54 Ewert and Sunder. "Trading Networks"; iidem, "Modelling Maritime Trade Systems".
55 Duncan Watts, "Networks, Dynamics, and the Small-World Phenomenon," *American Journal of Sociology* 105 (1999), 493–527; Selzer and Ewert. "Verhandeln und Verkaufen"; Ewert and Selzer, *Institutions of Hanseatic Trade*.
56 Selzer and Ewert. "Verhandeln und Verkaufen"; Ewert and Selzer, "Wirtschaftliche Stärke"; iidem, *Institutions of Hanseatic Trade*.
57 Ewert and Selzer, "Wirtschaftliche Stärke"; iidem, *Institutions of Hanseatic Trade*.

58 Mark Schonewille, *Risk, Institutions and Trade. New Approaches to Hanse History,* Working Paper (Nijmegen: Univ. Nijmegen, 1998).
59 Jenks, Stuart. "Small is Beautiful: Why Small Hanseatic Firms Survived in the Late Middle Ages," in *The Hanse in Medieval and Early Modern Europe,* edited by Justyna Wubs-Mrozewicz and Stuart Jenks (Leiden and Boston: Brill, 2013), pp. 191–214.
60 Ewert and Selzer, "Wirtschaftliche Stärke"; iidem, *Institutions of Hanseatic Trade.*
61 Stuart Jenks, "Hansisches Gästerecht," *Hansische Geschichtsblätter* 114 (1996), 2–60.
62 Jenks, "War die Hanse kreditfeindlich?".
63 Ewert and Selzer, "Wirtschaftliche Stärke"; iidem, *Institutions of Hanseatic Trade.*

Bibliography

Primary sources

Carl Mollwo (ed.). *Das Handlungsbuch von Hermann und Johann Wittenborg.* Leipzig: Dyk, 1901.
Hans Nirrnheim (ed.). *Das Handlungsbuch des Vicko von Geldersen.* Hamburg: Voss, 1895.
Michail P. Lesnikov and Walter Stark (eds.). *Die Handelsbücher des Hildebrand Veckinchusen: Kontobücher und übrige Manuale (Quellen und Darstellungen zur hansischen Geschichte, Neue Folge 67).* Cologne: Böhlau, 2013.
Wilhelm, Stieda (ed.). *Hildebrand Veckinchusen. Briefwechsel eines deutschen Kaufmanns im 15. Jahrhundert.* Leipzig: S. Hirzel, 1921.

Secondary literature

Adamczyk, Dariusz. "The Use of Silver by the Norsemen of Truso and Wolin: The Logic of the Market or Social Prestige?," in *Social Norms in Medieval Scandinavia,* edited by Jakub Morawiec, Aleksandra Jochymek and Grzegorz Bartusik, pp. 19–34. Leeds: Arc Humanities Press, 2019.
Adamczyk, Dariusz. "How and why did Dirhams flow to Scandinavia during the Ninth Century?," *Quaestiones Medii Aevi Novae* 23 (2018), 139–151.
Adamczyk, Dariusz. "Fernhandelsemporien, Herrschaftszentren, Regional- und Lokalmärkte: Die ökonomischen Funktionen von Silber, oder wie lässt sich der Grad der Monetarisierung in den frühmittelalterlichen Gesellschaften des Ostseeraumes 'messen'?," in *Economies, Monetisation and Society in the West Slavic Lands AD 800–1200,* edited by Tateusz Bogucki and Marian Rębkowski, pp. 115–136. Szczecin: Wydawnictwo IAE PAN, 2013a.
Adamczyk, Dariusz. "Wollin und sein Hinterland im kontinentalen und transkontinentalen Beziehungsgeflecht um das Jahr 1000," in *Geschichte, um zu verstehen. Traditionen, Wahrnehmungsmuster, Gestaltungsperspektiven Carl-Hans Hauptmeyer zum 65. Geburtstag,* edited by Heike Düselder, Detlef Schmiechen-Ackermann, Thomas Schwark, Martin Stöber and Christiane Schröder, pp. 299–317. Bielefeld: Verlag für Regionalgeschichte, 2013b.
Arthur, W. Brian. "Competing Technologies, Increasing Returns, and Lock-in by Historical Events," *The Economic Journal* 99 (1989), 116–131.
Bell, Adrian R., Chris Brooks, and Tony K. Moore, "The Non-Use of Money in the Middle Ages," in *Money and its Use in Medieval Europe. Three Decades on Essays in Honour of Professor Peter Spufford (Royal Numismatic Society Special Publication 52),* edited by Martin Allen and Nicolas J. Mayhew, pp. 137–151. London: Royal Numismatic Society, 2017.

Cordes, Albrecht. *Wie verdiente der Kaufmann sein Geld? Hansische Handelsgesellschaften im Spätmittelalter (Handel, Geld und Politik 2)*. Lübeck: Schmidt-Römhild, 2000.

Cordes, Albrecht. "Einheimische und gemeinrechtliche Elemente im hansischen Gesellschaftsrecht des 15.–17. Jahrhunderts. Eine Projektskizze," in *"kopet uns werk by tyden." Beiträge zur hansischen und preußischen Geschichte. Festschrift für Walter Stark zum 75. Geburtstag*, edited by Nils Jörn, Detlef Kattinger and Horst Wernicke, pp. 67–71. Schwerin: Thomas Helms Verlag, 1999.

Cordes, Albrecht. *Spätmittelalterlicher Gesellschaftshandel im Hanseraum (Quellen und Darstellungen zur hansischen Geschichte, Neue Folge 45)*. Cologne: Böhlau, 1998.

David, Paul A. "Why are Institutions the 'Carriers of History'? Path Dependence and the Evolution of Conventions, Organizations and Institutions," *Structural Change and Economic Dynamics* 5 (1994), 205–220.

David, Paul A. "Clio and the Economics of QWERTY," *American Economic Review* 75 (1985), no. 2, 332–337.

Dollinger, Philippe. *Die Hanse*, 4 edn. Stuttgart: Kröner, 1989.

Edwards, Jeremy and Sheilagh C. Ogilvie. "What Lessons for Economic Development Can We Draw from the Champagne Fairs?," *Explorations in Economic History* 49 (2012), 131–148.

Ewert, Ulf Christian. "Collective Goods in the Middle Ages," in *Methods in Premodern Economic History: Case Studies from the Holy Roman Empire, c. 1300 – c. 1600*, edited by Ulla Kypta, Julia Bruch and Tanja Skambraks, pp. 64–67. London: Palgrave Macmillan, 2019a.

Ewert, Ulf Christian. "Pfadabhängigkeit und 'Lock-in' – Fernhandelspraxis im Hanseraum jenseits italienischer Vertragsstandards," in *Italien als Vorbild? Ökonomische und kulturelle Verflechtungen europäischer Metropolen am Vorabend der "ersten Globalisierung" (1300–1600)*, edited by Jörg Oberste und Susanne Ehrich, pp. 151–166. Regensburg: Schnell & Steiner GmbH, 2019b.

Ewert, Ulf Christian and Stephan Selzer. *Institutions of Hanseatic Trade: Studies on the Political Economy of a Medieval Network Organisation*. Frankfurt/Main: Peter Lang, 2016.

Ewert, Ulf Christian and Stephan Selzer. "Chapter 5: Social Networks," in *A Companion to the Hanseatic League (Brill's Companions to European History 8)*, edited by Donald J. Harreld, pp. 162–193. Leiden and Boston: Brill, 2015.

Ewert, Ulf Christian and Stephan Selzer. "Wirtschaftliche Stärke durch Vernetzung. Zu den Erfolgsfaktoren des hansischen Handels," in *Praktiken des Handels. Geschäfte und soziale Beziehungen europäischer Kaufleute in Mittelalter und früher Neuzeit*, edited by Mark Häberlein and Christof Jeggle, pp. 39–69. Konstanz: UVK Verlagsgesellschaft, 2010.

Ewert, Ulf Christian and Stephan Selzer. "Netzwerkorganisation im Fernhandel des Mittelalters: Wettbewerbsvorteil oder Wachstumshemmnis?," in *Unternehmerische Netzwerke. Eine historische Organisationsform mit Zukunft?*, edited by Hartmut Berghoff and Jörg Sydow, pp. 45–70. Stuttgart: Kohlhammer, 2007.

Ewert, Ulf Christian, and Marco Sunder. "Modelling Maritime Trade Systems: Agent-based Simulation and Medieval History," *Historical Social Research* 43 (2018), no. 1, 110–143.

Ewert, Ulf Christian, and Marco Sunder. "Trading Networks, Monopoly, and Economic Development in Medieval Northern Europe: An Agent-based Simulation of Early Hanseatic Trade," in *Raumbildung durch Netzwerke? Der Ostseeraum zwischen Wikingerzeit und Spätmittelalter aus archäologischer und geschichtswissenschaftlicher*

Perspektive (Zeitschrift für Archäologie des Mittelalters, Beiheft 23), edited by Sunhild Kleingärtner and Gabriel Zeilinger, pp. 131–153. Bonn: Rudolf Habelt, 2012.

Greif, Avner. *Institutions and the Path to the Modern Economy: Lessons from Medieval Trade.* New York: Cambridge University Press, 2006.

Greif, Avner. "Chapter 52: Economic History and Game Theory," in *Handbook of Game Theory with Economic Explanations*, vol. 3 edited by Robert Aumann and Sergiu Hart, pp. 1989–2004. Amsterdam: North Holland, 2002a.

Greif, Avner. "Institutions and Impersonal Exchange. From Communal to Individual Responsibility," *Journal of Institutional and Theoretical Economics* 158 (2002), 168–204, 2002b.

Greif, Avner. "The Fundamental Problem of Exchange. A Research Agenda in Historical Institutional Analysis," *European Review of Economic History* 4 (2000), 251–284.

Greif, Avner. "On the Political Foundations of the Late Medieval Commercial Revolution: Genoa During the Twelfth and Thirteenth Centuries," *Journal of Economic History* 94 (1994), 271–287.

Greif, Avner, Paul Milgrom, and Barry R. Weingast. "Coordination, Commitment, and Enforcement: The Case of the Merchant Guild," *Journal of Political Economy* 41 (1994), 745–776.

González de Lara, Yadira. "The Secret of Venetian Success: A Public-order, Reputation-based Institution," *European Review of Economic History* 12 (2008), 247–285.

Guidi-Bruscoli, Francesco. "The Florentines and European 'Capitals' at the Dawn of the 'First Globalisation'," in *Italien als Vorbild? Ökonomische und kulturelle Verflechtungen europäischer Metropolen am Vorabend der "ersten Globalisierung"(1300–1600) (Forum Mittelalter. Studien 16)*, edited by Jörg Oberste and Susanne Ehrich, pp. 137–150. Regensburg: Schnell & Steiner GmbH, 2019.

Hammel-Kiesow, Rolf. *Die Hanse.* München: C.H. Beck, 2000.

Rolf Hammel-Kiesow and Stephan Selzer (eds.) *Hansischer Handel im Strukturwandel vom 15. zum 16. Jahrhundert (Hansische Studien 25).* Trier: Porta Alba Verlag, 2016.

Huang, Angela and Alexandra Sapoznik. "Fremdes Geld. Auswärtige Kapitalbeziehungen des Braunschweiger Rentenmarktes im 15. und 16. Jahrhundert," *Vierteljahrschrift für Sozial- und Wirtschaftsgeschichte* 106 (2019), no. 1, 29–66.

Irsigler, Franz. "Der hansische Handel im Spätmittelalter," in *Die Hanse. Lebenswirklichkeit und Mythos. Eine Ausstellung im Museum für Hamburgische Geschichte in Verbindung mit der Vereins- und Westbank*, edited by Jörgen Bracker, pp. 518–532. Lübeck: Museum für Hamburgische Geschichte; Vereins- und Westbank, 1989.

Irsigler, Franz. "Der Alltag einer hansischen Kaufmannsfamilie im Spiegel der Veckinchusen-Briefe," *Hansische Geschichtsblätter* 103 (1985), 75–99.

Jahnke, Carsten. "Lübeck: Early Economic Development and the Urban Hinterland," in *A Companion to Medieval Lübeck (Brill's Companions to European History 18)*, edited by idem, pp. 226–252. Leiden–Boston: Brill 2019.

Jahnke, Carsten. *Die Hanse.* Stuttgart: Reclam, 2014.

Jenks, Stuart. "Small is Beautiful: Why Small Hanseatic Firms Survived in the Late Middle Ages," in *The Hanse in Medieval and Early Modern Europe (The Northern World 60)*, edited by Justyna Wubs-Mrozewicz and Stuart Jenks idem, pp. 191–214. Leiden and Boston: Brill, 2013.

Jenks, Stuart. "Transaktionskostentheorie und die mittelalterliche Hanse," *Hansische Geschichtsblätter* 123 (2005), 31–42.

Jenks, Stuart. "Hansisches Gästerecht," *Hansische Geschichtsblätter* 114 (1996), 2–60.

Jenks, Stuart. "War die Hanse kreditfeindlich?," *Vierteljahrschrift für Sozial- und Wirtschaftsgeschichte* 69 (1982), 305–337.

Kleingärtner, Sunhild. *Die frühe Phase der Urbanisierung an der südlichen Ostseeküste im Frühmittelalter (Studien zur Archäologie des Ostseeraums 13)*. Neumünster: Wachholtz, 2013.

Kluge, Mathias Franc. "Zwischen Metropole, Fürst und König: Die Venedische Handelsgesellschaft der Kaufleute Veckinchusen und ihr Niedergang," *Hansische Geschichtsblätter* 131 (2013), 33–76.

Koppe, Gert. "Hans Wynekes Revaler Handlungsbuch (1490–1497). Ein Beitrag zur Ausbildung hansischer Kaufleute," in *Menschen – Märkte – Meere. Bausteine zur spätmittelalterlichen Wirtschafts- und Sozialgeschichte zwischen Hamburg, Lübeck und Reval (Contributiones 6)*, edited by Stephan Selzer, pp. 123–179. Münster: Verlag für Wissenschaft, 2018.

Kypta, Ulla. "Die Hanse und die Krise des Spätmittelalters. Überlegungen zum Zusammenspiel von wirtschaftlichem und institutionellem Wandel," in *Wirtschaftskrisen als Wendepunkte*, edited by Dariusz Adamczyk and Stephan Lehnstaedt, pp. 159–184. Osnabrück: fibre, 2015.

Mickwitz, Gunnar. *Aus Revaler Handelsbüchern. Zur Technik des Ostseehandels in der ersten Hälfte des 16. Jahrhunderts (Societas Scientiarum Fennica. Commentationes Humanarum Litterarum IX/5)*. Helsingfors: Akademische Buchhandlung, 1938.

Mickwitz, Gunnar. "Neues zur Funktion hansischer Handelsgesellschaften," *Hansische Geschichtsblätter* 62 (1937), 191–201.

Milgrom, Paul R., Douglass C. North, and Barry R. Weingast. "The Role of Institutions in the Revival of Trade: The Law Merchant, Private Judges, and the Champagne Fair," *Economics and Politics* 2 (1990), 1–23.

North, Douglass C. *Institutions, Institutional Change and Economic Performance*. Cambridge and New York: Cambridge University Press, 1990.

North, Michael. "Kreditinstrumente in Westeuropa und im Hanseraum," in *"kopet uns werk by tyden." Beiträge zur hansischen und preußischen Geschichte. Festschrift für Walter Stark zum 75. Geburtstag*, edited by Nils Jörn, Detlef Kattinger and Horst Wernicke, pp. 43–46. Schwerin: Thomas Helms Verlag, 1999.

Ogilvie, Sheilagh C., and André W. Carus. "Chapter 8: Institutions and Economic Growth in Historical Perspective," in *Handbook of Economic Growth*, vol. 2A, edited by Philippe Aghion and Steven Durlauf, pp. 405–514. Amsterdam: North Holland, 2014.

Ogilvie, Sheilagh C. "'Whatever is, is right'? Economic Institutions in Pre-industrial Europe," *Economic History Review* 60 (2007), 649–684.

Orłowska, Anna Paulina, Johan Pyre. *Ein Kaufmann und sein Handelsbuch im spätmittelalterlichen Danzig. Darstellung*. Cologne: Böhlau, 2020.

Orłowska, Anna Paulina. "Handel in einem Kaufmannsnetz: Der Danziger Johann Pyre," in *Vertraute Ferne. Kommunikation und Mobilität im Hanseraum*, edited by Joachim Mähnert and Stephan Selzer, pp. 32–39. Husum: Husum Druck- und Verlagsgesellschaft, 2012.

Paravicini, Werner. *Die Preussenreisen des europäischen Adels, Part 2 (Beihefte der Francia 17/2)*. Sigmaringen: Thorbecke, 1995.

Schonewille, Mark. Risk, Institutions and Trade. *New Approaches to Hanse History*. Working Paper. Nijmegen: Univ. Nijmegen, 1998.

Seggern, Harm von. "The 'Niederstadtbuch'. A Source of History of Private Life of Lübeckers around 1500," in *A Companion to Medieval Lübeck (Brill's Companions to European History 18)*, edited by Carsten Jahnke, pp. 352–371. Leiden and Boston: Brill, 2019.

Selzer, Stephan. *Die mittelalterliche Hanse*. Darmstadt: Wissenschaftliche Buchgesellschaft, 2010.

Selzer, Stephan and Ulf Christian Ewert. "Nord- und Ostsee, 500–1600," in *Globale Handelsräume und Handelsrouten von der Antike bis zur Gegenwart*, edited by Markus A. Denzel and Mark Häberlein. Berlin: De Gruyter, 2021.

Selzer, Stephan and Ulf Christian Ewert. "Die Neue Institutionenökonomik als Herausforderung an die Hanseforschung," *Hansische Geschichtsblätter* 123 (2005), 7–29.

Selzer, Stephan and Ulf Christian Ewert. "Verhandeln und Verkaufen, Vernetzen und Vertrauen. Über die Netzwerkstruktur des hansischen Handels," *Hansische Geschichtsblätter* 119 (2001), 135–161.

Slaski, Witold von. *Danziger Handel im 15. Jahrhundert auf Grund eines im Danziger Stadtarchiv befindlichen Handlungsbuches geschildert.* Heidelberg: Beisel, 1905.

Sprandel, Rolf. "Die Konkurrenzfähigkeit der Hanse im Spätmittelalter," *Hansische Geschichtsblätter* 102 (1984), 21–38.

Sprandel, Rolf. *Das mittelalterliche Zahlungssystem nach hansisch-nordischen Quellen des 13.–15. Jahrhunderts (Monographien zur Geschichte des Mittelalters 10)*. Stuttgart: Anton Hiersemann, 1975.

Stark, Walter. "Über Handelstechniken auf dem Brügger Markt um die Wende vom 14. zum 15. Jahrhundert," in *Hansekaufleute in Brügge, Part 4: Beiträge der Internationalen Tagung in Brügge April 1996*, edited by Nils Jörn, Werner Paravicini and Horst Wernicke, pp. 97–107. Frankfurt/Main: Peter Lang, 2000.

Stark, Walter. "Über Techniken und Organisationsformen des hansischen Handels im Spätmittelalter," in *Der hansische Sonderweg? Beiträge zur Sozial- und Wirtschaftsgeschichte der Hanse (Quellen und Darstellungen zur hansischen Geschichte, Neue Folge 39)*, edited by Stuart Jenks and Michael North, pp. 191–201. Cologne, Weimar and Vienna: Böhlau, 1993.

Stark, Walter. *Untersuchungen zum Profit beim hansischen Handelskapital in der ersten Hälfte des 15. Jahrhunderts*. Weimar: H. Böhlaus Nachfolger, 1985.

Stark, Walter. "Über Platz- und Kommissionshändlergewinne im Handel des 15. Jahrhunderts," in *Autonomie, Wirtschaft und Kultur der Hansestädte (Hansische Studien 6/Abhandlungen zur Handels- und Sozialgeschichte 34)*, edited by Konrad Fritze, Eckehard Müller-Mertens and Walter Stark, pp. 130–146. Weimar: Böhlau, 1984.

Steinbach, Sebastian. "What is Money?," in *Methods in Premodern Economic History: Case Studies from the Holy Roman Empire, c. 1300 – c. 1600*, edited by Ulla Kypta, Julia Bruch and Tanja Skambraks, pp. 132–145. London: Palgrave Macmillan, 2019.

Stieda, Wilhelm. *Hansisch-venetianische Handelsbeziehungen im 15. Jahrhundert. Festschrift der Landes-Universität Rostock zur zweiten Säcularfeier der Universität Halle a. S.* Rostock: Dr. v. Adler's Erben, 1894.

Stromer, Wolfgang von. "Der innovatorische Rückstand der hansischen Wirtschaft," in *Beiträge zur Wirtschafts- und Sozialgeschichte des Mittelalters. Festschrift für Herbert Helbig zum 65. Geburtstag*, edited by Knut Schulz, pp. 204–217. Cologne and Vienna: Böhlau 1976.

Sydow, Jörg, Georg Schreyögg and Jochen Koch. "Organizational Path Dependence: Opening the Black Box," *Academy of Management Review* 34 (2009), 689–709.

Thierfelder, Hildegard. *Rostock-Osloer Handelsbeziehungen im 16. Jahrhundert. Die Geschäftspapiere der Kaufleute Kron in Rostock und Bene in Oslo (Abhandlungen zur Handels- und Sozialgeschichte 1)*, pp. 194–207. Weimar: H. Böhlaus Nachfolger, 1958.

Watts, Duncan. "Networks, Dynamics, and the Small-World Phenomenon," *American Journal of Sociology* 105 (1999), 493–527.

6 Monetisation and economic inequality among peasants in medieval Poland

Piotr Guzowski

Introduction

In his work on the modernisation of the medieval society, David Levine wrote that "Money spoke a language that all rulers understood".[1] The perspective of the elite dominates almost all currents of medieval research, which is largely due to the availability of sources, but also plays a major role in looking at economic history. Chris Wickham emphasises the role of elites, whose attitude is to be crucial for the understanding of economic development:

> Here the key problem is demand for goods. In any society that does not depend on mass buying-power, the people who determined the basic scale and patterns of demand were elites [...]. Peasantries and the poor were not yet a sufficiently consistent, prosperous market for economies of scale to exist just for them, particularly given the absence of sophisticated and responsive structures for the movement of goods.[2]

This is why the focus is on royal and ducal courts, the farms of magnates and urban patricians. Luxury consumption has become a form of scientific fetish to explain all transformations, not only economic, but political and systemic alike.

Meanwhile, the pre-industrial economy, both feudal and capitalist, was peasant economy. The vast majority of the population worked in agriculture, and it goes without saying that more than half of the production was also made in this sector of the economy; moreover, mainly on family farms. There also existed a state which opposed kinship-based power systems, and there existed urban centres and stable relations between urban and rural life.[3] Some researchers noted "the spontaneous slow technical progress of which traditional societies are capable". Accumulated experience can lead to the introduction and adoption of new techniques, which can certainly occur within a village and in a peasant on an estate, which has its own economic advantages: the possibility of a more rational use of resources and more efficient deployment of labor".[4] Unfortunately, the aforementioned theoretical foundations of both a pessimistic and optimistic look at the importance of the peasant economy can hardly be regarded as thoroughly analysed through the lens of medieval and even early modern sources. In the case of Polish historiography, the general resentment towards exploring the economic history of the former epochs overlaps with the conviction, existing from the times of Tchaïanov that the overriding principle of self-sufficiency prevailed among peasants. In any case, the principle was also supposedly characteristic of other social groups of the country that was perceived as peripheral and backwards, from the ducal elite in the early Piast state[5] to the early modern-day gentry.[6]

Hence, it is not surprising that archaeologists and numismatists have demonstrated a greater interest in medieval economy than historians in recent years. They discuss the monetisation of the Polish land economy, which in their deliberations stands for a situation where "the majority of transactions used a coin of a fixed value rather than silver scrap in pieces or by weight".[7] Unfortunately, most of them[8] mistakenly identify monetisation with the money economy. Also, in this case, the authors are focused on the elites and hardly ever consider the extent of monetisation of particular sectors of the economy or the availability of money for different social groups.

This article, therefore, aims to look at the processes of monetisation and participation in the money economy of the most numerous social groups, e.g. peasants living in medieval Poland. Commercialisation processes leading to the development of economic inequality among peasants in the late Middle Ages will also be subject to an analysis. In my deliberations, I will refer to the terminology developed in research on medieval English economy. I use James Bolton's definition of monetised economy and money economy. In the first case,

> Money is used as standard of value, and in limited way for exchange, in buying and selling and in the payment of rents and taxes. But self-sufficiency, payments in kind and barter for both goods and services persist on large scale.[9]

Among the peasant population, land is also used in exchange for service or labour services, and there are relatively few coins in circulation. The mere appearance and circulation of coins do not make an economy a market economy. For market economy to be born, a number of factors, not only economic in nature, are indispensable, such as growth of population and markets, the advancement of law, the spread of literacy and numeracy and, above all, the creation of a strong political centre along with the monetary policy. As Bolton pointed out, population growth was a driving force behind demand and led to market growth, the development of trade and emergence of cities. This involved simplifying the exchange process, building infrastructure (roads, bridges) and reducing the costs of trade. The more frequent use of money required a clarification of the accounting system, weights and measures, not only associated with the monetary system, but in all branches of the economy. The development of trade influenced the spread of new financial instruments such as loans, bonds and, over time, the development of tax and rent systems. All this enforced the introduction of legal regulations to govern transactions. This was in the interest of and part of the responsibility of the state, which both created the legal framework for the development of the market and guaranteed the quality of coins, the symbol of the state's power. The introduction of taxes in cash influenced the popularity of money use and stimulated the circulation of money. The state also developed institutions playing a major role in the money economy, such as fairs. In such circumstances, the economy became the money economy; in other words, one in which bullion money commonly served as legal tender, a means of hoarding, a measure of value and an element of a loan.[10] Transformations of this type were of evolutionary in nature, accompanied by commercialisation meaning (according to a broad definition) an increase in the commercial activity of the society measured by the increase in the number of entities engaged in trade, the growth of urban centres and the amount of money on the market.[11]

Specific issues related to monetisation, money economy and commercialisation of the Polish medieval economy and peasants in particular, understood in this manner, were addressed several times, but the outcome was mostly presented in the Polish language.[12]

The first stage of monetisation (tenth–twelfth centuries)

When the Polish state appeared on the political arena in the second half of the tenth century, it became part of the weight-money economy (*Gewichtsgeldwirtschaft*). Unlike the west-European, post-Carolingian Münzgeldwirschaft, where coins were standard legal tender, in Central and Eastern Europe as well as in Scandinavia,

> Coins were used in the 10th–11th centuries for the most part not as money. They counted as bullion, which in the form of fragments and pieces was weighed or processed into bars (and ornaments). The goods were therefore paid for not with a coin as such, but with a unit of weight of bullion.[13]

In the exchange system based on the value of bullion, different forms of bullion were used, one of them being coins and another one being bars or ornaments. All these objects had a monetary function, and at the same time were part of the system of measurements and weights. Thus, the denarius could be a coin as well as a weight and account unit.[14] This system was an elite one, requiring not only simple counting skills, but also measuring tools and even expert knowledge.

Obviously, the peasant population participated to a small extent in the system. Around the year 1000 the peasants constituted about 95% of the population[15] in Poland, although fractions of coins found during excavations in proto-urban centres testify to the existence of basic trade among those outside the elite.[16] In general, however, the monetisation of lower social groups must have been connected with the development of local mint production. It is essential to know the scale of coin production in a given country to estimate the level of monetisation. Researchers of the medieval English economy, thanks to an excellent source base, are able to approximate the value of money supply as well as the average number of times a certain coin passed from hand to hand (velocity of circulation).[17] In the case of Polish lands this is impossible. Owing to source limitations, it is easier to pose the question to what extent peasant farms had to be monetised and commercialised in order to function in the medieval Polish economy rather than the question how the peasant economy was monetised and commercialised. Obviously, it is helpful to be familiar with the development of local coin production, especially with the estimation of its scale in particular periods.

The beginnings of minting in our country date back to the first years of Bolesław Chrobry's reign, around 995,[18] yet the scale of this ruler's entire production (until 1025) is estimated to have amounted to only about 130,000 denarii.[19] There was then a break in official minting activities for several decades, which resulted in copied coins, imitating German and Anglo-Saxon specimens.[20] Even more important were the Saxon cross denarii (German: Randpfenning), found more often in Polish than German treasures, in huge quantities, about 50,000 on the territory of Poland alone.[21] They were minted from 965 to 1105/20, and contributed to the monetisation of the Saxon–Slavic border, especially after 1040.[22] In the case of Poland, the resumption and intensification of coin production was connected with the reign of Bolesław Szczodry (1058–1079), and the number of denarii minted during his twenty-year reign is estimated at 4–5 million pieces.[23] Even more – about 1 million pieces a year were minted in the times of Władysław II (1138–1146).[24] The production of the Polish mints by no means matched the activity of mints in the neighbouring Bohemia, in which until the turn of the tenth and eleventh centuries about 7.5 million denarii were minted,[25] and in the years 1120–1125 the Bohemian mints were releasing about 2 million denarii annually.[26]

As Sławomir Gawlas noted, "It was essential to undertake local minting production in a sustainable manner for the monetisation of internal exchange".[27] It also influenced the development of the local money circulation sphere, characterised by a large dispersion of resources, as opposed to the long-lasting sphere of large international trade transactions. In addition, forcing the population of the country to use coins in settlements with the state apparatus was the easiest way to generate money transfers from the local to the state sphere. For Poland, however, the basic burden of the population towards the state until the end of the twelfth century was in kind; it was paid in the form of specific amounts of grain, honey, marten hides, hay, pigs and cattle.[28] There were still additional charges, such as duties and tolls, which at the end of the twelfth century usually included tariffs in kind, although cash payments also existed. As Roman Grodecki wrote:

> ...for example, in the tariff of Kołobrzeg in 1159 (two denarii per wagon), in the tariff of the customs chamber in Pomnichów on the River Vistula at the end of the 12th century: 1 denarius per empty wagon, 2 denarii per one item of horned cattle, 1 denarius per 2 pigs, 6 denarii per slave, 12 denarii per wagon containing cloth.[29]

The fines, whose relentless enforcement is reported by Wincenty Kadłubek, were also a source of cash.[30] If there was a shortage of cash on the market, according to Tadeusz Lalik, the state apparatus (mint workers or mints) was supposed to sell coins for the products of the local economy sought after at the duke's court and thus introduce new coins into circulation.[31]

A tithe was the most important of the other burdens that could be borne in cash by the rural population. In Western Pomerania, as early as in the middle of the twelfth century, it was partially paid in coins,[32] but in the lands within the range of the Piast rule, the first traces of a monetary tithe, paid individually by different categories of population, are only recorded for the beginning of the thirteenth century.[33] A common monetary tribute was also St. Peter's denarius (Peter's Pence) that was to be paid in Poland as early as from the second half of the eleventh century on the hearth, but later sources indicate that the payment could also be collected in grain.[34] There are no sources that would contain information about monetary settlements of the servant population with the ducal administration. The first records about rents paid in cash in the grand estates date back to as late as 1204, when the Trzebnica document was issued. The system of payments to the benefit of the property was diverse, and the monetary rents were not the most popular form – "out of the entire population, about 120 families paid in kind, 20 in cash and 10 families paid a mixed tariff".[35]

Despite the fact that the monetary obligations of Poland's inhabitants were by no means large, households had some opportunities to participate in the monetisation of the economy. As Stanisław Trawkowski noticed, this was, to a large extent, due to:

> an increase in the exchange of surplus production on a rural farm in the emerging local market and a slow conversion of these surpluses into deliberately produced commodity as shown by data from the late 12th and first half of the 13th century. The fact that even a small part of the agricultural and livestock production was intended for the market, so that it could be considered a commodity, had to change the way to look at the whole economy.[36]

Increased agricultural production and population growth in the early Middle Ages influenced the establishment and functioning of the market for staples. Documentary sources from the beginning of the thirteenth century contain remarks that certain regulations of the dukes were announced *in foro*.[37] Fairs were regular gatherings of people and, in the economic setting of producers, consumers and intermediaries, they played a fundamental role in the monetisation process. "The local names such as Środa (Wednesday), Czwartek (Thursday) or Piątek (Friday) indicate weekly functioning of the fairs on days whose names are already linked to the Christian calendar",[38] and thus the names must have been created some time after the adoption of the new religion, not earlier than in the mid-eleventh century. The relatively early functioning of fairs, from which tithes were paid in each castellany within the Archbishopric of Gniezno, is confirmed by the Gniezno bull of 1136.[39] The research carried out by Karol Maleczyński and Karol Buczek demonstrates a strong connection between the fair network and the fortified settlements network along with the exclusive right to establish fairs and obtain income from them [*regale targowe*].[40] Tadeusz Lalik estimated that at the end of the twelfth century there were about 250 fairs in Poland, not only ducal ones, but also those belonging to church institutions.[41]

The inn was an important institution closely related to the fair. In any case, the expressions *forum cum taberna* and *forum et taberna* appearing in the documents indicate an almost genetic link between the two institutions, although inns obviously also existed outside the fairs, most frequently in places related to the transport infrastructure: at crossings, bridges, duty and toll collection points. According to Irena Cieślowa,

> On the basis of the information on the inns found in the bull of 1136 it can be [...] concluded that there were inns in towns and other centres already in this early period, and the inns were generally known and widespread.[42]

The inns were located in the estate of the Benedictines of Tyniec as well as the Cistercians in Ląd, Canons in Trzemeszno and a number of other places that were put together in a collection that was quite impressive at the time.[43] Admittedly, inns located outside the fairs, in villages distant from the key transport routes, could accept as payment commodities from the locals, but it still holds true that the commonness of inns indicates an advanced process of monetisation of the peasant economy as well.

Indirectly, the phenomenon of *renovatio monetae* – in other words, the withdrawal of old coins from circulation by rulers and their replacement by new issues, which were of lower quality in the long run – provides evidence of the fact that coins reached different groups of the population meeting during the exchange at fairs or inns. The first cases of deployment of the *renovatio monetae* policy in Poland are connected with the times of Bolesław Krzywousty, who probably resorted to this procedure three times during his long reign.[44] Władysław II also carried out the money exchange three times, but during only eight years of his reign. After Bolesław Kędzierzawy reduced the frequency of coin exchange, the system was again developed by Mieszko Stary, whose policy was perceived as extremely onerous.[45] The coin renovation policy was associated with the introduction of single-sided coins, such as bracteates. Initially, the Polish bracteates were of a solemn and propaganda nature and were connected with the cult of St. Wojciech.[46] The breakthrough in the popularisation of bracteates as circulating money in Poland came thanks to the bracteate reform of Mieszko III, who from 1173 minted such coins not only in the central mint,[47] but also in regional ones.[48]

The mass production of bracteates, which were perishable and therefore frequently replaced, could quickly take the monetisation process to the level of non-elite consumption and even lead to a habit of the coins being used by all social groups. On the other hand, during the replacement of money profit was made at the expense of the people's resources and may have discouraged the use of circulating money.[49] Despite the potentially contradictory consequences, the practice of periodic exchange of money proves the existence of spheres of the economy that went beyond the autarkic model and were at least marginally involved in the exchange of goods, in which coins played a major role. As Zbigniew Żabiński rightly pointed out, *renovatio monetae* "would not have been feasible without such an economy".[50] On the other hand, however, the effectiveness of such a practice, allowing for the withdrawal from circulation of the entire issue of the former coin, meant that there was relatively little money in coins on the market, and hence the circulation could be controlled by the clerical apparatus.

The second stage of monetisation – the model of German colonisation and its consequences (thirteenth–fifteenth centuries)

The key changes in the monetisation of the Polish economy, including the peasant economy, are connected with the introduction of German law, reorganisation of agricultural production and the conversion of feudal benefits from in kind to monetary.[51] The point of departure was the model of the so-called Stadt-Landkolonisation, first implemented by the individual rulers of the fragmented country and church institutions, and then imitated by the mighty. "As part of this model, there were plans to organise entire property complexes for which commercial (*villae forenses*), court and administrative centres were designated."[52] From the peasants' point of view, it was important to implement the *domeine bipartite* concept, according to which the land belonging to the landlord was divided into two parts. The first part was the direct economic resource base of the landlord, while the second one was divided for peasant use into plots which were to provide food for the peasant family and to earn a surplus which could be given to the landlord in the form of a fee, or sold so that rent could be paid to the landlord in cash.[53] Changes in the way of land management were also connected with the reorganisation of fields and the cultivation system, i.e. the introduction of the three-field crop rotation. The organisational modernisation was accompanied by the introduction of technical innovations and the spread of the iron harrow, heavy plough, wider use of the horse collar and horses on the peasant farms as well as the development of breeding. All these changes resulted in an increase in agricultural production and, along with increasingly wider specialisation, enabled the creation of municipal towns, such as markets for peasant goods and services.

The modernisation impulses, broadening the monetisation of the peasant economy, came from three directions. Firstly, dukes, along with lay and clerical landlords, sought to "maximise income by providing peasant farms with outlets on the local market".[54] By obtaining a surplus and monetising it, the peasants could pay their obligations to the dukes and landlords in a monetary form. Secondly, the rulers, initially of the fragmented duchies and later of the reconstructed Kingdom of Poland, were able set about achieving their fiscal goals. It was easier for them to achieve the goals in urban centres by supervising trade and its facilities (fairs, inns, butchers' shops and stalls, cloth halls).[55] However, the villages were directly impacted by coin replacements (mainly bracteates) that were frequent in the fourteenth century, and the salt monopoly. In the middle of the fourteenth century, a plough tax paid in money was also imposed. We do not know its amount, but it was considered to be very burdensome.[56] St. Peter's Pence was also paid in the form of money, in the amount of one denarius per capita, along with small church fees in some cases. The tithe is unlikely to have been paid in cash. Thirdly, monetisation processes could take place through commercialisation. During the thirteenth century, 230 there were towns in Poland, and in the fourteenth century another 265.[57] Thanks to the analysis of St. Peter's Pence accounts, we know that in about 1340, the share of the non-rural population in the society was 14%.[58] The appearance of the mark accounting system and the addition of a thick coin in the form of a *groschen*, used to determine the amount of the rent paid by peasants, to the assortment of bracteates and denarii in circulation demonstrates the development of markets in which peasants had to participate. The fact of writing down the rules of land use and feudal charges (in privileges) or functioning according to the law of German rural self-government was also of great significance in peasant economic activity.

Despite the undoubted increase in the level of monetisation of the peasant economy in the thirteenth and fourteenth centuries, it cannot be asserted that representatives of the largest social group functioned in the money economy on a daily basis. A large part of the urban population with predominant medium and small towns was engaged in agriculture. The clergy and knights did not create an outlet for agricultural products either, as they had their own crops and fees received in kind, or tithes paid in grain. Limited outlets did not guarantee that the peasants had a large commercialisation potential. According to Andrzej Wyczański, peasant farms with an area of about 1 *mansus* (16.8 hectares), with much better technical and organisational capabilities (three-field crop rotation, horses, plough, harrows) than in the early Middle Ages were able to generate a grain production surplus worth about 16 groschen after sale.[59] Even though as much as that is added from the sale of other agricultural crops (fruit and vegetables), livestock products (cheese, eggs, meat) or services, only a minimum level of engagement in market production can be discerned. Fiscalism, characteristic of Kazimierz Wielki, was, after his death, restricted by Louis the Hungarian in 1374 to a plough tax in the amount of 2 or 4 groschen from a peasant's mansus.[60] The reconstruction of the Kingdom of Poland by Władysław Łokietek did not mean the start of permanent minting of the local coins, although Polish denarii appeared in circulation.[61] On the other hand, the monetary reform of Kazimierz Wielki, modelled on the monetary system of the Czech groschen, which meant the introduction of Polish groschen and *kwartniki* into circulation, ended in failure. According to papal sources, in some parishes, the collectors collecting 1 denarius per capita as St. Peter's Pence had to agree for the alms to be paid in grain.

The modernisation of the peasant economy, initiated owing to colonisation and conducive to monetisation and commercialisation, was deepened in the second half of the fourteenth and fifteenth centuries. Despite the lack of continuity in mint production during the reign of Władysław Jagiełło and his sons, Władysław III and Kazimierz Jagiellończyk, the royal mints issued far more than ever before. The preserved fragmented accounts show that in 1391 the mint of Krakow issued 484,000 so-called denarii, and for 18 months, from mid-1393 onward, it minted 1,050,000 *kwartniki*, which amounts to 4.3 million denarii.[62] In the following years of Władysław Jagiełło's reign, a half-*grosz* coin was also minted on an unprecedented scale.[63] The real emission boom occurred during the time of Władysław Warneńczyk, when, between 1434 and 1435, silver was used in the mint of Krakow, allowing for the production of between 53 million and 61 million denarii[64]. In addition to denarii (money), the basic type among Polish coins was also a half-*grosz*, and initially a small *kwartnik* (*trzeciak*). In the territory of Ruthenia, at the turn of the fourteenth and fifteenth centuries, *kwartniki* were minted, and in Prussia, after the start of the Thirteen Years' War, *szelągi* (solidi). Crown denarii and half-*grosze* were issued until the monetary reform 1528/29.[65]

Despite temporary interruptions in the activity of the main mint in the country, including in Krakow during the periods 1414–1431, 1440–1456, 1466–1480 and about 1498–1502, and the irregular work of the mints in Wschowa, Poznań, Lviv, Toruń, Elbląg and Gdańsk,[66] in the opinion of Stanisława Kubiak, "the already very advanced domestic mint production at that time satisfied the domestic money market to a sufficient degree".[67]

The market was most likely concentrated mainly in towns, still developing at a high pace. During the fifteenth century, 201 new towns were located in the country, but a higher rate of money circulation and a greater weight of money had to affect the peasant economy, too. Luckily enough, the village court records appeared as early as at the end of the Middle Ages. They recorded the cases that were resolved before the peasant courts. The majority of the records concerned land transactions between peasants and the related very primitive rural credit consisting in the sale of plots on instalments. Transactions of this type did not involve intermediaries; peasants buying a plot of land, homestead or house paid a certain part of the fixed price first and agreed to pay the rest usually in annual instalments. Hence, they were able to plan their economic activity and estimate the size of potential resources. They were by no means large, though; in the fifteenth century, the user of a single-mansus plot of land (16.8 hectares) was able to earn about 3 marks per year from the sale of grain production surplus.[68] The income from other peasant activities was probably as much as that. The average value of peasant land transactions was from 1 to 5 marks,[69] and the annual instalment of the loan most frequently amounted to 1 mark.[70] Thus, in the fifteenth century, the peasants were able to earn a few marks a year and allocate them for small or larger investments. The level of monetisation of their economy exceeded the minimum required by the state apparatus, and the settlement in money had to be common enough for the village court books to record the so-called estimation (*taksowanie*) of the deceased peasants' assets in money (determining the succession to be distributed among the heirs).

The fiscal apparatus decided several times in the first half of the fifteenth century to impose an extraordinary land tax on the peasant population, usually amounting to 12 groschen per mansus, which is much more than the fixed plough tax of 2 or 4 groschen. In the second half of the century, it was actually imposed on a regular basis, every two years on average, and at the end of the century a poll tax was also chosen once.

Peasant farms were not taxed at a high level. The rents paid to the landlords cost the peasants slightly more than the burden to the benefit of the state. A growth of the rents can be observed in the late Middle Ages. While in the mid-fourteenth century the most common rate was 12 groschen per mansus, a hundred years later it was half a mark (24 groschen). The fifteenth century location documents from the areas of Małopolska and Red Ruthenia also note the spread of a lump-sum tithe (4–12 groschen per mansus), although payments to a church institution remained mostly in kind.[71] The tithe did not force the majority of peasants to become more engaged in the monetary economy, although individuals among the peasants could be observed to make excellent use of the possibility to buy out tithes from the Church, either at the parish level or at the level of the bishopric or chapter, offered by the decisions of the diocesan and provincial synods already from the fourteenth century, and by state legislation.[72]

Economic inequality among peasants in the late Middle Ages

The progressing monetisation and commercialisation of the peasant economy had to lead to the appearance of economic inequality in the villages on a wider scale. It is true that Polish historical literature emphasises that economic diversification among peasants appeared with the second serfdom already in the early modern period, but its traces can be found as early as at the turn of the fifteenth and six-teenth centuries.[73] Due to the fact that the peasant economy relied on the land, it is worth looking at the information about the acreage that was in the hands of peasants. The location privileges of the colonisation period were based on the standard size of the plots of land given to peasants, with an area of one mansus. Data on the size of peasant land plots from the oldest surviving inventories of royal (Pol. *starostwo*) and bishop estates from the turn of the Middle Ages and modern times are compiled for the purposes of this text. A total of 2,862 peasant farms from the following royal estates were taken into account: Brześć (1494), Sambor (1495), Przemyśl (1497), Płock (1498), Przedecz (1502), Sanok (1523) and the villages of Płock chapter (1512).[74] They were divided into typically rural farms, but a group of peasant farms from the suburbs or urban areas was also isolated. Only peasant users individually named in the sources were considered. Undoubtedly, the quality of the results was greatly influenced by the way the inventory was made and by the precision of the writers. When describing peasant farms from the point of view of rent collection, the writers tried to round up the data to whole *mansuses*, halves or quarters to be able to calculate peasant obliga-tions more easily (Table 6.1).

The level of inequality is nowadays determined by the Gini coefficient express-ing the numerical inequality of distribution of goods or income.[75] Its value may range from 0 to 1, where 0 means uniformity of distribution, and 1 means cases where one observation has a positive value. An increase in the value of the coef-ficient means an increase in the inequality of distribution. When the village was located, its owners probably tried to organise it in such a way that there would be relative equality among peasant farmers, facilitating the calculation and collec-tion of burdens for the landlord. The more time passed following the establish-ment of the village or its shift to German law, the more complicated the structure of land users became. In the case of villages slightly distant from the centres of the properties, the Gini coefficient ranged from 0.104 in royal and church estates in Mazovia to 0.310 in Przemyśl royal estate. The low level of differentiation in Płock estates (royal and church) is undoubtedly affected by the largest source record schematism. Gini coefficient above 0.2 also applied to the villages of Sam-bor royal estates, Brześć royal estates, Sanok royal estates and Przedecz royal estates, hence different regions of the country (Table 6.2).

A higher Gini coefficient applied to peasant farms located in the suburbs or in urban land. It amounted to 0.382 in the towns and suburbs of the Brześć starosty and exceeded 0.3 in the vicinity of Sambor and Przedecz (Table 6.3).

Table 6.1 Peasant farms

Estate	Year	Number of farms
Brześć royal estate	1494	478
Płock royal estate	1498	99
Płock chapter estate	1512	424
Przedecz royal estate	1502	393
Przemyśl royal estate	1497	483
Sambor royal estate	1495	336
Sanok royal estate	1523	649

Source: The Central Archives of Historical Records in Warsaw, ASK I, manuscript 21: Inwentarz starostwa sanockiego 1523 [Inventory of starosty of Sanok 1523]; ASK I, manuscript 41: Inwentarz dóbr kapituły płockiej 1512 [Inventory of estates of Płock chapter 1512]; ASK LVI, manuscript 204: Inwentarz starostwa przedeckiego 1502 [Inventory of starosty of Przedecz 1502]; ASK LVI manuscript 250: Inwentarz starostwa samborskiego 1494 [Inventory of starosty of Sambor 1494]; *Inwentarz starostwa przemyskiego 1494–1497* [Inventory of starosty o Przemyśl 1494–97], edited by Michail Hruszewski, in *Zapiski Naukowo Towaristwa Imieni Szewczenka* 19, (1897), 1–24; *Inwentarz dóbr starostwa brzeskiego na Kujawach z roku 1494* [Inventory of Starosty of Brześć in Kuiavia in 1494], edited by Wiesław Posadzy, Henryk Kowalewicz, in *Studia i Materiały do Dziejów Wielkopolski i Pomorza,* vol. 2, part 2 (Warszawa: Państwowe Wydawnictwo Naukowe, 1956) 355–398. *Inwentarz starostwa płockiego w 1498 r.* (Inventory of Starosty of Płock in 1498), in *Lustracje województwa płockiego 1565–1789,* edited by Anna Sucheni-Grabowska, Stella M. Szachelska, (Warszawa: Państwowe Wydawnictwo Naukowe, 1965), 147–161.

Table 6.2 Gini coefficient for peasant farms for non-suburban villages

Estate	Number of farms	Gini coefficient	Lower band	Upper band
Brześć royal estate 1494	351	0.251	0.226	0.275
Płock royal estate 1498	99	0.104	0.063	0.146
Płock church estate 1512	424	0.189	0.167	0.211
Przedecz royal estate 1502	174	0.216	0.188	0.247
Przemyśl royal estate 1497	483	0.31	0.298	0.337
Sambor royal estate 1495	177	0.230	0.203	0.258
Sanok royal estate 1523	649	0.258	0.241	0.273

Source: as Table 6.1.

The relatively low level of economic diversification is undoubtedly influenced by the fact that inventory sources make it possible to compare only the owners of hereditary plots of land: 60–80% of the village population.

The analysis of the inventory data provides quite a static picture of the variation in the size of the land acreage in peasants' hands, yet it should be borne in mind that there was a land market among peasants, they were affected by the decisions of the landlords allowing the settlement of new peasants in the village, and certain inheritance rules were in force, which were conducive to the monetisation of the economy – the property was usually taken over by one heir, who was obliged to

Table 6.3 Gini coefficient for peasant farms for suburban villages

Estate	Number of farms	Gini coefficient	Lower band	Upper band
Brześć royal estate 1494	127	0.382	0.343	0.412
Przedecz royal estate 1502	219	0.329	0.282	0.371
Sambor royal estate 1495	159	0.314	0.278	0.346

Source: As Table 6.1.

repay the remaining heirs in cash. Very interesting data to capture the dynamics of the financial situation of the rural population are provided by the example of the inhabitants of two villages from the turn of the Middle Ages and modern times, Kłobuck and Zawada, described by Andrzej Wyczański.[76] The researcher used annual information on tithe payments and compiled data on changes over the years 1465–1516 (Figure 6.1). Half a century of the economic history of these villages was by no means affected by any breakthrough moments, yet the Gini coefficient showed a significant level of differentiation even in the short term.

In his research, Jacek Wiesiołowski presented a slightly different way of demonstrating economic diversity in the late medieval villages.[77] He used the information about estimations of peasant property carried out for the purposes of court cases pending before the Gniezno consistory in the fifteenth century. The peasants taking part in the estimations declared their belonging to a specific

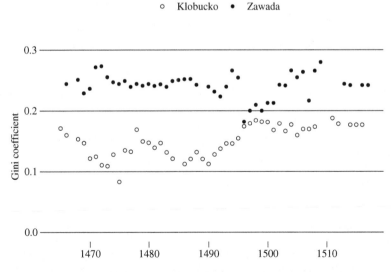

Figure 6.1 Gini coefficient for peasant farms in Klobucko and Zawada villages. Source: Andrzej Wyczański, "Rolnicy Kłobucka i Zawady w latach 1465–1517" [Peasants from Klobuck and Zawada in the years 1465–1517], in *Społeczeństwo staropolskie*, vol. 3 (Warszawa: Państwowe Wydawnictwo Naukowe, 1983), 47.

Table 6.4 The size of peasant property in the hearings before the Gniezno consistory

Wealth in marks	Servants	Crofters	Craftsmen	Peasants	Village mayors	Total	% of the group
40–200				23	25	48	8
16–30			5	95	9	109	18
9–15	2		13	184	3	202	33
5–8		4	5	64		73	12
1–4	31	50	4	22		107	18
<1	65	3	1			69	11
	98	57	28	388	37	608	100

Source: Jacek Wiesiołowski, "Rozwarstwienie ludności wiejskiej w świetle zeznań świadków w konsystorzu gnieźnieńskim w trzeciej ćwierci XV wieku" [The stratification of the rural population in the light of the witnesses' testimony in Gniezno consistory in the third quarter of the 15th century], *Społeczeństwo Polski Średniowiecznej*, vol. 5, (Warszawa: Wydawnictwo Naukowe PWN, 1992), 289.

group of village inhabitants and determined the value of their property in money by themselves (Table 6.4).

Obviously, the value of the property declared by the peasants is difficult to verify. In comparison with other regions of the country it seems to be definitely overestimated, yet it must be borne in mind that it was peasants from the relatively prosperous Greater Poland that were mostly heard by the Gniezno consistory. If we try to recalculate and present the data processed and initially grouped by Jacek Wiesiołowski by means of the Gini coefficient, we will receive a much higher result than in the case of the data obtained from the inventories. The Gini coefficient is as high as 0.716 with a 95% confidence interval of 0.691–0.729. The result might be even higher if we were to use non-grouped data for the calculations.

Contrary to the data obtained from the inventory of goods, which only refer to a simple variable such as the acreage, we can assume that peasants took into account other elements in their declarations, such as the quality of land, working animals at their disposal, available tools, assets resulting from other, non-agricultural economic activities (such as services), savings or accumulation effects. In addition to ordinary peasant landowners, Wiesiołowski included in his research the village mayors, who surpassed the other peasant villagers in wealth (often the mayors were also noblemen), but also servants or rural craftsmen.

Conclusion

Regardless of whether the level of economic diversification will be assessed through the lens of data on the acreage of peasant farms or the declaration of the value of peasant assets, there is no doubt that economic inequality existed among the peasant population as early as in the late Middle Ages, even before the second serfdom. There were several reasons for their emergence, which Werner Rösener defined in a universal way against the background of the economic history of peasants throughout the continent. He pointed out that the decisive factors were:

- the demographic situation of the region (and access to land);
- diversity in the legal situation of villagers, whose status could evolve as the royal estate economy developed and landowners gained legal advantage;
- different share of peasants in the market economy, which was influenced by factors such as the level of urbanisation or exports;
- the possibilities of obtaining income from non-agricultural economy, including crafts and services, which was of particular significance for the poorer part of the rural society;
- inheritance habits;
- the level of technological and economic development of the region; and
- legal restrictions on migration and market demand for peasant labour in the city.[78]

Each of these factors was present in late medieval Poland and is well worth a separate study. It should also be emphasised at this point that the location of the village was not a one-off event, but a process extended over a number of years, in which peasants could negotiate individual settlement conditions and plot sizes. In Polish villages, there was a land market in which typical phenomena could be observed; the land in villages distant from urban commercial centres was relatively cheap. After several years of work as servants on peasant farms or in manor houses, young men of peasant origin were able to buy plots sufficient to support their families. Land trade was also supported by the peasant inheritance system. Although officially, from the mid-fourteenth century, state legislation imposed some restrictions on leaving the village, the restrictions did not close the way to migration, not only to the town, but also to other rural areas. Finally, the hide system, assuming that a mansus is a *terra unius familie*, favoured the individualisation of the peasant economy. Corvée and subjection, emerging at the turn of the fifteenth century, may have intensified the processes of economic diversification among peasants, but without giving rise to the phenomenon itself. The organisation of the emerging manor required the existence of landless peasants (gardeners, crofters, lodgers) as well as large and medium-sized farms with human resources and working animals.[79]

From the vantage point of research into the monetisation of the peasant economy, the participation of peasants in the market economy was extremely important among the causes of inequality. This is clearly visible in the much higher Gini coefficient for peasants living near towns than for those living in villages far away from urban centres. In fact, the rents paid by peasants in money, typical of the German colonisation model, first appeared near commercial centres and only with time did they spread to other rural areas. With a relatively uniform system of German law in force in most rural areas, similar principles of organisation of social and economic life regulated by location privileges and a similar system of inheritance, it is the deepening monetisation and commercialisation of the peasant economy that contributed to economic inequality, but also to visible economic development. However, monetisation was a long-term process. Until the end of the twelfth century, the largest social group was able to participate in money turnover at a minimum level. The breakthrough in this area and the extension of the social range of monetisation is connected with the German colonisation and the resulting agrarian revolution. It enforced the engagement in market production and thus also initiated the process of commercialisation of the economy. Although monetisation deepened in the fifteenth century, full money economy among peasants evolved as late as in the early modern period.

Notes

1 David Levine, *At the Dawn of Modernity: Biology, Culture, and Material Life in Europe after the Year 1000* (Berkeley: University of California Press, 2001), p. 46.

2 Chris Wickham, "Rethinking the Structure of the Early Medieval Economy," in *The Long Moring of Medieval Europe. New Directions in Early Medieval Studies*, edited by Jennifer R. Davies and Michael McCormick (Aldershot: Ashgate, 2008), pp. 22–23.

3 Daniel Thorner, "Peasant Economy as Category in Economic History," in *Peasants and Peasant Societies,* edited by Teodor Shanin (Hardmonsworth: Penguin Books Ltd, 1971), p. 203.

4 Angeliki E. Laiou, "The Early Medieval Economy: Data, Production, Exchange and Demand," in *The Long Morning of Medieval Europe,* p. 100; See also: Karl G. Persson, *Pre-industrial Economic Growth. Social Organisation and Technological Progress* (Oxford: OUP, 1988); Paul Millet, "Production to Some Purpose," in *Economies Beyond Agriculture in the Classical World*, edited by David J. Mattingly and John Salmon (London: Routledge, 2001), pp. 17–48.

5 Karol Modzelewski, *Organizacja Gospodarcza Państwa Piastowskiego X–XIII Wiek*, 2. edn., (Poznań: Wydawnictwo Poznańskiego Towarzystwa Przyjaciół Nauk, 2000), pp. 200, 203; Przemysław Urbańczyk, *Trudne początki Polski* (Wrocław: Wydawnictwo Uniwersytetu Wrocławskiego, 2008), p. 171.

6 Witold Kula, *Teoria ustroju feudalnego*, 2 edn. (Warszawa: Książka i Wiedza, 1983), p. 195.

7 Mateusz Bogucki, "Główne etapy upieniężnienia rynków na ziemiach polskich we wczesnym średniowieczu," in *Upieniężnienie. Kiedy moneta staje się pieniądzem. Materiały z XIV Ogólnopolskiej Sesji Numizmatycznej*, edited by Borys Paszkiewicz (Nowa Sól: Muzeum Miejskie w Nowej Soli, 2011), p. 71.

8 One notable exception are the works of Dariusz Adamczyk: See: Dariusz Adamczyk, *Monetarisierungsmomente, Kommerzialisierungszonen oder fiskalische Währungslandschaften? Edelmetalle, Silberverteilungsnetzwerke und Gesellschaften in Ostmitteleuropa (800-1200)*, (Wiesbaden: Harrassowitz, 2020), pp. 213–221, 227–240; Dariusz Adamczyk, "Pieniądz czy strategiczny instrument władzy? Obieg kruszcu w społeczeństwie piastowskim przełomu XI i XII wieku, załamanie w dopływie denarów z Saksonii a ekspansja Bolesława Krzywoustego na Pomorze" [Money or a strategic instrument of power? Circulation of the precious metals in the Piast society at the turn of the 11th and 12th centuries, the collapse in the inflow of denarii from Saxony and the territorial expansion by Bolesław Krzywousty in Pomerania], *Przegląd Zachodniopomorski* 32 (2017), 143–167.

9 James L. Bolton, *Money in the Medieval English Economy, 973–1489* (Manchester: Manchester University Press, 2012), p. 22; James L. Bolton, "What is Money? What is a Money Economy? When did a Money Economy Emerge in Medieval England?", in *Medieval Money Matters*, edited by Diana Wood (Oxford: Oxbowbooks, 2004), p. 4.

10 Bolton, "What is money", pp. 8–9; Bolton, *Money in the Medieval Economy*, pp. 22–39.

11 Mark Bailey, "The Commercialisation of the English Economy, 1086–1500," *Journal of Medieval History* 24, (1998), no. 3, 307–309.

12 Sławomir Gawlas, "Komercjalizacja Jako Modernizacja Europeizacji Peryferii," in *Ziemie polskie wobec zachodu. Studia nad rozwojem średniowiecznej Europy*, edited by Sławomir Gawlas and Roman Czaja (Warszawa: DIG, 2006), pp. 25–116; Piotr Guzowski, *Chłopi i pieniądze na przełomie średniowiecza i czasów nowożytnych* (Kraków: Avalon, 2008); Piotr Guzowski, "Upieniężnienie Gospodarki Wiejskiej (chłopskiej i szlacheckiej) na przełomie średniowiecza i czasów nowożytnych", in *Upieniężnienie*, pp. 105–118; Piotr Guzowski, "Money economy and economic growth: the case of medieval and early modern Poland", *Questiones Medii Aevi Novae* 18 (2013), 243–255; Piotr Guzowski, "Karolińska rewolucja gospodarcza na wschodzie Europy (do końca XII wieku)," in *Granica wschodnia cywilizacji zachodniej w średniowieczu*, edited by Zbigniew Dalewski (Warszawa: Instytut Historii PAN, 2014), pp. 115–169.

13 Dariusz Adamczyk, "Od dirhemów do fenigów. Reorientacja bałtyckiego systemu hand-lowego na przełomie X i XI wieku", *Średniowiecze Polskie i Powszechne* 4 (2007), 15–16.

14 Christoph Kilger, "Wholeness and Holiness: Counting, Weighing and Valuing Silver in the Early Viking Period," in *Means of Exchange. Dealing with Silver in the Viking Age*, edited by Dagfinn Skre (Aarhus: Aarhus Universitetsforlag, 2008), pp. 254–271.

15 Henryk Łowmiański, *Podstawy gospodarcze formowania się państw słowiańskich* (Warszawa: Państwowe Wydawnictwo Naukowe, 1953), pp. 235–236; Henryk Łowmiański, *Początki Polski. Z dziejów Słowian w I tysiącleciu n.e.*, vol. 3 (Warszawa: Państwowe Wydawnictwo Naukowe, 1967), p. 312; Tadeusz Ładogórski, "Zaludnienie ziem polskich w czasach Bolesława Chrobrego," *Roczniki Dziejów Społecznych i Gospodarczych* 50 (1989), 21–29.

16 Stanisław Suchodolski. "Zasoby pieniężne szarego człowieka w Polsce wczesnośredniowiecznej," in *Człowiek w społeczeństwie średniowiecznym*, edited by Roman Michałowski (Warszawa: DIG, 2004), pp. 151–158.

17 Michael Dolley, *The Norman Conquest and the English Coinage* (London: Spink, 1966); Paul Latimer, "The quantity of money in England 1180–1247: a model," *Journal of European Economic History* 32 (2003), no. 3, pp. 637–662; Bolton, *Money*, pp. 3–17; Nick J. Mayhew, "Coinage and money in England,1086–1500," in *Medieval Money Matters*, pp. 72–86; Martin Allen, *Mints and Money in Medieval England* (Cambridge: CUP, 2012), pp. 294–376.

18 Stanisław Suchodolski, *Początki mennictwa w Europie Środkowej, Wschodniej i Północnej* (Wrocław: Zakład Narodowy im. Ossolińskich, 1971), p. 96; Stanisław Suchodolski, "Początki rodzimego mennictwa", in *Ziemie polskie w X wieku i ich znaczenie w kształtowaniu się nowej mapy Europy*, edited by Henryk Samsonowicz (Kraków: Universitas, 2000), pp. 351–360.

19 Ryszard Kiersnowski, *Pieniądz kruszcowy w Polsce średniowiecznej*, (Warszawa: Państwowe Wydawnictwo Naukowe, 1960), pp. 264–266.

20 Ibidem, pp. 232–237; Bogucki, "Etapy", pp. 84–85.

21 Kiersnowski, *Pieniądz*, pp. 196–197; Bogucki, "Etapy", pp. 88.

22 Christoph Kliger, *Pfenningmärkte und Währungslandschaften. Monetarisierungen im Sächsisch-Slawischen Grenzland ca. 965–1120* (Stockholm: Almkqvist & Wiksll, 2000), pp. 99–110, 143–160.

23 Stanisław Suchodolski, "Z badań nad techniką bicia monet w Polsce we wczesnym średniowieczu," *Wiadomości Numizmatyczne* 3 (1959), 38; Stanisław Suchodolski, *Mennictwo polskie XI i XII wieku* (Wrocław: Zakład Narodowy im. Ossolińskich, 1973), p. 99.

24 Suchodolski, *Mennictwo polskie,* p. 100.

25 Suchodolski, *Początki*, p. 96.

26 Suchodolski, *Mennictwo polskie*, p. 100.

27 Gawlas, *Komercjalizacja*, p. 84.

28 Karol Buczek, "Powołowe – poradlne – podymne," in *Studia z dziejów ustroju społeczno-gospodarczego Polski piastowskiej*, vol. 2, edited by Karol Buczek (Kraków: Societas Vistulana, 2008), pp. 231–248; Modzelewski, *Organizacja*, pp. 144–152. Karol Modzelewski, "Skarbowść: okres prawa książęcego (X–XIII in *Encyklopedia historii gospodarczej Polski do 1945* r., vol. 2, edited by Antoni Mączak (Warszawa: Wiedza Powszechna, 1981), pp. 264–268.

29 Roman Grodecki, "Początki pieniężnego skarbu państwowego w Polsce," in *Polityka pieniężna Piastów*, edited by Roman Grodecki (Kraków: Avalon, 2009), p. 343.
30 Tadeusz Lalik, "O cyrkulacji kruszców w Polsce X–XII wieku," *Przegląd Historyczny* 58 (1967), no. 1, 20–23.
31 Ibidem, 20.
32 Karol Buczek, "Z badań nad organizacją gospodarki w Polsce wczesnofeudalnej," in *Studia z dziejów*, vol. 2, edited by Buczek, p. 35.
33 Piotr Górecki, *Parishes, Tithes and Society in Earlier Medieval Poland c.1100–c.1250* (Philadelphia: American Philosophical Society, 1993), p. 97.
34 Tadeusz Gromnicki, *Świętopietrze w Polsce*, (Kraków: Drukarnia A. Kozianskiego, 1908), pp. 21–24.
35 Karol Maleczyński, "Epoka feudalna (od połowy XII do połowy XIII w.)," in *Historia Śląska*, vol.1, edited by Karol Maleczynski (Wrocław: Zakład im Ossolińskich, 1966), p. 269.
36 Stanisław Trawkowski, "Troska o pożywienie," in *Kultura Polski średniowiecznej*, edited by Jerzy Dowiat (Warszawa: Państwowy Instytut Wydawniczy, 1985), p. 31.
37 Tadeusz Lalik, "Regale targowe książąt wschodniopomorskich w XII–XIII w." *Przegląd Historyczny* 56, (1965), no. 2, 173.
38 Maria Bogucka and Henryk Samsonowicz, *Dzieje miast i mieszczaństwa w Polsce przedrozbiorowej* (Wrocław: Zakład Narodowy im. Ossolińskich, 1986), p. 37.
39 Łowmiański, *Początki Polski*, vol. 6, part 2, pp. 677–679.
40 Karol Maleczyński, *Najstarsze targi w Polsce i stosunek ich do miast przed kolonizacja na prawie niemieckim* (Lwów: Towarzystwo Naukowe, 1926); Karol Buczek, *Targi i miasta na prawie polskim* (Wrocław: Zakład Narodowy im. Ossolińskich, 1968).
41 Tadeusz Lalik, "Märkte des 12. Jahrhunderts in Polen," in *L'artisanat et la vie urbaine en Pologne médiévale* (Warszawa: Państwowe Wydawnictwo Naukowe, 1962), p. 366.
42 Irena Cieślowa, "Taberna wczesnośredniowieczna na ziemiach polskich," in *Studia wczesnośredniowieczne*, vol. 4 (Wrocław: Zakład Narodowy im. Ossolińskich, 1958), p. 167.
43 Cieślowa, "Taberna", pp. 174–177; Stanisław Trawkowski, "Taberny płockie na przełomie XI i XII wieku," *Przegląd Historyczny* 53 (1963), no. 3, 742.
44 Stanisław Suchodolski, "Renovatio Monetae in Poland in the 13th Century," *Wiadomości Numizmatyczne* 5, (1961), 57–75.
45 Marian Plezia, "W sprawie częstotliwości wymiany monety w Polsce na początku XIII w.," *Wiadomości Numizmatyczne* 29 (1985), 221–223; Stanisław Suchodolski, "Polityka mennicza a wydarzenia polityczne w Polsce we czesnym średniowieczu," in *Numizmatyka średniowieczna. Moneta źródłem archeologicznym, historycznym i ikonograficznym*, edited by Stanisław Suchodolski (Warszawa: TRIO, 2012), p. 347.
46 Ibidem, p. 326.
47 Jan Piniński, "Brakteaty gnieźnieńskie Mieszka Starego z lat 1173–1177," *Wiadomości Numizmatyczne* 9 (1965), no. 2, 85–104.
48 Borys Paszkiewicz, "Najstarsze brakteaty śląskie. Katalog brakteatów Mieszka Młodego i Bolesława Wysokiego", *Wrocławskie Zapiski Numizmatyczne* 2 (2006), 3–9.
49 Wiesław Kopicki, "Czy renovatio monetae w średniowieczu oznaczało psucie pieniądza?," in *Psucie pieniądza w Europie Środkowo-Wschodniej od antyku po czasy współczesne: Białoruś-Litwa-Łotwa-Polska-Słowacja-Ukraina*, edited by Krzysztof Filipow (Warszawa: Polskie Towarzystwo Numizmatyczne, 2006), pp. 73–76.
50 Zbigniew Żabiński, *Systemy pieniężne na ziemiach polskich* (Wrocław: Zakład Narodowy im. Ossolińskich, 1981), p. 37.
51 Zdzisław Kaczmarczyk, Michał Szczaniecki, "Kolonizacja na prawie niemieckim w Polsce a rozwój renty feudalnej," *Czasopismo Prawno-Historyczne* 3 (1951), 59–83.
52 Gawlas, "Komercjalizacja", p. 97.
53 Michael Mitterauer, *Why Europe? The Medieval Origins of Its Special Path*, transl. G. Chaplle, (Chicago: The University of Chicago Press, 2010), p. 8.
54 Gawlas, "Komercjalizacja", p. 98.
55 Ibidem, p. 103.

56 Jacek S. Matuszewski, *Przywileje i polityka podatkowa Ludwika Węgierskiego w Polsce*, (Łódź: Uniwersytet Łódzki, 1983), pp. 173–184.

57 Bogucka, Samsonowicz, *Dzieje miast*, p. 84.

58 Tadeusz Ładogórski, *Studia nad zaludnieniem Polski XIV wieku* (Wrocław: Zakład im Ossolińskich, 1958), pp. 145–152.

59 Andrzej Wyczański, "Gospodarka wiejska w Polsce XIV wieku w ujęciu liczbowym," *Roczniki Dziejów Społecznych i Gospodarczych* 62 (2002), 167–187.

60 Matuszewski, *Przywileje*, pp. 173–184.

61 Borys Paszkiewicz, "Mennictwo Władysława Łokietka," *Wiadomości Numizmatyczne* 30 (1986), no. 1–2, 95–97.

62 Marian Gumowski, *Dzieje mennicy krakowskiej* (Poznań: Drukarnia Rolnicza Poradnika Gospodarskiego, 1927), pp. 38–39.

63 Stanisława Kubiak, *Monety pierwszych Jagiellonów (1386–1444)* (Wrocław: Zakład Narodowy im. Ossolińskich, 1970), pp. 152–161.

64 Kubiak, *Monety*, p. 132; M. Gumowski, *Dzieje*, p. 49.

65 Stanisława Kubiak, "Monety koronne z drugiej połowy XV w.," *Wiadomości Numizmatyczne* 42 (1998), no. 3–4, 117–181.

66 Gumowski, *Dzieje*, pp. 36–76; Ryszard Kiersnowski, *Wstęp do numizmatyki polskiej wieków średnich* (Warszawa: Państwowe Wydawnictwo Naukowe, 1964), p. 169; Stanisława Kubiak, "Monety Jagiellonów w Królestwie Polskim w latach 1386–1506," in *Problematika Mincovníctva Jagelovcov*, edited by Eva Kolníková (Nitra-Svit: Slovenská numizmatická spoločnost, 1988), pp. 85–97; Borys Paszkiewicz, "Monety koronne Władysława Jagiełły między Wschową i Krakowem?," *Biuletyn Numizmatyczny* 358 (2010), no. 2, 107–120. Sebastian Pawlikowski, *Półgrosze koronne Władysława II Jagiełły* (Łódź: Amsterdam, 2018), pp. 17–40.

67 Stanisława Kubiak, "Udział monet zagranicznych w obiegu pieniężnym w Królestwie Polskim w XV wieku," in *Nummus et Historia: Pieniądz Europy Średniowiecznej*, edited by Stefan K. Kuczyński and Stanisław Suchodolski (Warszawa: PTAiN, 1985), p. 280.

68 Piotr Guzowski, "Changing Economy – Models of Peasant Budgets in 15th and 16th century Poland," *Continuity and Change* 20 (2005), no. 1, 9–26.

69 Piotr Guzowski, "The Peasant Land Market in Late Medieval and Early Modern Poland, Fifteenth and Sixteenth Centuries," in *Property Rights, Land Markets and Economic Growth in the European Countryside (13th–20th Centuries)*, edited by Gerard Béaur, Phillipp R Schofield Jean-Michel Chevet and Maria-Teresa Perez-Picazo (Turnhout: Brepols, 2013), pp. 219–237.

70 Piotr Guzowski, "Village court records and peasant credit market in fifteenth- and sixteenth-century Poland," *Continuity and Change* 29 (2014), no. 1, 115–141.

71 Guzowski, *Chłopi i pieniądze*, p. 41.

72 Franciszek Sikora, "Kmieć szlachcicem. Wilkowie z Pawlikowic w XV w.," in *Heraldyka i okolice*, edited by Andrzej Rachuba, Sławomir Górzyński and Halina Mańkowska (Warszawa: DIG 2002), pp. 399–417.

73 Ireneusz Ihnatowicz, Antoni Mączak and Benedykt Zientara, *Społeczeństwo polskie od X do XX wieku* (Warszawa: Książka i Wiedza, 1979), pp. 259, 265.

74 Archiwum Główne Akt Dawnych w Warszawie, ASK I, manuscript 21: Inwentarz starostwa sanockiego 1523; ASK I, manuscript 41: Inwentarz dóbr kapituły płockiej 1512; ASK LVI, manuscript 204: Inwentarz starostwa przedeckiego 1502; ASK LVI manuscript 250: Inwentarz starostwa samborskiego 1494; *Inwentarz starostwa przemyskiego 1494–1497*, edited by Michail Hruszewski, *Zapiski Naukowo Towaristwa Imeni Szewczenka* 19 (1897), 1–24; *Inwentarz dóbr starostwa brzeskiego na Kujawach z roku 1494*, edited by Wiesław Posadzy and Henryk Kowalewicz, in *Studia i Materiały do Dziejów Wielkopolski i Pomorza*, vol. 2, part 2 (Warszawa: Państwowe Wydawnictwo Naukowe, 1956), pp. 355–398. *Inwentarz starostwa płockiego w 1498 r.*, in *Lustracje województwa płockiego 1565–1789*, edited by Anna Sucheni-Grabowska and Stella M. Szachelska (Warszawa: Państwowe Wydawnictwo Naukowe, 1965), pp. 147–161.

75 Guido Alfani, "Wealth inequalities and population dynamics in northern Italy during the early modern period," *Journal of Interdisciplinary History* 40 (2010), pp. 513–549; Guido Alfani and Francesco Ammannati, "Long-term trends in economic inequality: The case of the Florentine state, c.1300–1800," *Economic History Review* 70 (2017), no. 4, 1072–1102; Carlos Santiago-Caballero, "Income inequality in central Spain, 1690–1800," *Explorations in Economic History*, 48 (2011), 83–96; Jord Hanus, "Real inequality in the early modern Low countries: the city of 's Hertogenbosch, 1500–1660," *Economic History Review* 66 (2013), no. 3, 733–756.
76 Andrzej Wyczański, "Rolnicy Kłobucka i zawady w latach 1465–1517," in Społeczeństwo staropolskie, vol. 3, edited by Andrzej Wyczański (Warszawa: Państwowe Wydawnictwo Naukowe, 1983), pp. 29–48.
77 Jacek Wiesiołowski, "Rozwarstwienie ludności wiejskiej w świetle zeznań świadków w konsystorzu gnieźnieńskim w trzeciej ćwierci XV wieku", Społeczeństwo Polski Średniowiecznej, vol. 5, edited by Stefan K. Kuczyński (Warszawa: Wydawnictwo Naukowe PWN, 1992), pp. 277–297.
78 Werner Rösener, *Peasants in the Middle Ages*, transl. A. Stützer, (Urbana: University of Illinois Press, 1992), pp. 192–193.
79 Piotr Guzowski, "The Role of Enforced Labour in the Economic Development of Church and Royal Estates in 15th and 16th-century Poland," in *Serfdom and Slavery in the European Economy 11th–18th centuries*, edited by Simonetta Cavaciocchi, (Firenze: Firenze University Press, 2014), pp. 216–223; Piotr Guzowski, "Monetarny kontekst wprowadzenia pańszczyzny na przełomie średniowiecza i czasów nowożytnych," in: *Inter Ducatum et Regnum. Studia ofiarowane Profesorowi Janowi Tęgowskiemu w siedemdziesiątą rocznicę urodzin*, edited by Piotr Guzowski, Marzena Liedke and Krzysztof Boroda (Białystok: Instytu Badań nad Dziedzictwem Kulturowym Europy, 2018), pp. 183–202.

Bibliography

Primary sources

Unprinted sources

Archiwum Główne Akt Dawnych w Warszawie [The Central Archives of Historical records in Warsaw]
ASK I, manuscript 21: Inwentarz starostwa sanockiego 1523 [Inventory of starosty of Snok 1523]
ASK I, manuscript 41: Inwentarz dóbr kapituły płockiej 1512 [Inventory of estates of Plock chapter 1512]
ASK LVI, manuscript 204: Inwentarz starostwa przedeckiego 1502 [Inventory of starosty of Przedecz 1502]
ASK LVI manuscript 250: Inwentarz starostwa samborskiego 1494 [Inventory of starosty of Sambor 1494]

Printed sources

Inwentarz dóbr starostwa brzeskiego na Kujawach z roku 1494 Inventory of Starosty of Brześć in Kuiavia in 1494, edited by Wiesław Posadzy and Henryk Kowalewicz, in *Studia i Materiały do Dziejów Wielkopolski i Pomorza*, vol. 2, part 2, pp. 355–398. Warszawa: Państwowe Wydawnictwo Naukowe, 1956.

Inwentarz starostwa płockiego w 1498 r. (Inventory of Starosty of Płock in 1498), in*Lustracje województwa płockiego 1565–1789*, edited by Anna Sucheni-Grabowska and Stella M. Szachelska, pp. 147–161. Warszawa: Państwowe Wydawnictwo Naukowe, 1965.

Inwentarz starostwa przemyskiego 1494–1497 [Inventory of starosty o Przemyśl 1494–97], edited by Michail Hruszewski, in *Zapiski Naukowo Towaristwa Imieni Szewczenka* 19 (1897), 1–24.

Secondary literature

Adamczyk, Dariusz. "Od dirhemów do fenigów. Reorientacja bałtyckiego systemu handlowego na przełomie X i XI wieku," [From dirhems to pfennings. The reorientation of the Baltic trade system at the turn of the tenth century] *Średniowiecze Polskie i Powszechne* 4 (2007), 15–27.

Adamczyk, Dariusz. "Pieniądz czy strategiczny instrument władzy? Obieg kruszcu w społeczeństwie piastowskim przełomu XI i XII wieku, załamanie w dopływie denarów z Saksonii a ekspansja Bolesława Krzywoustego na Pomorze" [Money or a strategic instrument of power? Circulation of the precious metals in the Piast society at the turn of the 11th and 12th centuries, the collapse in the inflow of denarii from Saxony and the territorial expansion by Bolesław Krzywousty in Pomerania], *Przegląd Zachodniopomorski* 32 (2017), 143–167.

Adamczyk, Dariusz. *Monetarisierungsmomente, Kommerzialisierungszonen oder fiskalische Währungslandschaften? Edelmetalle, Silberverteilungsnetzwerke und Gesellschaften in Ostmitteleuropa (800-1200)*. Wiesbaden: Harrassowitz, 2020.

Alfani, Guido. "Wealth inequalities and population dynamics in northern Italy during the early modern period," *Journal of Interdisciplinary History* 40 (2010), 513–549.

Alfani, Guido and Francesco Ammannati. "Long-term trends in economic inequality: the case of the Florentine state, c.1300–1800," *Economic History Review* 70 (2017), no. 4, 1072–1102.

Allen, Martin. *Mints and Money in Medieval England*. Cambridge: CUP, 2012.

Bailey, Mark. "The Commercialisation of the English economy, 1086–1500," *Journal of Medieval History* 24 (1998), no. 3, 307–309.

Bogucka, Maria and Henryk Samsonowicz. *Dzieje miast i mieszczaństwa w Polsce przedrozbiorowej* [History of cities and townspeople in pre-partition Poland].Wrocław: Zakład Narodowy im. Ossolińskich, 1986.

Bogucki, Mateusz. "Główne etapy upieniężnienia rynków na ziemiach polskich we wczesnym średniowieczu," *The main stages of the monetisation of markets on Polish lands in the early Middle Ages in Upieniężnienie. Kiedy moneta staje się pieniądzem. Materiały z XIV Ogólnopolskiej Sesji Numizmatycznej [Monetisation. When a coin becomes money. Materials from the XIV Polish National Numismatic Session]*, edited by Borys Paszkiewicz, pp. 69–90. Nowa Sól: Muzeum Miejskie w Nowej Soli, 2011.

Bolton, James L. *Money in the Medieval English Economy, 973–1489*. Manchester: Manchester University Press, 2012.

Bolton, James L. "What is Money? What is a money economy? When did a money economy emerge in medieval England?," in *Medieval Money Matters*, edited by Diana Wood, pp. 1–15. Oxford: Oxbowbooks, 2004.

Buczek, Karol. "Powołowe – poradlne – podymne," *[Ox tax, Plough tax, Hearth tax] in Studia z dziejów ustroju społeczno- gospodarczego Polski piastowskiej [Studies in the history of the social and economic system of Piast Poland], vol. 2, edited by Karol Buczek*, pp. 231–248. Kraków: Societas Vistulana, 2008a.

Buczek, Karol. *Targi i miasta na prawie polskim [Fairs and cities under Polish law]*. Wrocław: Zakład Narodowy im. Ossolińskich, 1968.

Buczek, Karol. "Z badań nad organizacją gospodarki w Polsce wczesnofeudalnej [Studies on the organisation of the early-feudal economy in Poland]," in *Studia z dziejów ustroju społeczno- gospodarczego Polski piastowskiej [Studies in the history of the social and economic system of Piast Poland], vol. 2, edited by Karol Buczek*, pp. 17–60. Kraków: Societas Vistulana, 2008b.

Cieślowa, Irena. "Taberna wczesnośredniowieczna na ziemiach polskich," [Taberna in Polish lands in early Middle Ages] in *Studia wczesnośredniowieczne [Studies in Early Medieval history], vol. 4*, edited by Alexander Gieysztor. Wrocław: Zakład Narodowy im. Ossolińskich, 1958, 159–225.

Dolley, Michael. *The Norman Conquest and the English Coinage*. London: Spink, 1966.

Gawlas, Sławomir. Komercjalizacja jako modernizacja europeizacji peryferii, [Commercialisation as a mechanism for the Europeanisation of peripheries] in *Ziemie polskie wobec zachodu. Studia nad rozwojem średniowiecznej Europy [The Polish lands versus the West: studies on the development of medieval Europe]*, edited by Sławomir Gawlas and Roman Czaja. Warszawa: DIG, 2006, 25–116.

Górecki, Piotr. *Parishes, Tithes and Society in Earlier Medieval Poland c.1100–c.1250*. Philadelphia: American Philosophical Society, 1993.

Grodecki, Roman. "Początki pieniężnego skarbu państwowego w Polsce," *[The beginnings of the state treasury in Poland] in Polityka pieniężna Piastów [Piast monetary policy]*, edited by Roman Grodecki, pp. 335–371. Kraków: Avalon, 2009.

Gromnicki, Tadeusz. *Świętopietrze w Polsce [Saint Peter's Pence in Poland]*, Kraków: Drukarnia A. Koziańskiego, 1908.

Gumowski, Marian. *Dzieje mennicy krakowskiej [History of the Mint of Cracow]*. Poznań: Drukarnia Rolnicza Poradnika Gospodarskiego, 1927.

Guzowski, Piotr. "Changing Economy – Models of Peasant Budgets in 15th and 16th century Poland," *Continuity and Change* 20 (2005), no. 1, 9–26.

Guzowski, Piotr. *Chłopi i pieniądze na przełomie średniowiecza i czasów nowożytnych [Peasants and money at the turn of the Middle Ages]*. Kraków: Avalon, 2008.

Guzowski, Piotr. "Karolińska rewolucja gospodarcza na wschodzie Europy (do końca XII wieku)", [The Carolingian economic revolution in eastern Europe (until the end of the 12th century)] in *Granica wschodnia cywilizacji zachodniej w średniowieczu [The eastern border of western civilisation in the Middle Ages]*, edited by Zbigniew Dalewski, pp. 115–169. Warszawa: Instytut Historii PAN, 2014a.

Guzowski, Piotr. "Monetarny kontekst wprowadzenia pańszczyzny na przełomie średniowiecza i czasów nowożytnych", [The monetary context of the introduction of serfdom at the turn of the Middle Ages and modern Times] in *Inter Ducatum et Regnum. Studia ofiarowane Profesorowi Janowi Tęgowskiemu w siedemdziesiątą rocznice urodzin [Inter Ducatum et Regnum. Studies offered to Professor Jan Tęgowski on his seventieth birthday anniversary]*, edited by Piotr Guzowski, Marzena Liedke and Krzysztof Boroda, pp. 183–202. Białystok: Instytu Badań nad Dziedzictwem Kulturowym Europy, 2018.

Guzowski, Piotr. "Money economy and economic growth: the case of medieval and early modern Poland," *Questiones Medii Aevi Novae18* (2013a), 243–255.

Guzowski, Piotr. "The Peasant Land Market in Late Medieval and Early Modern Poland, Fifteenth and Sixteenth Centuries," in *Property Rights, Land Markets and Economic Growth in the European Countryside (13th–20th Centuries)*, edited by Gerard Béaur, Phillipp R Schofield Jean-Michel Chevet and Maria-Teresa Perez-Picazo, pp. 219–237. Turnhout: Brepols, 2013b.

Guzowski, Piotr. "The Role of Enforced Labour in the Economic Development of Church and Royal Estates in 15th and 16th-century Poland", in *Serfdom and Slavery in the European Economy 11th–18th centuries*, edited by Simonetta Cavaciocchi, pp. 216–223. Firenze: Firenze University Press, 2014b.

Guzowski, Piotr. "Upieniężnienie gospodarki wiejskiej (chłopskiej i szlacheckiej) na przełomie średniowiecza i czasów nowożytnych", [Monetisation of rural economy (peasant and gentry) at the turn of the Middle Ages] in *Upieniężnienie. Kiedy moneta staje się pieniądzem. Materiały z XIV Ogólnopolskiej Sesji Numizmatycznej [Monetisation. When a coin becomes money. Materials from the XIV Polish National Numismatic Session]*, edited by Borys Paszkiewicz, pp. 105–118. Nowa Sól: Muzeum Miejskie w Nowej Soli, 2011.

Guzowski, Piotr. "Village court records and peasant credit market in fifteenth- and sixteenth-century Poland," *Continuity and Change* 29 (2014c), no. 1, 115–141.

Hanus, Jord. "Real inequality in the early modern Low countries: the city of Hertogenbosch, 1500–1660," *Economic History Review* 66 (2013), no. 3, 733–756.

Ihnatowicz, Ireneusz, Antoni Mączak and Benedykt Zientara. *Społeczeństwo polskie od X do XX wieku [Polish society from the tenth to twentieth century]*.Warszawa: Książka i Wiedza, 1979.

Kaczmarczyk, Zdzisław. Szczaniecki, Michał. Kolonizacja na prawie niemieckim w Polsce a rozwój renty feudalnej, [Colonisation under German law in Poland and development of feudal rent] *Czasopismo Prawno-Historyczne* 3 (1951), 59–83.

Kiersnowski, Ryszard. *Pieniądz kruszcowy w Polsce średniowiecznej [Bullion money in medieval Poland]*. Warszawa: Państwowe Wydawnictwo Naukowe, 1960.

Kiersnowski, Ryszard. *Wstęp do numizmatyki polskiej wieków średnich [Introduction to Polish Numismatics of the Middle Ages]*. Warszawa: Państwowe Wydawnictwo Naukowe, 1964.

Kilger, Christoph. "Wholeness and Holiness: Counting, Weighing and Valuing Silver in the Early Viking Period," in *Means of Exchange. Dealing with Silver in the Viking Age*, edited by Dagfinn Skre, pp. 254–271. Aarhus: Aarhus Universitetsforlag, 2008.

Kliger, Christoph. *Pfenningmärkte und Währungslandschaften. Monetarisierungen im Sächsisch-Slawischen Grenzland ca. 965–1120*. Stockholm: Almkqvist &Wiksll, 2000.

Kopicki, Wiesław. "Czy renovatio monetae w średniowieczu oznaczało psucie pieniądza?", [Did renovatio monetae in the Middle Ages mean debasement of coinage?] in *Psucie pieniądza w Europie Środkowo-Wschodniej od antyku po czasy współczesne: Białoruś-Litwa-Łotwa-Polska-Słowacja-Ukraina [Debasement of coinage in central and eastern Europe from antiquity to modern times: Belarus-Lithuania-Latvia-Poland-Slovakia-Ukraine]*, edited by Krzysztof Filipow, pp. 73–76. Warszawa: Polskie Towarzystwo Numizmatyczne, 2006.

Kubiak, Stanisława. "Monety Jagiellonów w Królestwie Polskim w latach 1386–1506", [Coins of the Jagiellons in the Kingdom of Poland between 1386 and 1506] in *Problematika Mincovníctva Jagelovcov*, edited by Eva Kolníková, pp. 85–97. Nitra–Svit: Slovenská numizmatická spoločnost, 1988.

Kubiak, Stanisława. "Monety koronne z drugiej połowy XV w.," [Crown coins from the second half of the 15th century] *Wiadomości Numizmatyczne* 42 (1998), no. 3–4, 117–181.

Kubiak, Stanisława. *Monety pierwszych Jagiellonów (1386–1444) [Coins of the first Jagiellons: 1386–1444]*. Wrocław: Zakład Narodowy im. Ossolińskich, 1970.

Kubiak, Stanisława. "Udział monet zagranicznych w obiegu pieniężnym w Królestwie Polskim w XV wieku" [Share of foreign coins in monetary circulation in the Kingdom of Poland in the 15th century], in *Nummus et Historia: Pieniądz Europy Średniowiecznej*

[Nummus et Histoira. Coins of Medieval Europe], edited by Stefan K. Kuczyński and Stanisław Suchodolski, pp. 277–287. Warszawa: PTAiN, 1985.

Kula, Witold. *Teoria ekonomiczna ustroju feudalnego [The economic theory of the feudal system]*, 2 edn. Warszawa: Książka i Wiedza, 1983.

Laiou. Angeliki "The Early Medieval Economy: Data, Production, Exchange and Demand", in *The Long Moring of medieval Europe. New Directions in Early Medieval Studies*, edited by Jennifer R. Davies and Michael McCormick, pp. 99–106. Aldershot: Ashgate 2008.

Lalik, Tadeusz. "Märkte des 12. Jahrhunderts in Polen", in *L'artisanat et la vie urbaine en Pologne médiévale*, edited by Alexander Gieysztor et al., pp. 364–367. Warszawa: Państwowe Wydawnictwo Naukowe, 1962.

Lalik, Tadeusz. "O cyrkulacji kruszców w Polsce X–XII wieku," [On the circulation of bullion in Poland of the tenth–twelfth centuries] *Przegląd Historyczny* 58 (1967), no. 1, 1–27.

Lalik, Tadeusz. "Regale targowe książąt wschodniopomorskich w XII–XIII w.," [East Pomeranian Duke's rights to fairs in the 12th–13 centuries] *Przegląd Historyczny* 56 (1965), no. 2, 171–201.

Latimer, Paul. "The quantity of money in England 1180–1247: a model," *Journal of European Economic History* 32 (2003), no. 3, 637–662.

Levine, David. *At the dawn of modernity: biology, culture, and material life in Europe after the year 1000*. Berkeley: University of California Press, 2001.

Ładogórski, Tadeusz. *Studia nad zaludnieniem Polski XIV wieku [Studies on the population of Poland in the 14th century]*. Wrocław: Zakład im Ossolińskich, 1958.

Ładogórski, Tadeusz. "Zaludnienie ziem polskich w czasach Bolesława Chrobrego" [Population of Polish lands in the times of Bolesław Chrobry], *Roczniki Dziejów Społecznych i Gospodarczych* 50 (1989), 21–29.

Łowmiański, Henryk. *Początki Polski. Z dziejów Słowian w I tysiącleciu n.e. [The beginnings of Poland. History of the Slavs in the first millennium AD.]*, vol. 1–6 (Warszawa: Państwowe Wydawnictwo Naukowe), 1963–85.

Łowmiański, Henryk. *Podstawy gospodarcze formowania się państw słowiańskich [Economic fundamentals of the formation of Slavic states]*.Warszawa: Państwowe Wydawnictwo Naukowe, 1953.

Maleczyński, Karol. "Epoka feudalna (od połowy XII do połowy XIII w.)," [The feudal era (from mid-12th to mid-13th century)], in *Historia Śląska [History of Silesia] vol.1*, edited by Karol Maleczynski, pp. 145–237. Wrocław: Zakład im Ossolińskich, 1966.

Maleczyński, Karol. *Najstarsze targi w Polsce i stosunek ich do miast przed kolonizacja na prawie niemieckim [The oldest trade fairs in Poland and their attitude to cities before colonisation under German law]*, Lwów: Towarzystwo Naukowe, 1926.

Matuszewski, Jacek S. *Przywileje i polityka podatkowa Ludwika Węgierskiego w Polsce [Privileges and tax policy of Louis I of Hungary in Poland]*. Łódź: Uniwersytet Łódzki, 1983.

Mayhew, Nick J. "Coinage and money in England, 1086–1500," in *Medieval Money Matters*, edited by Diana Wood, pp. 72–86. Oxford: Oxbowbooks, 2004.

Millet, Paul. "Production to some Purpose," in *Economies beyond agriculture in the Classical World*, edited by David J. Mattingly and John Salmon, pp. 17–48. London: Routledge, 2001.

Mitterauer, Michael. *Why Europe? The Medieval Origins of Its Special Path, transl. G. Chaplle*. Chicago: The University of Chicago Press, 2010.

Modzelewski, Karol. *Organizacja gospodarcza państwa piastowskiego X–XIII wiek [Economic organisation of the Piast State in the 10–13th centuries]*, 2 edn., Poznań: Wydawnictwo Poznańskiego Towarzystwa Przyjaciół Nauk, 2000.

Modzelewski, Karol. "Skarbowść: okres prawa książęcego (X–XIII w.)", [Fiscal system in the period of princely law (10th–13th c.)] in *Encyklopedia historii gospodarczej Polski do 1945 r. [Encyclopedia of Polish economic history until 1945] vol. 2*, edited by Antoni Mączak, pp. 264–268. Warszawa: Wiedza Powszechna, 1981.

Paszkiewicz, Borys. "Mennictwo Władysława Łokietka," [Minting of Władysław Łokietek] *Wiadomości Numizmatyczne* 30 (1986), 3–108.

Paszkiewicz, Borys. "Monety koronne Władysława Jagiełły między Wschową i Krakowem?," [Crown Coins of Władysław Jagiełło between Wschowa and Kraków] *Biuletyn Numizmatyczny* 358 (2010), no. 2, 107–120.

Paszkiewicz, Borys. "Najstarsze brakteaty śląskie. Katalog brakteatów Mieszka Młodego i Bolesława Wysokiego" [The oldest Silesian bracteates. Catalogue of the bracteates of Mieszko Młody and Bolesław Wysoki]. *Wrocławskie Zapiski Numizmatyczne* 2 (2006), 3–9.

Pawlikowski, Sebastian. *Półgrosze koronne Władysława II Jagiełły [Crown half-groszes of Władysław II Jagiełło]*. Łódź: Amsterdam, 2018.

Persson, Karl. *Pre-industrial Economic Growth. Social Organisation and Technological Progress*. Oxford: OUP, 1988.

Piniński, Jan. "Brakteaty gnieźnieńskie Mieszka Starego z lat 1173–1177," [Gniezno Bracteates of Mieszko Stary from 1173–1177] *Wiadomości Numizmatyczne* 9 (1965), no. 2, 85–104.

Plezia Marian, "W sprawie częstotliwości wymiany monety w Polsce na początku XIII w.," [On the frequency of coin replacement in Poland in the early 13th century], *Wiadomości Numizmatyczne* 29 (1985), 221–223.

Rösener, Werner. *Peasants in the Middle Ages, transl. A. Stützer*. Urbana: University of Illinois Press, 1992.

Santiago-Caballero, Carlos. "Income inequality in central Spain, 1690–1800," *Explorations in Economic History* 48 (2011), 83–96.

Sikora, Franciszek. "Kmieć szlachcicem. Wilkowie z Pawlikowic w XV w.", [Peasant as nobleman. Wilk family of Pawlikowice in the 15th century] in *Heraldyka i okolice [Heraldry and associated sciences]*, edited by Andrzej Rachuba, Sławomir Górzyński and Halina Mankowska, pp. 399–417. Warszawa: DIG 2002.

Suchodolski, Stanisław. *Mennictwo polskie XI i XII wieku [The Polish Minting of the XI and XII century]*. Wrocław: Zakład Narodowy im. Ossolińskich, 1973.

Suchodolski, Stanisław. *Początki mennictwa w Europie Środkowej, Wschodniej i Północnej [The beginnings of minting in central, eastern and northern Europe]*. Wrocław: Zakład Narodowy im. Ossolińskich, 1971.

Suchodolski, Stanisław. "Początki rodzimego mennictwa", [Beginning of Polish Minting] in *Ziemie polskie w X wieku i ich znaczenie w kształtowaniu się nowej mapy Europy [Polish lands in the tenth century and their importance in shaping the new map of Europe]*, edited by Henryk Samsonowicz, pp. 351–360. Kraków: Universitas, 2000.

Suchodolski, Stanisław. "Polityka mennicza a wydarzenia polityczne w Polsce we czesnym średniowieczu," [Minting policy and political events in Poland in the Middle Ages] in *Numizmatyka średniowieczna. Moneta źródłem archeologicznym, historycznym i ikono-graficznym [Medieval numismatics. The coin is an archaeological, historical and icono-graphic source]*, edited by Stanisław Suchodolski, pp. 335–349. Warszawa: TRIO, 2012.

Suchodolski, Stanisław. "Renovatio monetae in Poland in the 13th century," *Wiadomości Numizmatyczne* 5 (1961), 57–75.

Suchodolski, Stanisław. "Z badań nad techniką bicia monet w Polsce we wczesnym średniowieczu" [Studies on the technique of minting coins in Poland in the early Middle Ages], *Wiadomości Numizmatyczne* 3 (1959), 23–40.

Suchodolski, Stanisław. "Zasoby pieniężne szarego człowieka w Polsce wczesnośredniowiecznej, [Money resources of ordinary people in early medieval Poland]" in *Człowiek w społeczeństwie średniowiecznym [Man in medieval society]*, edited by Roman Michałowski, pp. 151–158. Warszawa: DIG, 2004.

Thorner, Daniel. "Peasant Economy as category in Economic History," in *Peasants and Peasant Societies*, edited by Teodor Shanin, pp. 202–218. Hardmonsworth: Penguin Books Ltd, 1971.

Trawkowski, Stanisław. "Taberny płockie na przełomie XI i XII wieku, [Płock taverns at the turn of the 11 c.]" *Przegląd Historyczny* 53 (1963), no. 3, 731–744.

Trawkowski, Stanisław. "*Troska o pożywienie, [Care for food] in Kultura Polski średniowiecznej [Culture of medieval Poland]*", edited by Jerzy Dowiat, pp. 29–58. Warszawa: Państwowy Instytut Wydawniczy, 1985.

Urbańczyk, Przemysław. *Trudne początki Polski [Difficult beginnings]*.Wrocław: Wydawnictwo Uniwersytetu Wrocławskiego, 2008.

Wickham, Chris. "Rethinking the Structure of the Early Medieval Economy," in *The Long Moring of medieval Europe. New Directions in Early Medieval Studies*, edited by Jennifer R. Davies and Michael McCormick, pp. 19–32. Aldershot: Ashgate 2008.

Wiesiołowski, Jacek. "Rozwarstwienie ludności wiejskiej w świetle zeznań świadków w konsystorzu gnieźnieńskim w trzeciej ćwierci XV wieku", [The stratification of the rural population in the light of the witnesses' testimony in Gniezno consistory in the third quarter of the 15th century] in *Społeczeństwo Polski Średniowiecznej, vol. 5, edited by Stefan K. Kuczyński*, pp. 277–297. Warszawa: Wydawnictwo Naukowe PWN, 1992.

Wyczański, Andrzej. Gospodarka wiejska w Polsce XIV wieku w ujęciu liczbowym, [Rural economy in Poland in the 14th century in numerical terms] *Roczniki Dziejów Społecznych i Gospodarczych* 62 (2002), 167–187.

Wyczański, Andrzej. "Rolnicy Kłobucka i Zawady w latach 1465–1517", [Peasants from Klobuck and Zawada in the years 1465–1517] in *Społeczeństwo staropolskie, vol. 3, edited by Andrzej Wyczański, pp.* 29–48. Warszawa: Państwowe Wydawnictwo Naukowe, 1983.

Żabiński, Zbigniew. *Systemy pieniężne na ziemiach polskich [Money systems on Polish lands]*, Wrocław: Zakład Narodowy im. Ossolińskich, 1981. This chapter was prepared as part of the project: "Wealth inequalities in the Polish-Lithuanian Commonwealth and their socio-political consequences" financed by the National Science Centre Poland.

7 Toruń's burghers and silver/gold in the first half of the fifteenth century

Krzysztof Kopiński

In the first half of the fifteenth century, Toruń's economic position weakened in favour of the rapidly developing city of Gdańsk. In Toruń, however, there was no shortage of funds earned over the previous centuries that could be invested in various enterprises; there were also merchants and financial brokers who could take advantage of the opportunities that appeared there (including buying property in Wrocław, investing in mines in Hungary – today's Slovakia – and purchasing land and real estate). At that time there was also a Teutonic mint in Toruń, which was the most important mint workshop in the Teutonic state until 1410. But where did the silver and gold come from, and what role did these precious metals play? The purpose of this article is to identify the role of silver and gold in their various forms in medieval Toruń. It will be particularly important to think about the use and quantity of valuable items of silver and gold found in Toruń's sources. It should be clearly emphasised in this introduction that at that time whether or not coins played a major role in settlements is obviously undebatable.

In Toruń's sources relating to the first half of the fifteenth century, we encounter a large number of records about silver jewellery and items. It is difficult to assess unequivocally whether the latter were objects of everyday use or whether they only decorated individual households. The following should be mentioned:

- gems,[1]
- silver rings,[2] also gold-plated,[3] with precious stones,[4]
- a crown,[5] tiara,[6]
- a chain,[7]
- a rope,[8]
- belts,[9]
- a sheath for a dagger,[10]
- a decoration, fitting of the dagger,[11]
- buttons of various sizes, large and small, sometimes decorated, appearing separately or on dresses or even a bathrobe,[12]
- clothes hooks,[13]
- silver ribbons,[14] also gold-plated,[15]
- ribbon clips,[16]
- buckles, cuff links,[17]
- a woman's knife,[18]

- a salt cellar,[19]
- a cup,[20]
- ampoules,[21]
- crosses on episcopal gloves, given to the faithful to kiss (osculare),[22]
- a goblet,[23] goblet for roots,[24]
- a vase,[25]
- a pitcher,[26]
- a mug,[27] a cup,[28]
- spoons, forks,[29]
- dishes,[30]
- seals,[31]
- other equipment.[32]

It should be assumed that the above-mentioned silver objects, apart from their purely functional role, also constituted a way for Toruń's burghers to secure their property. At this point, special attention should be paid to the large numbers of silver buttons, which may have been equivalent to silver coins. We must remember that money was very often subjected to monetary reforms, which in the vast majority of cases lowered their mint rate rather than improving the silver content of the coin.

We also have a significant number of accounts referring to silver in melted form (*lotiges silber*), sometimes also referred to as pure.[33] Information also appears in the sources that the silver was bought in pieces (*stuecke*) of varying sizes.[34] It is also worth mentioning the entries, which provide a summary of the various silver items and also provide information on how much they weighed in the alloy of, for example, 16 ½ of a mark of silver.[35] Source records even state that the minor children of the deceased Langhe Hannos had 15 ½ marks in silver jewellery,[36] and in other cases there were 46 marks of jewellery.[37] Source materials also inform us about silver in the form of ore.[38]

Source records provide much information about the role of silver objects and silver in the life of Toruń's burghers in the Middle Ages. Relatively often was silver the subject of the most ordinary financial settlements,[39] or was the subject of property divisions.[40] In the latter case, it happened on several occasions that stepchildren and stepfathers/stepmothers, or legal guardians, settled accounts with adolescent children using an alloy of silver.[41] When, in 1412, the Foykencus brothers came of age (Fewkenkus, Vokenkus) and settled their accounts with each other, silver jewels were listed first.[42] In turn, when in 1423 representatives of the said family settled their accounts again, the list included gold rings (7 pieces, large and small), a coral rosary, followed by 1 silver belt, which weighed 7 silver *wiardunks* (*firdung*) of silver, followed by one smaller pearl crown as well as other items.[43]

Silver was also the subject of loans and their collateral. In 1418, Bertram II Ludenscheide borrowed 60 fines of silver from the capital of his minor son Johann Reusop, by guaranteeing a house in Jęczmienna Street.[44] In the same year, the widow of Johann Widenscheide borrowed 50 marks of silver from the minor children of Johann Reusop, perhaps his brother-in-law, on the security of a house in Szeroka Street and a shack.[45] In 1419, the subject of the pledge was an alloy of 9 ½ marks of silver in silver jewels.[46] In the same year of 1419, Laurence Stangenwald, a townsman of Toruń, testified that he had received 12 silver marks in jewellery from the minor nephews of his wife, in the knowledge of the city council and legal guardians. However, 11 marks of silver minus one dram (Pol. *łut*) (i.e. 1/16 of a mark) went to the Toruń Town Hall, because the outstanding silver remained in the hands of Barbara Stangenwaldynne and was intended for raising children.[47] In addition, in 1424 Barbara Stangenwaldynne received 2 marks and 3 ½ skojecs of silver in ore, in a scabbard with a dagger and drinking vessel.[48] In 1423, the debtors of Barbara Stangenwaldynne and her relatives were Henry von der Mersche (38 marks), Thomas Becker (70 marks) and Hartwig Hitfeld (28 marks), who borrowed a total of 136 marks of silver probably from the property of the minors who were looked after by the Toruń burgher.[49] At this point, one might be tempted to make another assumption that silver also served to secure the family's existence.

It seems that when drawing up inventories of movable property, attention was paid to the fact that certain items were made of precious metals. In 1428, the list of the property of a citizen of Toruń – Herman Trost contains information about "probably a silver forged dagger" (*degen wol mit silber beslagen*).[50] Elsewhere, the source reports about silver hooks as follows: "*und eyn paer mantel heffte, by eyn silber*".[51]

Somewhat less information is provided by the same sources about gold. Most often they mention jewellery and decorations, such as rings,[52] clasps.[53] However, some problems should be noted here. Rings and clasps are not always referred to as gold or silver in the sources, which excludes them from this study. Sometimes, it can only be assumed with a high degree of probability that rings might have been made of precious metals, since they are listed along with guilders and nobles, and then old money.[54] Other gold items include a gold-plated chasuble,[55] a gilded goblet,[56] a velvet hat with a gold ribbon,[57] and a cross.[58] As with silver, gold items were also meticulously weighed. In 1426, a clasp, a ring and a noble included one mark of gold.[59] Interestingly, in the same source reference, old money (most likely of silver)[60] weighed 3 marks. Coins were not specified in the record, but the weight was given immediately.

We have slightly less information for the examined period about gold. At this point, it should also be remembered that in Toruń there were masters of goldsmithery who produced for the needs of Prussian burghers, the nearby clergy, knights of Chełmno and the Teutonic Knights.[61] Toruń gold products also reached Kuyavia. An example here is the order made by the bishop of Włocławek Jan Kropidło, who commissioned Jan and Oswald, both goldsmiths of Toruń, to make monstrances and silver trays[62] for him.

Source records also mention gold, probably melted down. At the turn of 1448–1449 a certain Kotmannynne bought 11 ounces of gold[63] from Peter van der Netcze. The transaction was quite significant as over 342 grams of gold were involved. In 1451, a settlement took place in Toruń between Nicholas Opicz from Wrocław and Johann Bischoffheym, who was the representative of two residents of Wrocław – Alexander Banke and Martin Banke. The debt of 96 ½ gold Hungarian guilders (*gulden hungarische guldin*) was settled in gold and commodities (*an golde und an ware*). The commodities included 20 woollen fabrics and 9 oxen, while the gold comprised 19 Hungarian guilders and 8 Rhine guilders.[64] Another record from 1455 tells us that the compensation connected with the debt was to be made in gold and in money.[65] Probably at this point, on the basis of the above data, it should be considered whether, by any chance, there was a shortage of gold in Prussia at that time. In the meantime, we must remember that in 1454 the Thirteen Years' War broke out between Poland and the Teutonic Order, which might have been the reason for a monetary crisis related to payments in gold coins.

This might seem a trivial statement, but it must be remembered that precious metals were also found in coins minted in Prussia, or in foreign ones, which arrived there mainly through trade. In the State of the Teutonic Order in Prussia, the grand master Winrich von Kniprode (1351–1382) carried out a monetary reform around 1364. Initially, 1 Prussian (Chełmno) grzywna/mark = 24 skojccs = 45 half-skojecs = 192 firlings = 720 pfennigs (a bracteate – single-sided minted coins). As part of the second stage of the reform, the same grand master introduced around 1,380 shillings worth 12 pfennigs in exchange for half-skojecs and firlings. During the Polish–Lithuanian–Teutonic War of 1409–1411, the Teutonic Order started producing guilders using the Hungarian rate (Hungarian parameters).[66] This production lasted with breaks until 1425. At the initial stage, the coins produced were used to pay the Teutonic Order's mercenaries.[67] The unstable Prussian mark was definitely not suitable to pay the mercenary troops' wages at that time.

The Grunwald defeat and the monetary crisis of the Teutonic state arising from it in the following years, also due to high inflation, resulted in coins being minted in Prussia from silver of an increasingly inferior quality.[68] The situation was exacerbated by the necessity to pay a high ransom to the Polish-Lithuanian side for prisoners of war and the elevated fees for troops leaving the castles. The payment of 6 million Prague grosch was to be effectuated in this coin, which caused the Teutonic Order additional difficulty.[69] The crisis also forced the Teutonic authorities to introduce several ordinances on precious metals. On 14 February 1412, it was decided that the silver would only be melted in Chełmno, Toruń, Elbląg, Braniewo, Königsberg and Gdańsk. Goldsmiths were obliged to mark all silverware with their city signs and designations.[70] Since August 1412, townspeople had been prohibited from purchasing silver and gold coins. The ordinance stressed that Toruń's burghers could not buy old coins and silver in Gdańsk, while Gdańsk's residents could not do so in Toruń. Townspeople who made such purchases of old coins were required to deliver them to the mint, where they were to receive appropriate payment.[71] This procedure, however, did not seem to be approved of by religious serfs. In the complaints of the Prussian estates made against the Teutonic Knights in 1453, it reads that the grand master Henry von Plauen (1410–1413)

> forced many knights, squires and the cities to bring their silver ornaments to the mint, where they were given in return what they [Teutonic knights]

wanted; and the bodies and properties of those who refused to do it were affected by punishments, which had never been heard of before in all Christianity.[72]

This means that the Teutonic Knights failed to pay the correct equivalents for old silver and coins taken from their religious serfs. In this way, funds to cover the obligations associated with the Great War 1409–1411 were easily obtained.

At the end of 1412, the grand master introduced an order requiring that burghers of Toruń sell all silverware to the Teutonic commander at the same price as throughout Prussia. Silver bowls, jugs, cups and goblets were valued at 2 Prussian marks and 18 skojecs for an alloy of one mark while silver found in belts, chains, bells and clasps was valued at 2 marks and 15 skojecs for an alloy of one mark.[73] It seems that this exchange rate was more favourable for burghers, who were more willing to give away their silver jewellery and decorations to the Teutonic Order.[74]

On 4th November 1413, a regulation was issued which prohibited burghers, merchants and goldsmiths from buying silver and old money and remelting it. Silver should bear Toruń's or Gdańsk's mint markings. If the silver did not have such markings, it should be submitted for a chargeable marking to the minter.[75]

For a long time, the Teutonic Knights refrained from releasing mints, usually on the authority of the leaders[76] from their fraternity. After the monetary reform carried out in Prussia in 1415, the Prussian coin did not strengthen as much as had been expected. At the end of 1415, there was a decrease in the shilling's minting rate. The successive reduction of the silver content in Prussian coins in favour of copper was not conducive to the development of trade and in principle could be burdensome for all subjects.[77] In 1416, the new shilling was introduced in the Teutonic state with an exchange rate equal to two old shillings.[78] From that moment, sources regularly began to include the information about lighter Prussian marks of lower value – "geringe"[79] – and about good marks or good, new marks.[80] In the years 1416, 1418 and 1420, it was regularly reminded that the export of silver from Prussia was prohibited.[81] In addition, in 1420 goldsmiths and others were banned from smelting or contaminating new shillings. What is more, goldsmiths and others were forbidden to own secret furnaces and scales that were not tared. Goldsmiths also had to mark their products.[82] Certainly, there was a lack of silver in Prussia at that time, and the introduced bans were aimed at stopping the outflow of precious metals from the country, thus improving its economic situation. It seems that the restrictions on silver trade at that time must have adversely affected religious serfs. One more point is worth noting: namely, since the various bans on silver were reminded repeatedly, there might have been a serious problem with their compliance.

The strengthening of the Czech grosch did not contribute to the improvement of the situation in Prussia in the following years.[83] In this way, foreign coins such as Czech (Prague) grosches and Hungarian guilders were quite common in the State of the Teutonic Order in Prussia. In addition, the sources inform us about other coins circulating in Prussia: Rhine and Haarlem guilders, English and Flemish pounds, Polish marks, ducats and nobles.[84] This situation certainly caused numerous problems. The Teutonic officials themselves had problems calculating the value of various coins, and the sources of information for them in this regard were the Prussian burghers. On 30 July 1423, Johann Tiergart, the prosecutor general of the Teutonic Order in Rome, asked Toruń's councillors to send him information about the value of old coins.[85] A year later, in a letter of 20 July 1424, he himself informed the Toruń council about the coin rates.[86] The data on problems with the Czech grosch also come from 1424. Namely, Sigismund of Luxemburg along with the council of the city of Wrocław, explaining to the grand master Paul von Russdorf the issue of overdue payments to Toruń's burghers, informed about the fall of the Czech grosch and asked that rentiers in Prussia be content with this coin.[87] It seems that these various perturbations with domestic and foreign coins caused a greater interest in precious metals, which constituted a security of property independent of the economic and political situation.

In 1426, the grand master Paul von Russdorf informed the council of the Old Town of Toruń about the prohibition against goldsmiths and other people smelting used coins, and also forbade marking silver by unauthorised persons. Such a crime was to be punished with the most severe penalties. At the same time, the grand master banned the export of silver from Prussia.[88] This means that Prussian burghers tried to deal with these unfavourable economic trends by resorting to obtaining silver from old coins. This situation, however, met with a decisive reaction from the Teutonic Order, which, in fact, introduced a monopoly on trade in precious metals in their country.

The source reports from subsequent years inform us about the evolving unfavourable phenomena for the Prussian burghers in the monetary policy in Central and Eastern Europe. On 14th May 1426, the grand master Paul von Russdorf asked the Toruń council to send two councillors to the assembly in Elbląg (26th May) to deal with damages related to the inflow of money to Prussia.[89] However, in 1437, Paul von Russdorf in a letter to Toruń's councillors drew attention to Wrocław and Nuremberg merchants bringing the fake coins to Prussia. At the same time, the grand master asked that people bringing such money into the country be detained. Paul von Russdorf also informed that talks with the Polish envoys were underway in this matter.[90] Probably the last account should be combined with a slightly earlier letter from 1432 of the Polish King Władysław Jagiełło to the Wrocław council regarding the resolution passed in Sieradz, where the export of "domestic products" to Silesia was forbidden. This fact was justified with the desire to prevent the introduction of the bad coins to Polish territory.[91] Another document comes from 1442; we learn from it that the Toruń council took over 84 threescores of fake hellers from two Poles.[92] This type of information contributed to the fact that Toruń's burghers secured part of their profits in precious metals and objects made of them. This type of investment was more certain than securing their assets in coins containing small amounts of silver.

Finally, the question should be asked where the silver and gold used in Prussia came from. The answer should begin with a reminder that on 18 March 1403 the grand master Konrad von Jungingen, granted the city of Toruń the privilege of storage (Stapelrecht). The said storage law in Toruń covered wax, fur of animals, silk, and roots, and such metals as copper, lead, iron, mercury and silver and gold in ore. This meant that merchants coming to Toruń with the above-mentioned goods were obliged to expose them in this place and had to deal with their sale without the possibility of entrusting this activity to another person.[93]

It seems that silver most often went to Toruń through Silesia. It is worth mentioning here the transaction from 1407, when Heinrich Schurgast, a goldsmith, along with his guild, accused Herman Bars – a burgher from Toruń – in the court in Wrocław. Both Schurgast and Bars wanted to earn money on silver, which the Toruń burgher had delivered to the goldsmith from Wrocław from Nicholas Grutczenschreiber, a burgher from Legnica. In Toruń, however, Herman Bars was denied the marking of silver, explaining to him that it was not local silver, but silver that appeared here for the first time. The Toruń burgher had to pay a charge of 20 skojecs for the silver he possessed. Due to this fact, the planned undertaking incurred financial losses.[94]

In the years 1413–1419, some Wrocław residents – Sigismund Poznow, Nicholas Buntzlow and Sigismund Sitten – were in debt to Engilhart Nothafft, a Teutonic minter in Toruń. This debt was reimbursed in the following form: 100 silver marks, 135 old English nobles and 587 old Hungarian guilders ("*lilgener*"). This means that most probably some of the precious metals used in the Toruń mint were imported via Wrocław. The entire payment should certainly be considered very large. Finally, it also seems that the said mint also melted old gold coins for the Teutonic Order.[95] A few years later, the grand master prohibited Toruń's goldsmiths from the melting old coins, a job which was probably to be reserved for the Teutonic minters.

Opportunities for the residents of Toruń to obtain silver were from the fact that several of them actively participated in the implementation of the extensive economic plans of Sigismund of Luxembourg. In connection with the blockade of Venice in 1420, direct access to the Black Sea markets became very important for Sigismund's economic policy. In connection with this policy, it was decided to pave a new road to Kaffa, bypassing Venice. In 1420, Heinrich Ryman from Gdańsk and Nicholas II von der Linde from Toruń were sent in search of a new route for the expedition from Prussia.[96] It is worth adding here that Cunigunde, daughter of Nicholas II von der Linde, was the wife of Johann Falbrecht, the main shareholder of the powerful Silesian-Prussian company Falbrecht–Morser–Rosenfeld, which also actively participated in the implementation of the economic plans of Sigismund of Luxembourg.[97] In the years 1424–1425 and 1426–1428 Johann Falbrecht and David Rosenfeld were royal administrators and minters in the mining city of Kremnica in Hungary (today's Slovakia). In 1424 they were managers and minters in Košice. This function was also performed by Johann Falbrecht himself in the years 1427–1428 and in 1432. Then, in 1428 he was the administrator and minter in the mining town of Braszów (Romanian Braşow) in the province of Transylvania. In 1428 and in 1432 he was the administrator of the mining town of Smolnik. In 1431, Johann Falbrecht was referred to as the manager of all Hungarian copper mines ("Kupfergraf von Ungarn")[98]. Another shareholder – David Rosenfeld – was initially associated with the Grand Stewart of Königsberg (see below), then he became a juror (1405) and a councillor of Toruń (1406). In 1407, he probably moved to Chełmno to represent the said city at the assembly of Prussian cities in 1411. Shortly thereafter, he performed in Kraków, where he probably obtained the city rights. Around 1415 he moved to Wrocław. In 1417 he became the first councillor of Wrocław, while in 1418 he was elected to the Wrocław bench. After the riots that took place in the years 1418–1420 in Wrocław, he entered the Wrocław bench upon the appointment of Sigismund of Luxembourg. Probably around 1424, David Rosenfeld returned to Toruń.[99] Rosenfeld–Falbrecht owned mines and smelters in Hungary (today's Slovakia).[100]

The aforementioned company also introduced modern technologies related to extracting water from mines and smelting copper and silver in metallurgy.[101] It is also worth adding that Witchin Morser from Gdańsk, one of the main shareholders of the said company, was the owner of the copper ore mine in Falun (Sweden).[102] It should be remembered that copper and lead ore are the main sources of silver production. It seems that thanks to the above-mentioned Falbrecht–Morser-Rosenfeld company, the residents of Toruń took full advantage of the opportunities offered by trading precious metals. Perhaps one might even say that it was mainly through Toruń that the entire State of the Teutonic Order in Prussia was supplied with silver.

Johann Schweidniczer, a burgher from Kraków, and one of the most active Polish merchants participating in the trade of lead and copper also maintained strong ties with Toruń in the first half of the fifteenth century. Lead and copper ores were exported to Bohemia, Germany and (via Toruń and Gdańsk) to Flanders. In the years 1434–1456 Johann Schweidniczer leased an urbarium (*olbora*; in other words, a tax of 1/10 of the value of the excavated ores, paid to the King) along with the Olkusz commune. From 1442, Johann Schweidniczer moved to Toruń, where he helped his son Georg to begin his career in trading. It is worth adding that Johann Schweidniczer also had some connections with Witchin Morser from Gdańsk. In 1437, Albrecht IV Rebber settled Schweidniczer's debts to the children of the late Morser.[103]

Equally interesting is the case of Daniel Konitz, a burgher of Toruń, who in 1449 received from Johann von Lichtenstein, a minter of Toruń, 325 lighter Prussian marks for the purchase of an alloy of 50 silver marks to secure the valuables deposited with the commander of Toruń.[104] The money was sent to Kraków, where 50 silver marks and 11 skojecs were purchased. Unfortunately, for the next nine months, the minter did not receive the purchase from Daniel Konitz because of his absence. After this time, the settlement took place. Daniel Konitz demanded the compensation from the minter for the additionally purchased 11 skojecs of silver, while the minter demanded interest for the nine months of 75 Prussian marks blocking the pledge held by the commander.[105] The case of Daniel Konitz was pending over the next few years. In 1455, Daniel Konitz took claims of the minter's receivables deposited with Toruń's burghers, which included an alloy of 60 marks of silver deposited with Schweidniczer.[106] Johann and Georg Schweidniczer along with Daniel Konitz prove that some precious metals could have reached Prussia from the Polish lands through Kraków.

Silver was also sent to other Teutonic officials, not only minters, through the inhabitants of Toruń. The information about the sale of larger silver batches to

Table 7.1 Silver purchased in the years 1400–1402 by the grand steward from Königsberg from the Toruń burghers.

Toruń's burger	Weight an alloy of silver in marks	Price of silver for 1 mark	Size of the transaction
Gerhard Jungeweisse	212	2 marks 7 ½ skojecs	490 marks 1 firdungs
Herman von der Linden	[85.71]	2 marks 8 skojecs	200 marks
Albrecht Rebber	100	2 marks 8 skojecs 1 quarter	233 marks 2 firdungs
Total:	397.71		923 marks 3 firdungs

Source: *Handelsrechnungen*, p. 104.

the grand steward from Königsberg (see Table 7.1) by Toruń's burghers comes from the years 1399–1402. The total weight of an alloy of silver sold was 397.71 marks, and cost 923 Prussian marks and 3 wiarduneks. In the same years, David Rosenfeld and Herman Huxer, who were servants of the grand steward, also bought silver on a large scale. The said silver was then handed over to Ludike von der Heide and Hennyg Demeker, liegers (commissioners) of the grand steward in Veliky Novgorod. In total, an alloy of 1,473 marks and 23 ½ skojecs of silver was purchased for a huge amount of 3,453 Prussian marks and one *wiardunek* (see Table 7.2). The very grand steward of Königsberg was also active on the Toruń precious metal trading market; he purchased for Hennyg Demeker an alloy of 719 marks and 1.5 skojecs of silver valued at around 1681.5 Prussian marks (see Table 7.3). There is also information in the accounts of Teutonic stewards that silver settlements were sometimes carried out with the liegers/commissioners themselves. In this way, the purchase of 1,400 Prussian marks' worth of wax and leather from Toruń, was settled to the benefit of Lieger Ludike von der Heide.[107]

Table 7.2 Silver purchased in the years 1399–1402 by the inhabitants of Toruń – Herman Huxer and David Rosenfeld, servant of the grand steward from Königsberg, for his commissioners in Veliky Novgorod.

Toruń's burgher	Weight of an alloy of silver in marks	Price of silver for 1 mark	Size of the transaction
David Rosenfeld	302 marks 10 skojecs (24 pieces)	2 marks 8 skojecs	[about 705.72 marks]
Herman Huxer	289 marks without 5 skojecs	2 marks 8 skojecs	[about 673.84 marks]
Herman Huxer	546 marks 6 skojecs (62 small and big pieces)	2 marks 8 skojecs	1274.5 marks
Herman Huxer	336 marks 12 ½ skojecs (50 pieces)	2 marks 9 skojecs	799 marks 1 firdungs
Total	1473 marks 23 ½ skojecs	–	3453 marks 1 firdungs

Source: *Handelsrechnungen*, pp. 107–109.

Table 7.3 Purchases of silver in the years 1399–1402 made in Toruń directly by the great steward from Königsberg for Hennyg Demeker, steward's commissioner in Veliky Novgorod

Weight of silver in marks	Price of silver for 1 mark	Size of the transaction
46 marks 5 skojecs (1 piece)	2 marks 8 skojecs	[107.8 marks]
53 ½ marks 1 ½ skojecs (1 piece)	2 marks 8 skojecs	125 Prussian marks
440 marks 5 skojecs (30 small and big pieces)	2 marks 8 skojecs	1027 marks 4 skojecs without 10 denars
158 marks 5 skojecs	2 marks 8 ½ skojecs	372 ½ marks without 1 skojec
20 marks 21 skojecs	2 marks 8 ½ skojecs	49 marks 4 skojecs
In total 719 marks 1 ½ skojecs	–	In total [about 1681.5 marks]

Source: *Handelsrechnungen*, pp. 108–110.

Finally, these bills report a debt of an alloy of 100 marks of silver, which the grand steward of Königsberg paid for Tylman von Herken from Toruń to the Toruń minter.[108] It is worth noting the fairly stable exchange rate of the weight unit of mark to the accounting unit of mark in the years 1399–1402, which was significantly different from what happened to the Prussian coin after the Grunwald defeat.

To summarise, it should be stated that in Toruń in the first half of the fifteenth century, jewellery, valuables and various everyday items made of silver and gold were a means of securing capital, which was not insignificant due to the depreciation of the Prussian coin. Silver and gold were also frequently the subject of various property settlements and they also constituted collateral for loans. Certainly, the value of these precious metals and objects made from them was well understood. Especially merchants, participating in long-distance trade, had to be aware of the value of individual coins and the fineness of silver or gold. The deterioration of the national coin in Prussia after the Grunwald defeat along with the removal of silver from it, certainly increased interest in precious metals and foreign coins, both gold and silver, whose minting fineness stabilised. The Teutonic Order tried to control the circulation of silver in Prussia by means of its marking, at the same time banning its export from the country. The silver used in Toruń came primarily from Hungary (today's Slovakia) and was imported here through Wrocław (Silesia). Part of the silver could also reach Toruń from the Polish territories through Kraków. Large commercial companies whose shareholders were Toruń's burghers were involved in mining precious metals. Two of the most important recipients of silver brought to Toruń were the Teutonic minter and the grand steward of Königsberg. Some silver was also used for current trade or was used by local goldsmiths.

Notes

1 *Liber scabinorum Veteris Civitatis Thoruniensis 1363–1428*, edited by Kazimierz Kaczmarczyk (Toruń: Towarzystwo Naukowe w Toruniu, 1936) [hereinafter: *LS*], no. 1168, 1366; *Księga ławnicza Starego Miasta Torunia 1428–1456 [Liber scabinorum Veteris Civitatis Torunensis (1828–1456)]*, edited by Karola Ciesielska, Janusz Tandecki, part 1: *(1428–1443)* (Toruń: Towarzystwo Naukowe w Toruniu, 1992); part 2: *(1444–1456)* [hereinafter: *KłSMT (1428–1456)*] (Toruń: Towarzystwo Naukowe w Toruniu, 1993), no. 490, 1159, 1492; *Księgi małoletnich z lat 1376–1429*, edited by Krzysztof Mikulski and Janusz Tandecki (Toruń: Wydawnictwo Uniwersytetu Mikołaja Kopernika w Toruniu, 2002) [hereinafter: *Księgi małoletnich*], no. 138, 195; *Księga ławnicza Nowego Miasta Torunia (1387–1450)*, edited by Karola Ciesielska (Warszawa and Poznań: Państwowe Wydawnictwo Naukowe Oddział w Poznaniu, 1973) [hereinafter: *KłNMT (1387–1450)*], no. 2048.
2 *KłSMT (1428–1456)*, no. 1159, 1361, 1589.
3 Ibidem, no. 1589.
4 *Księgi małoletnich*, no. 118 (sapphire).
5 *KłSMT (1428–1456)*, no. 1056.
6 *KłNMT (1387–1450)*, no. 1978.
7 *KłSMT (1428–1456)*, no. 1014.
8 Ibidem, no. 279.
9 *LS*, no. 1761; *KłSMT (1428–1456)*, no. 243, 1056, 1533; *Księgi małoletnich*, no. 138, 194, 203; *KłNMT (1387–1450)*, no. 1771 (of the value of 3.5 good mark), 2254
10 *Księgi małoletnich*, no. 116.
11 Ibidem, no. 203.
12 *LS*, no. 1761 (6 three scores = 360); *KłSMT (1428–1456)*, no. 996, 1014, 1317, 1589, 1806; *Księgi małoletnich*, no. 118 (50 items with the lion's head, 65 items with lapis lazuli), 138; *KłNMT (1387–1450)*, no. 1454, 1727 (with the lion's head), 1771 (three scores of worse buttons), 1855, 1897 (three scores with the lion's head), 1982, 2116 (three scores with the lion's head), 2254.
13 *KłSMT (1428–1456)*, no. 1014, 1806; *KłNMT (1387–1450)*, no. 1305, 2190, 2363.
14 *KłNMT (1387–1450)*, no. 1413 and 1454 (both of the value of. 5.5 of the lighter (weight) mark.
15 *KłSMT (1428–1456)*, no. 1693.
16 *Księgi małoletnich*, no. 138.
17 Ibidem, no. 138; *KłNMT (1387–1450)*, no. 1317 (along with the travel dress).
18 *KłSMT (1428–1456)*, no. 1589.
19 Ibidem, no. 1024.
20 *KłNMT (1387–1450)*, no. 1317, 2305.
21 Ibidem, no. 1302 (the record for the altar in the Church of St. James in the New City of Toruń), no. 1317, 1653.
22 Ibidem, no. 1653.
23 *Księgi małoletnich*, no. 52, 138.
24 Ibidem, no. 138.
25 Ibidem, no. 118.
26 Ibidem, no. 138.
27 Ibidem.
28 Ibidem, no. 194.
29 Ibidem, no. 52, 138; *KłNMT (1387–1450)*, no. 1454, 2254
30 *Księgi małoletnich*, no. 117.
31 Ibidem, no. 194.
32 *KłSMT (1428–1456)*, no. 1014; *KłNMT (1387–1450)*, no. 2254.
33 *KłSMT (1428–1456)*, no. 473, 1322, 1803, 1806.
34 *Handelsrechnungen des Deutschen Ordens*, edited by Carl Sattler (Leipzig: Verlag von Duncker & Humbolt, 1886), pp. 107–110.

35 *Księgi małoletnich*, no. 138.
36 Ibidem, no. 112.
37 Ibidem, no. 137.
38 Ibidem, no. 116, in the subject index the term "silberynne glase" was translated as a silver glass. In this text we follow the solution to be found in the dictionary of the Grimm brothers, where the term "das Silberglas" was explained in the second meaning as "ein reiches silbererz, glaserz" (*Deutsches Wörterbuch*, edited by Jacob Grimm and Wilhelm Grimm, electronically in http://woerterbuchnetz.de/cgi-bin/WBNetz/wbgui_py?sigle=DWB&mode=Vernetzung&lemid=GS28710#XGS28710 [05.09.2018]); KłNMT (1387–1450), no. 2254 (here "silbern steine", which should be translated in a similar way).
39 *LS*, no. 1733 (the rent of an alloy of 50 marks of silver); 1811 (for the purchase of the house), 1824 (for the purchase of the house), 1894 (the settlement of an alloy of 38 marks of silver), 1950 (the purchase of a real estate – an alloy of 200 marks of silver).
40 *LS*, no. 1168, 1366, 1761; *KłNMT (1387–1450)*, no. 554, 572, 1698, 2028, 2056, 2255.
41 *LS*, no. 1366, 1502 (an alloy of 112 marks and 8 skojecs of silver), 1761 (i.e. 6 three scores silver buttons, two silver belts), 1917 (i.e. an alloy of 64 marks of silver along with a ship's chest decorated with silver jewels).
42 *Księgi małoletnich*, no. 118.
43 Ibidem, no. 120.
44 Ibidem, no. 186.
45 Ibidem, no. 187.
46 *LS*, no. 1427.
47 *Księgi małoletnich*, no. 115.
48 Ibidem, no. 116.
49 Ibidem, no. 117.
50 Ibidem, no. 203.
51 *KłNMT (1387–1450)*, no. 1305.
52 *Księgi małoletnich*, no. 115 (5 items), 118 (with sapphire), 120 (7 items), 137, 138 (10 items).
53 Ibidem, no. 137, 138, 194.
54 Ibidem, no. 203.
55 *KłNMT (1387–1450)*, no. 1653.
56 Ibidem, no. 2305.
57 Ibidem, no. 2254.
58 Ibidem, no. 2254.
59 *Księgi małoletnich*, no. 137.
60 Ibidem, no. 137
61 For the sake of exemplification: *LS*, see in the index the entries goldschläger, goldschmied; *KłSMT (1428–1456)*, see in the index the entry złotnik/goldsmith; *Księgi małoletnich*, see in the index the entry złotnik/goldsmith.
62 Tomasz Chrzanowski and Marian Kornecki, *Złotnictwo toruńskie. Studium o wyrobach cechu toruńskiego od wieku XIV do 1382 roku* (Warszawa: Państwowe Wydawnictwo Naukowe, 1988), p. 14.
63 *KłSMT (1428–1456)*, no. 1410.
64 *Ibidem*, no. 1607.
65 *KłSMT (1428–1456)*, no. 1778.
66 Borys Paszkiewicz, *Brakteaty – pieniądz średniowiecznych Prus* (Wrocław: Wydawnictwo Uniwersytetu Wrocławskiego, 2009), pp. 219, 222, 228, 231.
67 Ibidem; see also Oliver Volckart, *Die Münzpolitik im Ordensland und Herzogtum Preussen von 1370 bis 1550*, (Wiesbaden: Harrassowitz Verlag, 1996), p. 69.
68 Marian Gumowski, "Mennica toruńska," in *Dzieje Torunia. Praca zbiorowa z okazji 700-lecia miasta*, edited by Kazimierz Tymieniecki (Toruń: Towarzystwo Miłośników Historii w Poznaniu, 1933), p. 571.

69 Sławomir Jóźwiak, Krzysztof Kwiatkowski, Adam Szweda and Sobiesław Szybkowski, *Wojna Polski i Litwy z zakonem krzyżackim w latach 1409–1411* (Malbork: Muzeum Zamkowe w Malborku, 2010), p. 732.

70 *Acten der Ständetage Preussens unter der Herrschaft des Deutschen Ordens*, edited by Max Toeppen (Leipzig: Verlag von Duncker & Humbolt, 1878) [hereinafter: *ASP*], vol. 1, pp. 192–193, no. 152.

71 *ASP*, vol. 1, p. 203, no. 161.

72 *Związek Pruski i poddanie się Prus Polsce*, edited by Karol Górski (Poznań, Instytut Zachodni, 1949), p. 15, point 3; Paszkiewicz, *Brakteaty*, p. 231.

73 *ASP*, vol. 1, pp. 208–209, no. 169.

74 Marian Dygo, *Die Münzpolitik des Deutschen Ordens in Preußen in der ersten Hälfte des 15. Jahrhunderts* (Warszawa: Wydawnictwa Uniwersytetu Warszawskiego, 1987), p. 23.

75 *ASP*, vol. 1, p. 233, no. 184.

76 Marian Gumowski, "Polityka mennicza miast pruskich," *Zapiski Historyczne* 20 (1955), 257–259.

77 Irena Janosz-Biskupowa, "Materiały do dziejów lichwy w Prusach Krzyżackich," *Studia i Materiały do Dziejów Wielkopolski i Pomorza* 4 (1958), no. 1, 357.

78 Paszkiewicz, *Brakteaty*, p. 233; Volckart, *Die Münzpolitik*, p. 87.

79 *LS*, no. 1284 (1417), see also in the index the mark geringen geldes.

80 Ibidem, no. 1235 (1416), 1374, see also the index.

81 *ASP*, vol. 1, pp. 295, 318, 356.

82 Ibidem, pp. 356–357.

83 Volckart, *Die Münzpolitik*, pp. 79, 88–90; Emil Waschinski, *Die Münz- und Währungspolitik des Deutschen Ordens in Preussen, ihre historischen Probleme und seltenen Gepräge* (Göttingen: Der Göttinger Arbeitskreis, 1952), pp. 199–201, 245.

84 *LS*, the subject index; *KłSMT (1428–1456)*, the subject index.

85 Archiwum Państwowe w Toruniu, Akta miasta Torunia, Dokumenty i listy, Katalog I, entry no. 815; *Die Berichte der Generalprokuratoren des Deutschen Ordens an der Kurie*, vol. 3: *Johann Tiergart (1419–1428)*, edited by Hans Koeppen, vol. 3, half-vol. 1 (Göttingen: Vandenhoeck & Ruprecht, 1966), p. 325, no. 148; Andrzej Radzimiński and Janusz Tandecki, *Katalog dokumentów i listów krzyżackich Archiwum Państwowego w Toruniu*, vol. 1: *1251–1454* (Warszawa: Naczelna Dyrekcja Archiwów Państwowych, 1994), no. 153.

86 Archiwum Państwowe w Toruniu, Akta miasta Torunia, Dokumenty i listy, Katalog I, entry no. 813; *Die Berichte*, vol. 3, half-vol. 2 (Göttingen: Vandenhoeck & Ruprecht, 1971), p. 423, no. 202.

87 Geheimes Staatsarchiv Preussischer Kulturbesitz, Berlin-Dahlem, XX. Hauptabteilung, Ordensbriefarchiv [hereinafter: GStA PK, XX, OBA], no. 4306: "daz die behmische muncze so fere vergangen und undergedrucket ist, daz man der grossen nicht gehaben mag [...] du wollest mit deinen leutten bestellen, daz sy sich an solicher muncze genu-gen lassen"; *Regesta historico-diplomatica Ordinis S. Mariae Theutonicorum 1198–1525*, edited by Erich Joachim and Walther Hubatsch, Pars I, vol. 1 (Göttingen: Vandenhoeck & Ruprecht, 1948), no. 4306.

88 *ASP*, vol. 1, pp. 451–452, no. 351.

89 Archiwum Państwowe w Toruniu, Akta miasta Torunia, Dokumenty i listy, Katalog I, entry no. 830; Radzimiński, Tandecki, no. 160.

90 Archiwum Państwowe w Toruniu, Akta miasta Torunia, Dokumenty i listy, Katalog I, entry no. 894; Radzimiński, Tandecki, no. 178.

91 *Przyczynki do dziejów polskich z Archiwum Miasta Wrocławia*, edited by August Mosbach (Poznań: Towarzystwo Przyjaciół Nauk Poznańskie, 1860), p. 96; Kazimierz Myśliński, "Lublin a handel Wrocławia z Rusią w XIV i XV w.," *Rocznik Lubelski* 3 (1960), no. 12; Ludwig Petry, "Breslau und Krakau vom 13. bis 16. Jahrhundert. Zwei Städteschicksale auf Kolonialboden, "*Zeitschrift des Vereins für Geschichte und Alterthum Schlesiens (=Zeitschrift des Vereins für Geschichte und Schlesiens)* 68 (1934), 62.

92 Archiwum Państwowe w Toruniu, Akta miasta Torunia, Dokumenty i listy, Katalog I, entry no. 992; Radzimiński, Tandecki, no. 222.

93 *ASP*, Vol. 1, no. 66; *Hansisches Urkundenbuch*, edited by Karl Kunze, vol. 5 (Leipzig: Verlag von Duncker & Humbolt, 1899), no. 571; Janusz Tandecki, "Rozkwit toruńskiego ośrodka handlowego i produkcyjnego w latach 1350–1411," in *Historia Torunia*, edited by Marian Biskup, vol. 1 (Toruń: Towarzystwo Naukowe w Toruniu, 1999), pp. 188–189; Jürgen Sarnowsky, "Die Entwicklung des Handels der preußischen Hansestädte im 15. Jahrhundert, "in *Die preußischen Hansestädte und ihre Stellung im Nord- und Ostseeraum des Mittelalters*, edited by Zenon Hubert Nowak and Janusz Tandecki (Toruń: Uniwersytet Mikołaja Kopernika, 1998), pp. 62–64; Marian Magdański, *Organizacja kupiectwa i handlu toruńskiego do roku 1403* (Toruń: Nakładem Zarządu Miejskiego w Toruniu, 1939), p. 134.

94 Geheimes Staatsarchiv Preussischer Kulturbesitz, Berlin-Dahlem, XX. Hauptabteilung, Pergamenturkunden, no. 1767, 1958; *Regesta historico-diplomatica,* Pars II, no. 1767, 1958; Archiwum Państwowe we Wrocławiu [hereinafter: APW], Akta miasta Wrocławia [hereinafter: AmW], G5, 21, 51; APW, AmW, Dokumenty, 1425 (8 October 1417); Krzysztof Kopiński and Piotr Oliński, "Regesty dokumentów i wzmianek źródłowych do dziejów średniowiecznego Torunia i Prus w tzw. Zbiorze Klosego w Archiwum Państwowym we Wrocławiu, część 1–2," *Zapiski Historyczne* 68 (2003), no. 2–3, no. 145–160; no. 4, no. 107; see also GStA PK, XX, OBA, no. 2937; *Regesta historico-diplomatica,* Pars I, vol. 1, no. 2937; Jürgen Sarnowsky, *Die Wirtschaftsführung des Deutschen Orden in Preußen (1382–1454)* (Köln, Weimar and Wien: Böhlau Verlag, 1993), p. 68, fn. 34–35.

95 APW, AmW, G5, 16, 45: "das ander hette man im nicht wolt czeichen durch des willen, das is nicht als dorre was, als das irste".

96 *Hanserecesse. Die Recesse und andere Akten der Hansetage von 1256–1430,* Vol. VII, edited by Karl Koppmann (Leipzig: Verlag von Duncker & Humbolt, 1893), no. 277/14; Krzysztof Kopiński, *Gospodarcze i społeczne kontakty Torunia z Wrocławiem w późnym średniowieczu* (Toruń: Towarzystwo Naukowe w Toruniu, 2005), p. 35, fn. 182; Wolfgang Stromer, "Die Schwarzmeer- und Levante-Politik Sigismunds von Luxemburg und der Schwarzmeer-Handel oberdeutscher und hansischer Handelshäuser 1385–1453,"*Bulletin de l'Institut Historique Belge de Rome* 44 (1974), pp. 601–610 in particular 604.

97 See more about the company Bernd Ulrich Hucker, "Der Köln-Soester Fernhändler Johann von Lunen (1415–1443) und die hansischen Gesellschaften Falbrecht & Co. und v. d. Hosen & Co., " in *Soest, Stadt-Territorium-Reich. Festschrift zum 1000 jährigen Bestehen des Vereins für Geschichte und Heimatpflege Soest*, edited by Gerhard Köhn (Soest: Mocker & Jahn, 1981), pp. 383–421; Krzysztof Kopiński, "Mieszczanin Dawid Rosenfeld w dyplomatycznej i gospodarczej służbie zakonu krzyżackiego w Prusach w pierwszej połowie XV wieku, "*Zapiski Historyczne* 66 (2001), no. 2–3, 39–56; Erich Maschke, "Die Schäffer und Lieger des Deutschen Ordens in Preussen, "in idem, *Domus Hospitalis Theutonicorum. Europäische Verbindungslinien der Deutschordengeschichte* (Bonn-Bad Godesberg: Verlag Wissenschaftliches Archiv GMBH, 1970), p. 95.

98 Renáta Skorka and Boglárka Weisz, "A porosz kapcsolat. Johann Falbrecht és David Rosenfeld a magyar pénzügyigazgatásban, " in *Hatalom, adó, jog. Gazdaságtörténeti tanulmányok a magyar középkorról*, edited by Boglárka Weisz and István Kádas (Budapest: MTA BTK Történettudományi Intézetben, 2017), pp. 190, 201–202; Wolfgang Stromer, "Die Saigerhütten-Industrie des Spätmittelalters. Entwicklung der Kupfer-Silber-Scheidekünste zur 'ars coflatoria separantia argentum a cupro cum plumbo', "*Technikgeschichte* 62 (1995), no. 2, 196–197 (tab. 1); see also Krzysztof Kopiński, "Falbrecht Johann, "in *Toruński Słownik Biograficzny*, edited by Krzysztof Mikulski, vol. 4 (Toruń: Towarzystwo Miłośników Torunia, Uniwersytet Mikołaja Kopernika, 2004), pp. 71–73.

99 Krzysztof Kopiński, *Mieszczanin Dawid Rosenfeld*, pp. 39–56; Idem, "Rosenfeld Dawid," in *Toruński Słownik Biograficzny*, edited by Krzysztof Mikulski, vol. 4 (Toruń: Towarzystwo Miłośników Torunia, Uniwersytet Mikołaja Kopernika, 2004), pp. 196–199.

100 The Rosenfeld-Falbrecht received a loan against, i.e. 1/16 *adits*, divisions from mines, smelters and decks in Smolnik and other towns Ondrej R. Halaga, *Košice-Balt. Výroba a obchod v styku východoslovenských miest s Pruskom (1275–1526)* (Košice: Vychodoslovenské Vydavateľstvo pre Mestsky Vybor v Košicach, 1975), p. 281; see also Danuta Molenda, "Wywóz małopolskiego ołowiu przez Gdańsk do Europy Środkowej i Zachodniej w średniowieczu," in *Aetas media, aetas moderna. Studia ofiarowane profesorowi Henrykowi Samsonowiczowi w siedemdziesiątą rocznicę urodzin*, edited by Halina Manikowska, Agnieszka Bartoszewicz, and Wojciech Fałkowski (Warszawa: Instytut Historyczny Uniwersytetu Warszawskiego, 2000), p. 204.

101 Stromer, "Saigerhütten-Industrie," pp. 202–204; Hucker, "Soest", p. 390. In Wieliczka, modernisation in the mines was also introduced by the then żupnik/salt-mine manager – Venetian Piero Picoranos, with whom David Rosenfeld remained in the company in 1418: Kopiński, *Gospodarcze i społeczne kontakty*, p. 122, fn. 581.

102 Hucker, "Soest, "p. 394; Franz Irsigler, "Hansischer Kupferhandel im 15. und in der ersten Hälfte des 16. Jahrhunderts, "in *Hansische Geschichtsblätter* 97 (1979), 23; Stromer, "Saigerhütten-Industrie, "p. 202.

103 Krzysztof Mikulski, *Mikołaj Kopernik. Środowisko społeczne, pochodzenie i młodość* (Toruń: Wydawictwo Naukowe Uniwersytetu Mikołaja Kopernika, 2015), pp. 296–299; Danuta Molenda, *Polski ołów na rynkach Europy Środkowej w XIII–XVII wieku* (Warszawa: Wydawnictwo Instytutu Archeologii i Etnologii PAN, 2001), pp. 105–106; see also Jan Dąbrowski, "Krakow a Węgry w wiekach średnich," *Rocznik Krakowski*, 13 (1911), p. 229; Krystyna Pieradzka, "Przedsiębiorstwa kopalniane mieszczan krakowskich w Olkuszu od XV do pocz. XVII w., *Zeszyty Naukowe Uniwersytetu Jagiellońskiego, Historia,* 16 (1958), no. 3, 50–52.

104 Janosz–Biskupowa, "Materiały," pp. 358–359.

105 Ibidem, pp. 364–365.

106 Ibidem, p. 371.

107 *Handelsrechnungen*, p. 154.

108 Ibidem, p. 106–107.

Bibliography

Primary sources

Unprinted sources

Archiwum Państwowe w Toruniu, Akta miasta Torunia, Dokumenty i listy, Katalog I [The State Archive in Toruń, Files of the City of Toruń, Documents and letters, Catalogue I]

entry no. 813

entry no. 815

entry no. 830

entry no. 894

entry no. 992

Archiwum Państwowe we Wrocławiu, Akta miasta Wrocławia [The State Archive in Wrocław, Files of the City of Wrocław]

Dokumenty [Documents], 1425 (8 October 1417)

Sign. G5, 16, 45
Sign. G5, 21, 51
Geheimes Staatsarchiv Preussischer Kulturbesitz, Berlin-Dahlem, XX. Hauptabteilung
Ordensbriefarchiv, no. 2937
Ordensbriefarchiv, no. 4306
Pergamenturkunden, no. 1767, 1958

Printed sources

Max Toeppen (ed.) *Acten der Ständetage Preussens unter der Herrschaft des Deutschen Ordens*. Leipzig: Verlag von Duncker & Humbolt, 1878.

Jacob Grimm and Wilhelm Grimm (eds.) *Deutsches Wörterbuch*, electronically in http://woerterbuchnetz.de/cgi-bin/WBNetz/wbgui_py?sigle=DWB&mode=Vernetzung&lemid=GS28710#XGS28710 [05.09.2018].

Hans Koeppen (ed.) *Die Berichte der Generalprokuratoren des Deutschen Ordens an der Kurie: Johann Tiergart (1419–1428)*, vol. 3, half-vol. 1: 1419–1423. Göttingen: Vandenhoeck & Ruprecht, 1966; half-vol. 2: 1424–1428. Göttingen: Vandenhoeck & Ruprecht, 1971.

Carl Sattler (ed.) *Handelsrechnungen des Deutschen Ordens*. Leipzig: Verlag von Duncker & Humbolt, 1886.

Karl Koppmann (ed.) *Hanserecesse. Die Recesse und andere Akten der Hansetage von 1256–1430*, vol. VII. Leipzig: Verlag von Duncker & Humbolt, 1893.

Karl Kunze (ed.) *Hansisches Urkundenbuch*, vol. 5. Leipzig: Verlag von Duncker & Humbolt, 1899.

Karola Ciesielska (ed.) *Księga ławnicza Nowego Miasta Torunia (1387–1450) [The legal bench of the New City of Toruń]*. Warszawa and Poznań: Państwowe Wydawnictwo Naukowe Oddział w Poznaniu, 1973.

Karola Ciesielska and Janusz Tandecki (eds.) *Księga ławnicza Starego Miasta Torunia 1428–1456 [Liber scabinorum Veteris Civitatis Torunensis (1428–1456)]*, part 1: (1428–1443). Toruń: Towarzystwo Naukowe w Toruniu, 1992); part 2: (1444–1456). (Toruń: Towarzystwo Naukowe w Toruniu, 1993).

Krzysztof Mikulski, and Janusz Tandecki (eds.) *Księgi małoletnich z lat 1376–1429 [Books of the minors]*. Toruń: Wydawnictwo Uniwersytetu Mikołaja Kopernika w Toruniu, 2002.

Kazimierz Kaczmarczyk (ed.) *Liber scabinorum Veteris Civitatis Thoruniensis 1363–1428*. Toruń: Towarzystwo Naukowe w Toruniu, 1936.

August Mosbach (ed.). *Przyczynki do dziejów polskich z Archiwum Miasta Wrocławia [Contributions to the Polish history from the Archive of the City of Wrocław]*. Poznań: Towarzystwo Przyjaciół Nauk Poznańskie, 1860.

Radzimiński, Andrzej and Janusz Tandecki. *Katalog dokumentów i listów krzyżackich Archiwum Państwowego w Toruniu [Catalogue of Teutonic documents and letters, in the State Archive in Toruń]*, vol. 1: 1251–1454. Warszawa: Naczelna Dyrekcja Archiwów Państwowych, 1994.

Erich Joachim and Walther Hubatsch (eds.) *Regesta historico-diplomatica Ordinis S. Mariae Theutonicorum 1198–1525*, Pars I, vol. 1. Göttingen: Vandenhoeck & Ruprecht, 1948.

Karol Górski (ed.). *Związek Pruski i poddanie się Prus Polsce [The Prussian Confederation]*. Poznań: Instytut Zachodni, 1949.

Secondary literature

Chrzanowski, Tomasz and Marian Kornecki. *Złotnictwo toruńskie. Studium o wyrobach cechu toruńskiego od wieku XIV do 1832 roku [Goldsmithery in Toruń. A study on the guild products from the 14th century to 1832]*. Warszawa: Państwowe Wydawnictwo Naukowe, 1988.

Dąbrowski, Jan. "Kraków a Węgry w wiekach średnich," [Kraków and Hungary in the Middle Ages] *Rocznik Krakowski* 13 (1911), 187–250.

Dygo, Marian. *Die Münzpolitik des Deutscgenhen Ordens in Preußen in der ersten Hälfte des 15. Jahrhunderts*. Warszawa: Wydawnictwa Uniwersytetu Warszawskiego, 1987.

Gumowski, Marian. "Mennica toruńska," [Toruń mint] in *Dzieje Torunia. Praca zbiorowa z okazji 700-lecia miasta [History of Toruń: Collected work on the 700th anniversary of the city]*, edited by Kazimierz Tymieniecki, pp. 566–584. Toruń: Towarzystwo Miłośników Historii w Poznaniu, 1933.

Gumowski, Marian. "Polityka mennicza miast pruskich," [Minting policy of Prussian towns] *Zapiski Historyczne* 20 (1955), 257–294.

Halaga, Ondrej R. *Košice-Balt. Výroba a obchod v styku východoslovenských miest s Pruskom (1275–1526) [Košice-Balt: Production and Trade in the Contact Points with East Prussia from 1275 to 1526]*. Košice: Vychodoslovenské Vydavateľstvo pre Mestsky Vybor v Košicach, 1975.

Hucker, Bernd Ulrich. "Der Köln-Soester Fernhändler Johann von Lunen (1415–1443) und die hansischen Gesellschaften Falbrecht & Co. und v. d. Hosen & Co.," in *Soest, Stadt-Territorium-Reich. Festschrift zum 1000 jährigen Bestehen des Vereins für Geschichte und Heimatpflege Soest*, edited by Gerhard Köhn, pp. 383–421. Soest: Mocker & Jahn, 1981.

Irsigler, Franz. "Hansischer Kupferhandel im 15. und in der ersten Hälfte des 16. Jahrhunderts," *Hansische Geschichtsblätter* 97 (1979), 15–35.

Janosz-Biskupowa, Irena. "Materiały do dziejów lichwy w Prusach Krzyżackich," [Materials referring to the history of usury] *Studia i Materiały do Dziejów Wielkopolski i Pomorza* 4 (1958), no. 1, 355–372.

Jóźwiak, Sławomir, Krzysztof Kwiatkowski, Adam Szweda and Sobiesław Szybkowski. *Wojna Polski i Litwy z zakonem krzyżackim w latach 1409–1411 [The war of Poland and Lithuania against the Teutonic Order in the years 1409–1411]*. Malbork: Muzeum Zamkowe w Malborku, 2010.

Kopiński, Krzysztof. "Falbrecht Johann," in *Toruński Słownik Biograficzny [Toruń Biographies]*, edited by Krzysztof Mikulski, vol. 4, pp. 71–73. Toruń: Towarzystwo Miłośników Torunia, Uniwersytet Mikołaja Kopernika, 2004.

Kopiński, Krzysztof. "Rosenfeld Dawid," in *Toruński Słownik Biograficzny [Toruń Biographies]*, edited by Krzysztof Mikulski, vol. 4, pp. 196–199. Toruń: Towarzystwo Miłośników Torunia, Uniwersytet Mikołaja Kopernika, 2004.

Kopiński, Krzysztof. "Mieszczanin Dawid Rosenfeld w dyplomatycznej i gospodarczej służbie zakonu krzyżackiego w Prusach w pierwszej połowie XV wieku," [The burgher Dawid Rosenfeld in the diplomatic and economic service of the Teutonic Order in Prussia in the first half of the 15th century] *Zapiski Historyczne* 66 (2001), no. 2–3, 39–56.

Kopiński, Krzysztof. *Gospodarcze i społeczne kontakty Torunia z Wrocławiem w późnym średniowieczu [Economic and social contacts of Toruń with Wrocław in the late Middle Ages]*. Toruń: Towarzystwo Naukowe w Toruniu, 2005.

Kopiński, Krzysztof and Piotr Oliński, "Regesty dokumentów i wzmianek źródłowych do dziejów średniowiecznego Torunia i Prus w tzw. Zbiorze Klosego w Archiwum

Państwowym we Wrocławiu, część 1–2," [Regests of documents and references to the history of medieval Toruń and Prussia in the so-called Klose collection in the State Archives in Wrocław, part 1-2] *Zapiski Historyczne* 68 (2003), no. 2–3, 145–160.

Magdański, Marian. *Organizacja kupiectwa i handlu toruńskiego do roku 1403 [The organisation of Toruń's commerce and trade until 1403].* Toruń: Nakładem Zarządu Miejskiego w Toruniu, 1939.

Maschke, Erich. "Die Schäffer und Lieger des Deutschen Ordens in Preussen," in *Domus Hospitalis Theutonicorum. Europäische Verbindungslinien der Deutschordengeschichte* edited by Erich Maschke, pp. 69–103. Bonn-Bad Godesberg: Verlag Wissenschaftliches Archiv GMBH, 1970.

Mikulski, Krzysztof. *Mikołaj Kopernik. Środowisko społeczne, pochodzenie i młodość [Nicolaus Copernicus: Social environment, origin and youth].* Toruń: Wydawictwo Naukowe Uniwersytetu Mikołaja Kopernika, 2015.

Molenda, Danuta. *Polski ołów na rynkach Europy Środkowej w XIII–XVII wieku [Polish lead on the markets of Central Europe in the 13th–17th centuries].* Warszawa: Wydawnictwo Instytutu Archeologii i Etnologii PAN, 2001.

Molenda, Danuta. "Wywóz małopolskiego ołowiu przez Gdańsk do Europy Środkowej i Zachodniej w średniowieczu," [Exports of Lesser Poland lead through Gdańsk to Central and Western Europe in the Middle Ages] in *Aetas media, aetas moderna. Studia ofiarowane profesorowi Henrykowi Samsonowiczowi w siedemdziesiątą rocznicę urodzin [Aetas media, aetas moderna: Studies offered to Professor Henryk Samsonowicz on the seventieth anniversary of his birth],* edited by Halina Manikowska, Agnieszka Bartoszewicz, and Wojciech Fałkowski, pp. 199–209. Warszawa: Instytut Historyczny Uniwersytetu Warszawskiego, 2000.

Myśliński, Kazimierz. "Lublin a handel Wrocławia z Rusią w XIV i XV w.," [Lublin and the trade of Wrocław with Ruthenia in the 14th and 15th centuries] *Rocznik Lubelski* 3 (1960), no. 12; 5–36.

Paszkiewicz, Borys. *Brakteaty – pieniądz średniowiecznych Prus [Single-sided coins – the currency of medieval Prussia].* Wrocław: Wydawnictwo Uniwersytetu Wrocławskiego, 2009.

Pieradzka, Krystyna. "Przedsiębiorstwa kopalniane mieszczan krakowskich w Olkuszu od XV do pocz. XVII w.," [Mine enterprises of Kraków burghers in Olkusz from the 15th to the beginning of the 17th century] *Zeszyty Naukowe Uniwersytetu Jagiellońskiego, Historia*, 16 (1958), no. 3, 35–80.

Petry, Ludwig. "Breslau und Krakau vom 13. bis 16. Jahrhundert. Zwei Städteschicksale auf Kolonialboden," *Zeitschrift des Vereins für Geschichte und Alterthum Schlesiens (=Zeitschrift des Vereins für Geschichte und Schlesiens)* 68 (1934), 48–68.

Sarnowsky, Jürgen. "Die Entwicklung des Handels der preußischen Hansestädte im 15. Jahrhundert," in *Die preußischen Hansestädte und ihre Stellung im Nord- und Ostseeraum des Mittelalters*, edited by Zenon Hubert Nowak and Janusz Tandecki, pp. 51–78. Toruń: Uniwersytet Mikołaja Kopernika, 1998.

Sarnowsky, Jürgen. *Die Wirtschaftsführung des Deutschen Orden in Preußen (1382–1454).* Köln, Weimar and Wien: Böhlau Verlag, 1993.

Skorka, Renáta and Boglárka Weisz. "A porosz kapcsolat. Johann Falbrecht és David Rosenfeld a magyar pénzügyigazgatásban," [Prussian estates: Johann Falbrecht and David Rosenfeld in the Hungarian state financial administration] in *Hatalom, adó, jog. Gazdaságtörténeti tanulmányok a magyar középkorról [Power, tax, law. Studies in the economic history of medieval Hungary]* edited by Boglárka Weisz and István Kádas, pp. 181–207. Budapest: MTA BTK Történettudományi Intézetben, 2017.

Stromer, Wolfgang. "Die Saigerhütten-Industrie des Spätmittelalters. Entwicklung der Kupfer-Silber-Scheidekünste zur 'ars coflatoria separantia argentum a cupro cum plumbo'," *Technikgeschichte* 62 (1995), no. 2, 187–219.

Stromer, Wolfgang. "Die Schwarzmeer- und Levante-Politik Sigismunds von Luxemburg und der Schwarzmeer-Handel oberdeutscher und hansischer Handelshäuser 1385–1453," *Bulletin de l'Institut Historique Belge de Rome* 44 (1974), 601–610.

Tandecki, Janusz. "Rozkwit toruńskiego ośrodka handlowego i produkcyjnego w latach 1350–1411," [The prime of Toruń's trade and production centre] in *Historia Torunia [History of Toruń]*, edited by Marian Biskup, vol. 1, pp. 167–220. Toruń: Towarzystwo Naukowe w Toruniu, 1999.

Volckart, Oliver. *Die Münzpolitik im Ordensland und Herzogtum Preussen von 1370 bis 1550*. Wiesbaden: Harrassowitz Verlag, 1996.

Waschinski, Emil. *Die Münz- und Währungspolitik des Deutschen Ordens in Preussen, ihre historischen Probleme und seltenen Gepräge*. Göttingen: Der Göttinger Arbeitskreis, 1952.

8   The use of gold and silver in the praxis of a merchant in late medieval Gdańsk

Anna Paulina Orłowska

In this paper I want to examine the use of different financial tools in the context of monetisation in far trade in the basin of the Baltic Sea during the first half of the fifteenth century. I will analyse a wide range of payment methods, from bartering, to use of the commodity currencies, to balancing of liabilities and using promissory notes. The basis for this work is a merchant book of Johan Pyre, who was active in Gdańsk (Danzig) between 1421 and 1455. His partners originated from different economic zones – England, Flanders, Lithuania, Livonia and last but not least Prussia. Since the social and economic status of the vast majority of his partners was similar, as they were all involved in distant wholesale trade, I will analyse whether there were spatial differences in the use of the financial instruments in the context of monetisation. Monetisation is understood both as the use of silver and gold currencies as well as denominating the value of a transaction in a currency.

The merchant and his network

Johan Pyre (formerly known as Pisz or Piß) was a middle-range merchant in Gdańsk, acting quite typically for a merchant of the Hanseatic League. He traded mainly along an east–west axis, trading such commodities from the east as wax and furs, for western commodities like salt and cloth. Besides these four main categories of his merchandise, he offered a multitude of goods such as wood, herring, iron, copper, diverse foods and beverages, garments, and even amber.

The structure of his business activities was also quite typical for the time and place. He led his business on his own, without additional paid clerks, engaging in a multitude of short-term business relationships with similar merchants, a number of middle-term business bonds, and one very long business relationship. From the legal point of view these relationships combined different forms; the most important were *selscop* (also known as *societas*, a Northern counterpart to a *compagnia*) and *wedderlegynge* in which he engaged only as *socius dormens,* an investor as opposed to the travelling partner. He once mentioned a *vrye selscop*, which is a phenomenon for which there is no further historical description.

Pyre represented the type of merchant that evolved in the Hanseatic sphere in the late fourteenth and early fifteenth centuries: a sedentary far trade merchant, who commissioned his business activities outside the town to his partners and offered them the same services in his home town.[1] The merchandise was transferred between partners via ships. Also, money transfers were fulfilled in the same way or in some cases by partners, who travelled between cities for economic or political reasons.

Pyre mentioned nearly 1,000 people in his notes. His partners came from various regions. Since Pyre hardly ever left Gdańsk, he maintained contacts either during his partners' visits to Gdańsk or remotely using the letters and services provided by the captains of the vessels on which he shipped his goods. The partners from Prussia clearly predominated; in addition to burghers of Gdańsk, counterparts from the Prussian towns of Toruń (Thorn), Elbląg (Elbing), Braniewo (Brauensberg) and Kaliningrad (Königsberg) formed the biggest group among his partners. A second large group was made up of merchants from Livonia, primarily from Riga, but also from Tallinn (Reval). Pyre also maintained contacts with officials and employees of the Teutonic Order. In addition to his Prussian and Livonian partners, he also had further contacts that could be described as Hanseatic, in Bruges, Lübeck, Rostock, Kołobrzeg (Kolberg), Wrocław (Breslau) and Kraków (Cracow). Another significant group comprised of Englishmen, some of whom also settled in Gdańsk. The Dutch partners of Pyre were also clearly notable, which coincides with the general trend. The fifteenth century was a period in which their presence grew in the Baltic Sea basin, which had previously been dominated by the Hanseatic merchants.[2] Whilst this pattern is well known in the historical literature for the period, Pyre's book demonstrates a less well-documented rise in commercial activity by Lithuanians.

The merchant book and the bookkeeping

The primary source for this analysis is stored in the Gdańsk archive (Archiwum Państwowe w Gdańsku, APG) with the signature 300,R/F,4. It is a 113-page merchant book, which was written from 1421 to 1455. In previous literature, the author of the book was identified as Johan Pisz or Piß.[3] However, as I was able to prove, his name was Johan Pyre.[4]

The book was written in Middle–Low German and, as Doris Tophinke's research showed, the author used typical North German booking patterns.[5] However, the structure of his bookkeeping was less typical because Pyre used the so-called "method of opposite sides".[6] He described on the left page of the opened book the basic information about the business such as the name of the partner, the goods, their quantity, the date on which payment was due and also, in some cases, the date of the transaction. Further details of the transaction such as the paid rates and the name of a partner, who was involved in the payment, Pyre placed on the right-hand page, parallel to the first entry. Therefore, notes on subsequent transactions follow one another without gaps. This method allowed a much more efficient use of paper than did more traditional patterns. The end sums of the transactions were noted, as the North German booking patterns requires, at the end of the note, so that the comparison of sums was easy. Pyre also facilitated such comparison by using one booking currency. The booking currency for the entire length of Pyre's activity was the poor Prussian mark.

The currencies

Numerous coin types, both silver and gold currencies, can be found in Pyre's notations. Not all of these currencies were used equally as cash, some remained booking money only. Pyre used the mark of Riga rarely, only thirteen times in the first twenty years of doing business. He used them both as cash and as booking money. Since Pyre sometimes noted the type of coins he used, we can be sure that in these instances he was using cash. For example, in 1421 Pyre noted the sum of 1.5 mark of Riga in *ortegen* ('Item so hebbe yk noch Steven gedaen 1 ½ mk. Ryges an ortegen.'),[7] in other words, in small coins that were minted in Riga at the time.[8] In 1435 he sent mixed coins to his partner, primarily *groschen* but also some *schillings* from Riga: '35 op Ostern [17. April 1435]. Item doe sande yk Johan van dem Dyke bye scepper Jurgen Wylden in 1 sake 18 scok grossen unde 16 grossen unde 2 Ryges ß, dyt maket tohoeppe 64 mk. myn 2 ß. unde dyt slycht gerekent.'[9] However in some cases the mark of Riga was only booking money. In 1438 Pyre noted a contract for a salt delivery that was to take place in *Narvaw* (Narva). The value of this delivery was described in the coin of this port of destination; in mark of Riga: 'Item gecofft van Hynryk Vosse 10 last Bays solt toe der Narvaw to leverynden betakket vrye, dey last vor 43 mk. Ryges op Passchen [13. April [1438]] to betalen.'[10] However, the payment for this transaction was made in poor Prussian mark, which Pyre mentioned in the first entry on the right side: 'Item hiir op hebbe yk em betalt 41 mk. Prussche. Item betalt Hans op Johannis [24. Juni [1438]]110 mk.'[11]

Surprisingly, the local currency – Prussian mark – is the most difficult to examine. During the span of Pyre's business activities, the State of the Teutonic Order had de facto two currencies: the good Prussian mark and the poor Prussian mark.[12] The poor Prussian mark was the traditional one, and thus was used by merchants as booking money in order to preserve the continuity of accounting and to avoid mistakes. The good Prussian mark was introduced by the coinage reform of 1416, as the old coins had lost a lot of quality due to the economic struggles of the Teutonic Order after the Battle of Grunwald. The structure of the currency was preserved, so that 1 *mark* = 4 *viertel* = 24 s*cot* = 60 *schilling* = 720 *pfennig*, and only *schilling* (=*ß)* and *pfennig* (*=den.)* were coined. The official exchange rate of good and poor Prussian mark was 1:2. The replacement of the old coins was however very slow and uneven. As the coining of *schilling* was very expensive, only small amounts of these coins were minted. In the case of *pfennigs*, which allowed the mint a proper gain, the new *pfennig* dominated the market very quickly.[13] Since Pyre used the poor Prussian mark as booking money, it is not possible to determine whether any given transaction was actually carried out in this currency or whether it was completed in cash at all, as Pyre quite often omitted both pieces of information. A few examples demonstrate some of the challenges of interpretation. In 1422 Pyre described a payment by the writer of Toruń's mint was made in the *olde mark*, thus probably paid in old coins. 'Hiir op untffangen van Hynrycus de scriver muttemester to Thoren 50 olde mk. op Palmen [5. April [1422]].'[14] In 1423 he sent his partner a payment in mixed values: one of the coins was a single old *pfennig*: 'Item hiir op sande yk Gerd Slyter

5 dage vor Wynnachten [20. Dezember [1423]] [...] 17 schok grossen unde 18 grosse [...], 1 olden den. unde eyn sware nobel [...] und 2 Armlansche guld. [...]'[15] In 1437 he mentioned that he received a payment in both new and old *schilling*, which shows the long coexistence of two types of *schilling*: 'Item [100] nyer schyllynge. Item 1 older schyllyng.'[16] The poor Prussian mark was used in merchants' accountings, but in official documents the good Prussian mark was used. When Pyre bought a life annuity in 1454, he described very precisely that the maximum of the annuity was 15 good Prussian mark, and thus the same as 30 poor Prussian mark: 'Item op Domnyk [5. August [1454?]] doe rekende yk met Jacop Bluggen alle dynk slycht, doe bleff hey my schuldich 40 mk. unde 15 gude mk. op synem hus toe myle, dat ys 30 gerynge mk.'[17]

In the case of the *pound grote*, it is not clear whether Pyre ever received these coins physically or whether it remained for him purely booking money. Gdańsk merchants imported more goods from Bruges than they exported there. This sustained imbalance between income and expenditures led to a need for Gdańsk merchants to develop methods of transferring money to Bruges and maintain a system of credit in Bruges, where a local merchant kept an account for them. In his own notations, Pyre either described the value of the goods in Bruges or noted that the local merchant should credit his account there. For example, he noted that Hans Bakker sold the Lithuanian furs taken from Gdańsk in Bruges for about 42 *pound grote*. 'Item aldus staed myn dynk med Hans Bakker. Item int jar van 29 [1429]. Item doe hadde wye Lettauwes werk tohoepe, darvan ys geworden to myne parte 41 lb 2 ß 6 den'.[18] In another example, Pyre noted that when Gosswyn Wytte stayed in Gdańsk, Pyre paid him an equivalent of 12 *pound grote* in the local currency. Wytte then travelled to Bruges, where Pyre expected him to pay the 12 *pound grote* to Bertold Hemstede, Pyres' steady partner. 'Hiir op hebbe yk gecoft van Gosswyn Wyten 12 lb gr., ed lb vor 6 mk. unde 2 sc. unde dyt zal hey Bertolt Hemstede betalen dat eyrste, dar hey overkommt.'[19] Pyre could later use this money held on account by mailing to Bertold Hemstede a request to pay this sum to a further partner of Pyre's, who travelled to Bruges and was to make some purchases for Pyre. The Gdańsk merchant used such money transfers to even out the imbalance in his trade with Bruges. Such a money transfer, in which the partners in Prussia and Bruges paid in local currency, was described by Werner Paravicini as a form of cooperation between the Hanseatic merchants on the one hand and knights on the other hand, who travelled between Western and Eastern Europe in order to take part in crusades against Lithuania, so-called *Preußen-reisen*.[20] This cooperation collapsed after the Battle of Grunwald in 1410, but its remnants were still functioning in Pyre's time. In other examples, he bought the sum of 50 *pound grote* for 312.5 poor marks Prussian from Johan Reppyn, the Königsberg *Großschäffer* ('great administrator') who was planning to go to Bruges.

> Anno Domini 43 op sunte Mertyn [11. November 1443]. Item doe koffte yk van hern Johan Reppyn, den sceffer 50 lb gr., unde gaff vor ed lb 6 mk. unde 1 fer., unde Wenemer Overdiik sal ed gelt in Vlandern op boren. Summa ys 312 ½ mk.[21]

Reppyn was unable to deliver the 50 *pound grote* to Bruges as he was detained in Flanders due to debts of his representative.[22] This example demonstrated that Pyre used *pound grote* in contacts with his eastern partners in order to transfer money toward Flanders. He did not use it in any further contacts with his eastern partners.

The *groschen* played a completely different role in Pyre's activities. He used this heavy silver currency with a very stable monetary standard primarily in cash in order to settle obligations.[23] They were counted by schock (lat. sexagena grossorum), which equates to 60 pieces. He did not record which *groschen* he used – Bohemian, Meissner or Polish half-*groschen*. Unfortunately, there are also neither archaeological nor numismatic clues.[24] Remarks such as the one from 1433, according to which the 22.5 *schock groschen* (or 1,350 coins) sent to Hynryk Wesebom were sewn into a cloth, attesting to the fact that the transfer was made with coins.

> 14 dage noe Mychelis [13. Oktober [1433]]. […] Item doe sande yk hern Hynryk Wesebõm in scepper Jacop Kronen bye enen prester, dey heyt her Augustyn unde scholemester to der Ryge to wesenden: in 1 kanneffas beñget 22 ½ schok grossen.[25]

Augustyn, the schoolmaster from Riga, who took this parcel as he travelled with Jacop Kronen's ship, carried a considerable weight, since the package weighed about five kilograms.

The *groschen* were also used as booking money, especially in contacts with Vilnius: For example, in autumn 1436 Pyre sold two *Ypersche* cloths to Vilnius merchant Andreas Kopervysse, for which he counted 14 *schock groschen*. The value of the wax that Kopervysse was to supply was also calculated in this currency.

> Item soe ys my schuldich Andreas Kopervysse van dem Vylle vor 2 Ypersche als 1 swart 1 glasur blae, vor elk 14 scok unde darvor zal hey my was seynden, met dem eyrsten van dem vorjaer, unde vor elk sceppunt wasses 8 scõk.[26]

Groschen, both as booking money and as cash, was only used by Pyre in contacts with his eastern partners (with the exception of one transaction with a Nuremberg citizen). So, a clear separation of the currency areas can be drawn: While the *pound grote* was only used in contacts to the west and never in accounts in the east, both mark of Riga and *schock groschen* were only used in contacts in the east. *Groschen* was used in contacts with both Hanseatic and not Hanseatic partners and mark of Riga only within the Hanse. It is also noteworthy that no Lübeck coins were used. Occasionally, Pyre traded with silver, which was not minted into coins. It was probably in the form of bars, as the weight of silver pieces can be estimated using his description as roughly one kilogram. [27]

Pyre's use of gold currencies was different from the silver currencies. Gold is not the booking money; on the contrary: Some notes suggest that the transaction was carried out in gold coins, but it was booked using the booking currency: poor Prussian mark. An example here is the transaction with a burger of Elbląg

Hynryk van me Loe. Van me Loe bought *Nynevensche* cloth in September 1433 and was supposed to pay 105 poor Prussian mark for it. '8 dage vor Mychelis [21. September [1433]]. Item doe vercoffte yk Hynryk van me Loe van dem Elbyngen 14 Nynevensche, ed par vor 15 mk. Summa 105 mk.'[28] Pyre noted the payment of the first rate of 100 marks less a Rhenish guilder. 'Item hiir op untffangen 100 mk. myn 1 Rynsche guld.'[29] This currency change within a note indicates that van me Loe probably paid the sum of 100 poor Prussian mark in gold, in Rhenish guilders, but he lacked one gold coin. Another indication is the note at the end of the statement that there is still a poor Prussian mark missing. 'Item noch 1 mk.'[30] The value of Rhenish guilders was about 1 mark and 4 *schillings*, or 1.16 poor Prussian mark, so it comes to about the same, but Pyre maintained use of his booking currency.

It can therefore be assumed that most of the notations that mention gold coins relate to the gold coins actually used. The variety of gold coins in Pyre's business was large. However, the Rhineland and Hungarian guilders clearly dominated. The Rhenish guilders were used primarily in transactions with the eastern partners but also occasionally with western ones, such as a transaction with Rytczart Schottun[31] or in the settlement with Wenemer Overdiik,[32] who was active in both Bruges and Lübeck during this time. The Hungarian guilder cannot be observed in contacts to the west, or in contacts to the east; for example, the payment to the Königsberg *Großschäffer* ('great administrator') Johan Reppyn, from whom Pyre bought two tonnes of amber.[33] Business with a merchant from Kraków is also interesting: Peter Herseberch was using Hungarian guilders to pay off his debts from a cloth purchase 'Item hiir op untffangen 180 Ungersche guld., dey guld. vor 1 ½ mk. unde 4 sc. Summa 300 mk.'[34] – he could have had easier access to this currency because of the intensive contacts between Kraków merchants and Hungarians, which among other things drove a strong metal import.[35] It might make sense to compare Pyre's merchant book with the account book of Kraków merchant Hans Smet to compare the use of different currencies in commercial practice in these two Hanseatic cities.[36]

In addition to these two highly recognised currencies, Pyre used a number of other gold currencies. These were mainly coins from the Netherlands, namely from Utrecht, Arnheim and Moers, but also nobel, both Flemish and English as well as the so-called crowns. It should be mentioned that the number of English coins was very low, despite the intensive business relationship with the English merchants that Pyre kept. The use of these differentiated coins was based purely on the weight of gold. For instance, Pyre sent a payment with the help of a shipper, this payment consisted of a so-called Arnoldus guilder (a guilder of Arnheim), as well as a Flemish noble and 17 heavy ones. It was a mix of different currencies that were probably just available to Pyre, that added up to the necessary sum.

> Item em noch gesant by Alberd Bysscoppe 18 sware nobele, dar was eyn Vlamessche nobel mede, elke nobel stont 3 mk. myn 3 ½ ß, unde dey Vlamessche stant 3 mk. myn 8 ß. Item 1 Arnoldus guld. stant 17 sc. Summa van dessem golde ys 53 ½ mk. unde 2 sc. Summa to hoppe, dat yk em weder gesant hebbe, 67 mk. unde 9 sc.[37]

Another example is the payment to the city clerk Conradus Gumpert, which was transported by Hans Bekerwerter. The merchant took with him 12 Rhenish guilders, a light noble and 101 so-called light guilders, which again means the guilders from Arnheim.

> Item 8 dage nae sunte Johans to mydsomer [2. Juli [1440]]. Item doe sande yk Conradus bye Hans Bekerwerter in scepper Laurens Swarten in enen dok gebunden int eyrste 100 unde 1 lychte guld., elk stont 16 sc. unde 1 ß. Item 12 Rynsche guld., elk stont 1 mk. unde 9 sc. Item 1 lychte nobel stont 3 mk. unde 8 ß. Summa to hoeppe van dessem golde ys 88 mk. unde ½ mk. unde 9 ß, aldus blyfft mu Conradus schuldich 4 ß.[38]

In addition, we see the effectiveness of the use of gold coins, since the sum paid to Conradus was over 88 poor Prussian mark. The total weight of the coins was less than half a kilo. In comparison, the aforementioned consignment with *groschen*, which weighed about five kilograms, was only worth 68 marks. It was also possible to buy more money, as in the case of the *pound grote*. In 1426 Pyre wrote down the information from a letter sent that he paid Jacop Wyckeden and Hans Wezenberge 35 marks, for which they were to pay 12 heavy nobel to his partner, Peter van der Eyck, a Revaler. 'Item noch gedaen |-Hynryk-| Jacop Wyckeden unde Hans Wezenberge 35 mk., dar vor zal hey iu geven 12 sware nobel.'[39]

In the first two examples there were two coin names, both of which I attributed to the Dutch city of Geldern, namely Arnoldus guilders and light guilders. Pyre called the coins from this county "Arnhemisch" in the first years of its activity, after the city of Arnhem, the capital of the Duchy. However, because he noted the name of the city by year, the name varies greatly: *Arlansche, Armlemsche, Armlansche, Armlanische, Arnlansc[h]e*. It is not clear why he did not use the ruler's name, Rainald, on the coins. He used the term *Arnheimisch* consistently even after 1423 when the coins were given the name of the new ruler, Arnoldus. Perhaps his practice was based on the appearance of the coins, which did not change until 1429. Pyre did not begin to use the name Arnoldus-gulden until 1429, six years after the handover of the throne. In 1437 he noted the name 'new Arnoldus guilders' and in 1435 'new Armlanische', in parallel he used the shorter name 'new guilders'. In twelve transactions he used the name 'light guilder' and also these coins I identify as the coins of Arnheim due to their price. So, there are a total of six different names of this currency in Pyre's merchant book.

The coins of this currency were as changeable as their names. The quality of the embossing changed quickly, and of course, its value fell. Pyre, however, showed a conscious use of the coin. If we express the prices of the coin in Rhenish guilders and compare the prices of Pyre with those from city calculations from Deventer and Zutphen,[40] we can clearly see that the assessment of the value of the coin from Pyre was very close to that from Deventer and Zutphen. Pyre was therefore able to correctly assess the quality of the coin.

If we analyse the use of gold coins by Pyre during his whole business activity, we can see a clear pattern. A total of 204 mentions can be identified, which results

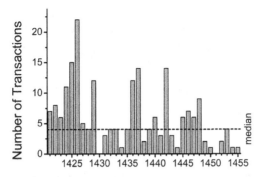

Figure 8.1 The number of transactions with gold coins per year.

in an average of 5.8 uses of gold per year, the median value is 4, with 45% of all mentions taking place in the first ten of the 35 years of Pyre's activity (Figure 8.1).

The difference in use of gold coins between the first ten years of Pyres business activities and following 25 years is massive. What caused that immense shift? What led to the intense use of gold coins in the first ten years? One hypothesis is that Pyre made use of differences in the price of gold between Gdańsk and Riga, where he sent the majority of the gold coins. However, this decade (1420–1430) was the only one in the entire century in which the gold–silver ratio in Flanders and Prussia favoured the export of gold to the west. Pyre did not take advantage of this trend. It would also be surprising if he would relinquish the incomes of such sales. In my opinion, the reason for the decline of the use of the gold coins by Pyre is a consequence of the character of the use of these coins. Pyre used them to discharge liabilities he had, especially bigger liabilities by distant partners. For the western partners he could use the mechanism of money purchase in Bruges described in the section on *pound grote*. In case of the eastern partners occasionally he had to close the liabilities in cash and used gold currencies as they were easier to transport.

"Paying with the closed wallet" – advanced means of payments

The transport of cash was cost-intensive and associated with a risk of loss due to robbery, or in the case of sea transport, piracy or ship accidents, and therefore was avoided. The development of different means of cashless payment such as bills of exchange and promissory notes as well as offsetting of liabilities in the European trade was intense in the Late Middle Ages[41] and described figuratively by German merchants as 'paying with closed wallet' ('bezahlen mit geschlosse-nem Geldbeutel').

In his activities, Pyre used offsetting of liabilities and promissory notes. These methods allowed him to settle the debts without using cash, or in some cases even the booking currency. Since Pyre primarily used his merchant book as an aid to memory rather than as a meticulous record of the details of every trade, he omitted many details. Nevertheless, it can be demonstrated that in the case of intensive contacts, usually no payments were made, but rather occasionally the mutual obligations were compared, and only the difference was paid. In 1423, after working in Gdańsk for a year and a half, he described, quite meticulously since he was still an inexperienced merchant, how the offsetting of liabilities was to be carried out: one sum of all liabilities should be deducted from the other.

> Item, dey ene summa tegen, dey ander geslagen, […] dyt gerekent met Johans van dem Hagen int jar 1423 15 dage nae sunt Mychele [13. Oktober 1423] soe blyve yk em sculdich in a[l] unde alle dynk slycht 460 mk. unde 19 sc.[42]

The same method was applied also when several partners were involved: In 1448 Pyre bought Russian wax from Tydeman op den Orde. The amount due was 91 poor Prussian mark.[43] Pyre noted that he paid it by deducting this sum from the money Tydeman should pay him as a rate from Wykbolt Thoymen. 'Item diit betalt Tydcman affgerekent an dem gelde van Wykbolt Thoymen wegen.'[44] Tydeman, therefore, did not bring Pyre the full amount of money in cash, but reduced it by the liability from the wax transaction. A liability could be passed between merchants multiple times. For example, when in 1453 Pyre sold cloth to the tailor Koseler,[45] he got one of his rates from Mathyas Sprynghorn, who owed Jacop Haserde, who owed Hans Hessen, who, in turn, probably owed Koseler himself. 'Hiir op untffangen bye Mathyas Sprynghorn van Jacop Haserde van Hans Hessen wegen 128 mk.'[46]

In order to develop the offsetting of liabilities, a merchant needed an established network. The more flexibly he wanted to execute his business – to be able to buy merchandise at different places, being able to pay at any given time or to pay any given sum of money – the bigger and more intensely interwoven the network had to be. The establishing of this network was one of the most important tasks in business life. If the merchant did not have a network developed enough to offset the liabilities, he had to transfer cash, which raised costs. The high number of Pyre's early gold transactions and the sudden drop after the first ten years shows how the development of a business network could reduce the need for cash transports.

The offsetting of liabilities could be fulfilled without use of money, even booking currency. Pyre describes in the year 1444 a number of transactions with wax between himself and Hynryk Vos, and in the end, using exactly the same wording as above mentioned, he sums up that after deducting of liabilities, Hynryk Vos's debt was eight shippounds, three liespounds and six and a half of mark pound. 'Item aldus, dey ene summa theghen, dey ander affgerekent, soe blycht my Hynryk Vos schuldich op Mychelis [29. September [1444]] thoe betalen 8 sceppunt unde 3 lb unde 6 ½ markpunt.'[47] Later, he recalculates this obligation into the booking currency; however, it is to be stressed that the calculation was made primarily in the commodity. The payment was fulfilled partially in wax.[48] This apparently surprising method of bookkeeping is easy to explain if we realise that the money of that time was commodity currencies. The distance between commodities such as gold and wax is less pronounced than between modern currencies and commodities.

The offsetting of liabilities was not only made in direct contact, but was also prescribed in writing. So as in autumn of 1432 Rogger Brugeney departed from Gdańsk, he left 3 marks with Pyre, which were supposed to be paid to Hans Segelande. 'Item zoe leyt my Rogger Brugney 3 mk., dey yk Hans Segelande solde geven.'[49] Segelande did not come to Gdańsk personally, but wrote a letter that the money should be paid to Hennyng Kaldevelde. 'Item desse 3 mk. hebbe yk gegeven Hennyng Kaldevelde nae utwysyng Hans Segelands breyven.'[50]

The letter mentioned in this case could have been a promissory note. It is one of 14 mentions of a letter (*breyff, breyve*) and six cases, where the grammar construction of the note in the merchant book allows us to assume that they were copied out of a letter sent to the business partner; however, it is not possible to determine whether these letters were promissory notes. The research on promissory notes is very complicated, as they were such an ordinary part of the business that they were not mentioned even if we can prove their use. A promissory note has been preserved between the pages of Pyre's merchant book. The issuer, Hynryk van Staden, promised on 15th August 1453 to pay 500 poor Prussian mark till the forthcoming Easter that he owed the payee, Johan Pyre, for cloth and wax.[51] The same transaction with Hynryk van Staden, who in mid-August 1453 bought cloth for 500 poor Prussian mark and should pay the sum till the forthcoming Easter, is described in the merchant book.[52] However, the remark in the book does not mention the existence of a promissory note. This example suggests that the number of promissory notes was much higher than we can determine on the basis of the merchant book.

Barter

The last group of payment methods that I would like to analyse is barter. Barter is 'trading goods or services for other goods or services'[53] without using money. The German equivalent 'Tauschhandel' means, however, the exchange of goods only,[54] and I will use this definition. I will focus on cases in which the payment was – or should have been – a commodity. I will define which partners were using the direct exchange of goods and the possible reasons for the choice of this payment method.

The pattern of the trade exchange with Lithuanian merchants is very clearly described in the merchant book and easy to reconstruct. The Lithuanian merchants came to Gdańsk in the fall and bought western products, usually cloths for which they should deliver eastern products such as wax in spring. The term of delivery was described as 'with the first free water' (*met den open water*) in other words, after the winter closure in sail, as the merchandise from Lithuania was transported to Gdańsk via ship. A transaction in this exchange looked like this one with Vilnius merchant Peter Gossevytze in September 1426, who bought eight cloths of high and middle quality and should deliver six and a half ship pounds of wax the next spring. Further Pyre should pay him at the Arthushof, the main place for merchant gatherings in Gdańsk, 30 silver coins.

26 op Mychelis [29. September 1426]. Item doe vercoffte yk eynem Russen van der Vylle, dey heyt Peter Gossevytze 6 kostel Ypersce, 3 blae unde

3 grõn, unde 2 Maboesche, darvor zal hey my geven op Passchen [20. April [1427]] 6 ½ sceppunt wasses unde yk zal em geven op dem hoeppe ½ schok grossen.[55]

This transaction is a very clear barter transaction, in which the worth of one of the merchandises is translated directly into the other without involving booking currency. The monetisation aspect of this transaction is only the delivery of silver coins to the eastern partner. This example evokes an impression, that the Lithuanian merchants – not only non-Hanseatic but also from the freshly baptised country – were not able to use more advanced means of payments and perhaps were unfamiliar with the level of abstraction required to use monetary values in calculating fair exchange. Let us analyse further contacts with Lithuanian merchants, starting with the already mentioned example. Andreas Kopervysse bought from Pyre cloth, the value of which was calculated in *schock groschen* and he should therefore send wax – the amount of wax was not explicitly listed, only the price per ship pound was defined as 8 *schock groschen*, so Kopervysse should calculate the size of delivery on this basis. This shows his ability to convert the value in the booking currency into the size of delivery and furthermore Pyre's trust that no further explanations were needed. Kopervysse should deliver 3.5 ship pounds. The delivery weighed only 2.8 ship pounds, the remaining 0.7 ship pounds were worth about 20 marks, but instead of paying them in cash Kopervysse demanded a further merchant from Gdańsk should pay to Pyre. Kopervysse therefore had an open credit in Gdańsk – he was able to use further financial instruments if he was not able to fulfil the delivery contract. In some cases, the barter was not mentioned in the description of the transaction, but the further notes on the transaction show the exchange of goods, as in the case of Mertyn Vysselvytsen and Mertyn Weperyk, who bought 42 cloths for 338 ¼ poor Prussian mark. In this case the payment in wax was not mentioned, the value of the merchandise is denoted not even in *schock groschen*, but in poor Prussian mark. The payment was fulfilled in wax, Vysselvytsen organised it in two deliveries. This model of barter can be observed in contacts with merchants from different regions – two Englishmen, Wylm Baldrye and Jon Sydey purchased fish oil for which they delivered two different types of cloth. 'Item soe ys my schuldich Wylm Baldrye unde Jõn Sydey [van] 34 vate seels unde tran, vor ed vat 8 mk. Summa ys 272 mk.'[56] 'Item untffangen 1 terlynk van 20 hele laken, ed laken vor 18 mk. Summa ys 360 mk. Item 2 keyrsey vor 17 mk.'[57] Robart Barrye, also an Englishman, bought seven pieces of wax in 1433, delivered also cloth.[58] Similar description can be found in a notice on Gdańsk merchant Hynryk van dem Berge, who oved Pyre 48 poor Prussian mark, which he paid in wax. 'Item ys my noch schuldich Hynryk van den Bergen van den Arrassche 48 mk. Untfangen an wasse.'[59] In all three cases the value of the purchased and delivered merchandise was stated in poor Prussian mark, and we cannot prove whether or not the barter was planned in advance or developed later. In some cases, the barter was planned in advance as in the case of a council of Gdańsk Hynryk van Staden, who also purchased cloths and should have delivered lead.

Op sunte Mertyn [11. November [1449]]. Item doe vercoffte yk hern Hynryk
van Staden 1 terlynk Tynsches, dar waren in 20 hele laken, ed laken vor 15 mk.
unde 1 fer., darvor sal hey my leveryren blye, den syntener vor 6 ½ fer. met
den eyrsten vorjar. Summa van den laken ys 305 mk.[60]

In summary, the same mechanism of the barter, as in contacts with Lithuanian
merchants, was used in contacts with English merchants and with Gdańsk, and
therefore Hanseatic merchants.

Barter could also be combined with advanced means of payment. As an
already elderly person, just two years before his death, in the year 1453 Pyre
sold 28 *Merdesch* cloths for 215 poor Prussian mark to Gdańsk merchant Leyffart
Blamendal.[61] This debt was turned into a life annuity, secured by the house of
Blamendal. 'Item diit sal hey my vortynssen op myn liffgedynge, wan yk dŏt sye,
soe sal ed ok dŏt syen.'[62] He delivered here a definition of life annuity – 'when
he is dead, it should also be dead'. It was one of three such transactions, as Pyre
sold in the same year 55 cloths to Peter Bemen,[63] who also should establish a life
annuity. 'Item vor desse 2 terlyng sal my Peter Bemen op syne hus laten scriven
toe mynen lyven 100 geryng mk.'[64] In the last case, Jacop Vligen bought twelve
pieces of wax for which he should pay circa 476 poor Prussian mark.[65] After
paying 150 mark, Vligen established a life annuity for Pyre comprising 229.5
poor Prussian mark, with a yearly payment of 26 poor Prussian mark. 'Item noch
sal hey my laten scriven op synem hus 26 mk. geryngen geldes, darvor sal yk em
affgerekend 229 ½ mk.'[66] The 11.3% annual interest rate was extremely high for
that time, as the common interest rate in Gdańsk in the mid-fifteenth century was
approximately 8.3%.[67] Given Pyre was probably already advanced in his years,
or that Jacop Vligen was not able to pay his debt on term, it was turned into the
life annuity, requiring Vligen to accept harsh conditions. Pyre's advanced age was
probably also the reason why he bought life annuities guaranteed in Gdańsk and
not in other towns, which was a common practice.[68]

Pyre's transactions diverge significantly from what we know solemnly from
the town books, as the purchase of life annuity in these three cases was not made
in money but with commodities. Unfortunately, we cannot compare these purchases with town books of Gdańsk from that period, as they are not decipherable,
so we do not know how the case was described in town books, nor if the payment
method was ever mentioned in them. It is possible, however, that this model was
much more common than we assume.

Further cases of such atypical barter are the purchases of ships. In the year
1443 Pyre sold yarn to shipper Tydeke Buk for 674 poor Prussian mark.[69]
One of the rates for this purchase was a sixteenth part of Buk's own ship –
Pyre mentioned that he was using the ship, so it probably lowered his cost of
shipping. 'Item noch untffangen, dat yk met em reydede, 1 sesteyndel scepps,
stont 225 mk.'[70] The shares of ships were sold not only by the shippers themselves – Hans Moldenhauwer sold to Pyre shares of a ship of Teygler and of
a ship of Ekgerd Jungen as partial payments for his purchases of yarn.[71] Pyre
also sold his parts of a ship of Ekgerd Jungen, which he purchased from Hans

Moldenhauwer and Thomas Hoewech to Everd Rynkenrode and Tydeman Monyk. Quite remarkable is the fact that he sold the parts at the same price for which he bought them.

Summary

To summarise the business activities of a late Middle Ages Hanseatic merchant, such as Pyre we can observe a number of different means of payments: he used offsetting of liabilities often, from the simplest ones, where he just compared his payables and receivables with one partner, to using receivables from one partner to pay the payables of another; to executing such offsetting of liabilities with a number of partners and partners from different towns. He also used promissory notes, in some cases again with a number of partners at once. He executed the offsetting of liabilities not only in gold and silver currencies but also in merchandise such as wax.

He used a number of gold and silver currencies, some of them primarily as booking money, some solely in cash form. The latter is the case of gold coins of bad quality, mainly minted in the Netherlands, which Pyre priced by their gold content – he was able to determine the percentage of gold in the coins. He mixed coins of different origins in order to get the sum he ought to pay to his partner. As he developed his business network, the number of gold transactions sunk rapidly. He used gold coins in contacts with both eastern and western partners. He used *schock groschen* in contacts with his eastern partners and *pound grote* in contacts with western partners.

Barter was the method he used with partners both from the east – such as merchants from Vilnius or Riga – as well as with partners from the west – such as Englishmen. The value of the merchandise exchanged in the transaction could be – but was not necessarily – defined in money. The shortages in the deliveries were covered rather by offsetting of liabilities than paid in money. In a few cases the payments were made in shares of ships or in life annuities.

If we define monetisation as a mental ability to convert the value of merchandise into currency, no differences among his partners can be observed. Regarding monetisation as the use of cash in transactions a major tendency to avoid it is to be observed. On one hand, it is connected with the higher costs of such payments, especially over distance; on the other hand, in the time of bouillon famine the access to the coins could be difficult, and alternative methods of payment were used instead.

Notes

1 Stuart Jenks, "Small is Beautiful: Why Small Hanseatic Firms Survived in the Late Middle Ages," in *The Hanse in Medieval and Early Modern Europe,* edited by Justyna Wubs-Mrozewicz and Stuart Jenks (Leiden: Brill, 2016), pp. 191–214; Ulla Kypta, "What is a Small Firm? Some Indications from the Business Organization of Late Medieval German Merchants," in *The Company in Law and Practice: Did Size Matter? (Middle Ages–Nineteenth Century),* edited by Dave De ruysscher, Albrecht Cordes, Serge Dauchy and Heikki Pihlajamäki (Leiden: Brill, 2017), pp. 10–33.

2 Wim P. Blockmanns, "Der holländische Durchbruch in der Ostsee," in *Der hansische Sonderweg? Beiträge zur Sozial- und Wirtschaftsgeschichte der Hanse*, edited by Stuart Jenks and Michael North, pp. 49–58 (Köln, Weimar and Wien: Böhlau, 1993), pp. 49–58.

3 Witold von Slaski, *Danziger Handel im XV. Jahrhundert auf Grund eines im Danziger Stadtarchiv befindlichen Handlungsbuches geschildert* (Heidelberg: C.F. Beisel Nachf., 1905); Walter Schmidt-Rimpler, *Geschichte des Kommissionsgeschäfts in Deutschland* (Halle an der Saale: Verlag der Buchhandlung des Waisenhauses, 1915); Walter Stark, *Untersuchungen zum Profit beim hansischen Handelskapital in der ersten Hälfte des 15. Jahrhunderts* (Weimar: Hermann Böhlaus Nachfolger, 1985); Walter Stark, "Kopet uns werk by Tyden. Historische Einführung," in *Die Handelsbücher des Hildebrand Veckinchusen. Kontobücher und übrige Manuale*, edited by Michail Lesnikov, Walter Stark and Albrecht Cordes (Köln und Wien: Böhlau, 2013), pp. XLVII–LVIII; Doris Tophinke, *Handelstexte. Zu Textualität und Typik kaufmännischer Rechnungsbücher im Hanseraum des 14. und 15. Jahrhundert* (Tübingen: Günter Narr Verlag, 1999), Ulf-Christian Ewert and Stephan Selzer. "Netzwerkorganisation im Fernhandel des Mittelalters: Wettbewerbsvorteil oder Wachstumshemmnis?," in *Unternehmerische Netzwerke. Eine historische Organisationsform mit Zukunft?*, edited by Hartmut Berghoff and Jörg Sydow (Stuttgart: Kohlhammer, 2007), pp. 45–70; Ewert, Ulf-Christian and Stephan Selzer. "Wirtschaftliche Stärke durch Vernetzung. Zu den Erfolgsfaktoren des hansischen Handels," in *Praktiken des Handels: Geschäfte und soziale Beziehungen europäischer Kaufleute in Mittelalter und früher Neuzeit*, edited by Mark Häberlein and Christof Jeggle (Konstanz: UVK Verlagsgesellschaft, 2008), pp. 39–70.

4 Anna Paulina Orłowska, *Johan Pyre. Ein Kaufmann und sein Handelsbuch im spätmittelalterlichen Danzig. Darstellung* (Köln: Böhlau Verlag, 2021).

5 Tophinke, *Handelstexte*, pp. 175–180.

6 Schmidt-Rimpler, *Geschichte des Kommissionsgeschäfts*, pp. 72–92.

7 Anna Paulina Orłowska, *Johan Pyre. Ein Kaufmann und sein Handelsbuch im spätmittelalterlichen Danzig. Edition*, (Köln: Böhlau Verlag, 2021) 5v 2.

8 Eugeniusz Mrowiński, *Monety Rygi* (Warszawa: Polskie Towarzystwo Archeologiczne i Numizmatyczne, Komisja Numizmatyczna, 1986), p. 15; Gunnar Haljak, *Livländische Münzen aus der Ordenszeit 13.–16. Jahrhundert* (Tallinn: As Verle, 1997), p. 98.

9 Orłowska, *Johan Pyre. Edition*, 18r 5.

10 Orłowska, *Johan Pyre. Edition*, 54 r 10.

11 Orłowska, *Johan Pyre. Edition*, 53v 10.

12 Borys Paszkiewicz, *Brakteaty – pieniądz średniowiecznych Prus*, (Wrocław: Wydawnictwo Uniwersytetu Wrocławskiego, 2009), pp. 233–236.

13 Paszkiewicz, *Brakteaty*, p. 234.

14 Orłowska, *Johan Pyre. Edition*, 110v 5.

15 Orłowska, *Johan Pyre. Edition*, 3r 7–8.

16 Orłowska, *Johan Pyre. Edition*, 21r 4.

17 Orłowska, *Johan Pyre. Edition*, 67r 6.

18 Orłowska, *Johan Pyre. Edition*, 14v 14.

19 Orłowska, *Johan Pyre. Edition*, 1v 10.

20 Werner Paravicini, "Edelleute, Hansen, Brügger Bürger. Die Finanzierung der Westeuropäischen Preußenreisen im 14. Jahrhundert," *Hansische Geschichtsblätter* 104 (1986), 5–20; Werner Paravicini, *Die Preußenreisen des europäischen Adels* (Sigmaringen: Thorbecke, 1989) vol. 2, pp. 210–308.

21 Orłowska, *Johan Pyre. Edition*, 50r 1.

22 Jürgen Sarnowsky, "Der Fall Thomas Schenkendorf: rechtliche und diplomatische Probleme um die Königsberger Großschäfferei des Deutschen Ordens," *Jahrbuch für die Geschichte Mittel- und Ostdeutschlands* 43 (1995), 187–275.

23 Karel Castelin, *Grossus Pragensis. Der Prager groschen und seine Teilstücke; 1300–1547; mit 2 gesonderten Beitr. 1, Preise der Goldmünzen in Böhmen in den Jahren 1300–1555, 2, Gegenstempel auf Prager groschen* (2nd edn. Braunschweig: Klinkhardt & Biermann, 1997).

Arthur Suhle, "Grosz," in *Wörterbuch der Münzkunde*, edited by Friedrich von Schrötter et al., (2nd edn. Berlin: De Gruyter, 1970), 234; Arthur Suhle, "Kwartnik," in ibidem, 338, Arthur Suhle, "Meißner groschen," in ibidem, 384–385.

24 Orłowska, *Johan Pyre. Darstellung*, p. 40; Karel Castelin. "Kontramarky pražských grošů. (Les contremarques des gros pragois)," *Numismatické listy* 17 (1973), 71–94.
25 Orłowska, *Johan Pyre. Edition*, 17r 2.
26 Orłowska, *Johan Pyre. Edition*, 95r 6.
27 Orłowska, *Johan Pyre. Edition*, 14r 1, 23r 5, 51r 1, 112r 11.
28 Orłowska, *Johan Pyre. Edition*, 101r 8.
29 Orłowska, *Johan Pyre. Edition*, 100v 8.
30 Orłowska, *Johan Pyre. Edition*, 100v 8.
31 Orłowska, *Johan Pyre. Edition*, 93v 9.
32 Orłowska, *Johan Pyre. Edition*, 27r 3.
33 Orłowska, *Johan Pyre. Edition*, 51r 4.
34 Orłowska, *Johan Pyre. Edition*, 93v 2.
35 Stanisław Kutrzeba, *Handel Krakowa w wiekach średnich na tle stosunków handlowych Polski* (Kraków: Nakładem Akademii Umiejętności, 1902), pp. 58–72.
36 *Regestra mercatoria. Rachunki kupców krakowskich z lat 1401–1510*, edited by Agnieszka Bartoszewicz and Marcin Starzyński (Kraków: Towarzystwo Miłośników Historii i Zabytków Krakowa, 2018).
37 Orłowska, *Johan Pyre. Edition*, 13r 4.
38 Orłowska, *Johan Pyre. Edition*, 24r 2.
39 Orłowska, *Johan Pyre. Edition*, 10r 7.
40 H. Enno van Gelder, "Gelder, H. Enno van. "Coins and accounts in the eastern Netherlands," in *Coinage in the Low countries: (880–1500); the 3. Oxford Symposium on Coinage and Monetary History*, edited by Nicholas Mayhew (Oxford: B.A.R., 1979), p. 210.
41 Markus A. Denzel, *Das System des bargeldlosen Zahlungsverkehrs europäischer Prägung vom Mittelalter bis 1914* (Stuttgart: F. Steiner, 2008), pp. 93–128.
42 Orłowska, *Johan Pyre. Edition*, 7v 12, 13.
43 Orłowska, *Johan Pyre. Edition*, 46r 9.
44 Orłowska, *Johan Pyre. Edition*, 45v 9.
45 Orłowska, *Johan Pyre. Edition*, 68r 1.
46 Orłowska, *Johan Pyre. Edition*, 67v 1.
47 Orłowska, *Johan Pyre. Edition*, 83r 5.
48 Orłowska, *Johan Pyre. Edition*, 82v 5.
49 Orłowska, *Johan Pyre. Edition*, 59r 13.
50 Orłowska, *Johan Pyre. Edition*, 58v 13.
51 Orłowska, *Johan Pyre. Edition*, 66v.
52 Orłowska, *Johan Pyre. Edition*, 67r 1.
53 Merriam-Webster, 2.
54 'im Tausch von Waren bestehender Handel', Duden.
55 Orłowska, *Johan Pyre. Edition*, 106r 8.
56 Orłowska, *Johan Pyre. Edition*, 86r 8.
57 Orłowska, *Johan Pyre. Edition*, 85v 8.
58 Orłowska, *Johan Pyre. Edition*, 101r 11, 100v 11.
59 Orłowska, *Johan Pyre. Edition*, 82r 7.
60 Orłowska, *Johan Pyre. Edition*, 74r 7.
61 Orłowska, *Johan Pyre. Edition*, 67r 3.
62 Orłowska, *Johan Pyre. Edition*, 65v 3.
63 Orłowska, *Johan Pyre. Edition*, 68r 5, 6.
64 Orłowska, *Johan Pyre. Edition*, 67v 5–6.
65 Orłowska, *Johan Pyre. Edition*, 67r 8.
66 Orłowska, *Johan Pyre. Edition*, 67v 8.

67 Marcin Grulkowski, "Grulkowski, Marcin. "Rynek renty w Głównym Mieście Gdańsku w świetle najstarszych ksiąg gruntowych w XIV–XV wieku," in *Studia i materiały do dziejów domu gdańskiego*, edited by Edmund Kizik. Gdańsk: Wydawnictwo Uniwersytetu Gdańskiego, 2009, p. 26.
68 Cezary Kardasz, *Rynek kredytu pieniężnego w miastach południowego pobrzeża Bałtyku w późnym średniowieczu (Greifswald, Gdańsk, Elbląg, Toruń, Rewel)* (Toruń: TNT, 2013).
69 Orłowska, *Johan Pyre. Edition*, 84r 3.
70 Orłowska, *Johan Pyre. Edition*, 83v 3.
71 Orłowska, *Johan Pyre. Edition*, 78r 9, 77v, 9.

Bibliography

Primary sources

Regestra mercatoria. *Rachunki kupców krakowskich z lat 1401–1510 [Accounts of Cracow merchants, 1401–1510]*, edited by Agnieszka Bartoszewicz and Marcin Starzyński. Kraków: Towarzystwo Miłośników Historii i Zabytków Krakowa, 2018.
Orłowska, Anna Paulina, Johan Pyre. *Ein Kaufmann und sein Handelsbuch im spätmittelalterlichen Danzig*. Edition. Köln: Böhlau, 2021.

Secondary literature

Blockmanns, Wim P. "Der holländische Durchbruch in der Ostsee," in *Der hansische Sonderweg? Beiträge zur Sozial- und Wirtschaftsgeschichte der Hanse*, edited by Stuart Jenks and Michael North, pp. 49–58. Köln, Weimar and Wien: Böhlau, 1993.
Castelin, Karel. "Kontramarky pražských grošů. (Les contremarques des gros pragois)," *Numismatické listy* 17 (1973), 71–94.
Castelin, Karel. *Grossus Pragensis. Der Prager groschen und seine Teilstücke; 1300–1547; mit 2 gesonderten Beitr. 1, Preise der Goldmünzen in Böhmen in den Jahren 1300–1555, 2, Gegenstempel auf Prager groschen*. 2nd edn. Braunschweig: Klinkhardt & Biermann, 1997.
Denzel, Markus A. *Das System des bargeldlosen Zahlungsverkehrs europäischer Prägung vom Mittelalter bis 1914*. Stuttgart: F. Steiner, 2008.
Duden. "Tauschhandel, "in https://www.duden.de/rechtschreibung/Tauschhandel (01.07.2020)
Ewert, Ulf-Christian and Stephan Selzer. "Netzwerkorganisation im Fernhandel des Mittelalters: Wettbewerbsvorteil oder Wachstumshemmnis?," in *Unternehmerische Netzwerke. Eine historische Organisationsform mit Zukunft?*, edited by Hartmut Berghoff and Jörg Sydow, 45–70. Stuttgart: Kohlhammer, 2007.
Ewert, Ulf-Christian and Stephan Selzer. "Wirtschaftliche Stärke durch Vernetzung. Zu den Erfolgsfaktoren des hansischen Handels," in *Praktiken des Handels: Geschäfte und soziale Beziehungen europäischer Kaufleute in Mittelalter und früher Neuzeit*, edited by Mark Häberlein and Christof Jeggle, pp. 39–70. Konstanz: UVK Verlagsgesellschaft, 2008.
Gelder, H. Enno van. "Coins and accounts in the eastern Netherlands," in *Coinage in the Low countries: (880–1500); the 3. Oxford Symposium on Coinage and Monetary History*, edited by Nicholas Mayhew, pp. 203–215. Oxford: B.A.R., 1979.
Grulkowski, Marcin. "Rynek renty w Głównym Mieście Gdańsku w świetle najstarszych ksiąg gruntowych w XIV–XV wieku," [The rent market in the Main Town Gdańsk in the light of cadastres in the fourteenth and fifteenth centuries] in *Studia i materiały do*

dziejów domu gdańskiego, edited by Edmund Kizik, pp. 21–98. Gdańsk: Wydawnictwo Uniwersytetu Gdańskiego, 2009.

Haljak, Gunnar. *Livländische Münzen aus der Ordenszeit 13.–16. Jahrhundert*. Tallinn: As Verle, 1997.

Kardasz, Cezary. *Rynek kredytu pieniężnego w miastach południowego pobrzeża Bałtyku w późnym średniowieczu [The market of monetary credit in towns of the southern Baltic coast in the late Middle Ages] (Greifswald, Gdańsk, Elbląg, Toruń, Rewel)*. Toruń: TNT, 2013.

Kutrzeba, Stanisław. *Handel Krakowa w wiekach średnich na tle stosunków handlowych Polski [The trade of Cracow in the Middle Ages at the background of trade relationships Polands]*. Kraków: Nakładem Akademii Umiejętności, 1902.

Jenks, Stuart. "Small is Beautiful: Why Small Hanseatic Firms Survived in the Late Middle Ages," in *The Hanse in Medieval and Early Modern Europe*, edited by Justyna Wubs-Mrozewicz and Stuart Jenks, pp. 191–214. Leiden: Brill, 2012.

Kypta, Ulla. "What is a Small Firm? Some Indications from the Business Organization of Late Medieval German Merchants," in *The Company in Law and Practice: Did Size Matter? (Middle Ages–Nineteenth Century)*, edited by Dave De ruysscher, Albrecht Cordes, Serge Dauchy and Heikki Pihlajamäki, pp. 10–33. Leiden: Brill, 2017.

Merriam-Webster. "Barter" in https://www.merriam-webster.com/dictionary/barter (01.07.2020)

Mrowiński, Eugeniusz. *Monety Rygi [The coins of Riga]*. Warszawa: Polskie Towarzystwo Archeologiczne i Numizmatyczne, Komisja Numizmatyczna, 1986.

Orłowska, Anna Paulina. *Johan Pyre. Ein Kaufmann und sein Handelsbuch im spätmittelalterlichen Danzig. Darstellung*. Köln: Böhlau, 2021.

Paravicini, Werner. "Edelleute, Hansen, Brügger Bürger. Die Finanzierung der Westeuropäischen Preußenreisen im 14. Jahrhundert," *Hansische Geschichtsblätter* 104 (1986), 5–20.

Paravicini, Werner. *Die Preußenreisen des europäischen Adels*. Sigmaringen: Thorbecke, 1989.

Paszkiewicz, Borys. *Brakteaty – pieniądz średniowiecznych Prus [Bracteates – money of Medieval Prussia]*. Wrocław: Wydawnictwo Uniwersytetu Wrocławskiego, 2009.

Sarnowsky, Jürgen. "Der Fall Thomas Schenkendorf: rechtliche und diplomatische Probleme um die Königsberger Großschäfferei des Deutschen Ordens," *Jahrbuch für die Geschichte Mittel- und Ostdeutschlands* 43 (1995), 187–275.

Schmidt-Rimpler, Walter. Geschichte des Kommissionsgeschäfts in Deutschland. *Halle an der Saale: Verlag der Buchhandlung des Waisenhauses*, 1915.

Slaski, Witold VON. *Danziger Handel im XV. Jahrhundert auf Grund eines im Danziger Stadtarchiv befindlichen Handlungsbuches geschildert*. Heidelberg: C.F. Beisel Nachf., 1905.

Stark, Walter. *Untersuchungen zum Profit beim hansischen Handelskapital in der ersten Hälfte des 15. Jahrhunderts*. Weimar: Hermann Böhlaus Nachfolger, 1985.

Stark, Walter. "Kopet uns werk by Tyden. Historische Einführung," in *Die Handelsbücher des Hildebrand Veckinchusen. Kontobücher und übrige Manuale*, edited by Michail Lesnikov, Walter Stark and Albrecht Cordes, pp. XLVII–LVIII. Köln and Wien: Böhlau, 2013.

Suhle, Arthur. "Grosz," in *Wörterbuch der Münzkunde*, edited by Friedrich von Schrötter et al., 243. 2nd edn. Berlin: De Gruyter, 1970a.

Suhle, Arthur. "Kwartnik," in *Wörterbuch der Münzkunde*, edited by Friedrich von Schrötter et al., 338. 2nd edn. Berlin: De Gruyter, 1970b.

Suhle, Arthur. "Meißner groschen," in *Wörterbuch der Münzkunde*, edited by Friedrich von Schrötter et al., 384–385. 2nd edn. Berlin: De Gruyter, 1970c.

Tophinke, Doris. *Handelstexte. Zu Textualität und Typik kaufmännischer Rechnungsbücher im Hanseraum des 14. und 15. Jahrhundert*. Tübingen: Günter Narr Verlag, 1999.

9   City and money during a war

Gdańsk debt during the Thirteen Years' War

Marcin Grulkowski

The issue of debts has played an important role in the studies on city finances in the Middle Ages and the early modern era.[1] Debts constituted one of the characteristics of city finances in the late Middle Ages.[2] German cities of that time developed instruments allowing municipalities to satisfy their increasing financial needs (annuity sale, loans, new taxes etc.). City participation in a war was one of the circumstances increasing the level of city debts. The Thirteen Years' War (1454–1466) proved to be the situation increasing the debt level of big Prussian cities. The financial policy of Gdańsk in that crucial period, however, has stirred little interest in researchers so far[3] – allegedly because of the lack of bookkeeping data from the Thirteen Years' War period in Gdańsk.[4] This opinion probably discouraged researchers from discussing this issue.[5]

The Thirteen Years' War became a conflict in which the financial potential of the participants determined the military successes or losses.[6] The military potential of the cities was not sufficient to win a victory over the Teutonic Order. That is why mercenaries played a crucial role in the conflict. An enormous increase of expenses forced Gdańsk and Prussia to use two different strategies: to impose new taxes and to contract various forms of debts. These activities are the subject matter of this article.

The policy of debt increase was used in Gdańsk mainly in the beginning of the war. Despite the uprising against the Teutonic Order skilfully conducted in February 1454 and the fact that Gdańsk forces seized control of the northern part of Gdańsk Pomerania, the war started to take an unfavourable direction. Without going into details of military operations, several forms of Gdańsk activities during the war can be enumerated here:

1) keeping garrisons in individual castles and towns of the northern part of Gdańsk Pomerania[7];
2) participation in the sieges of some fortresses, in particular Marienburg (Malbork), Stuhm (Sztum), and Konitz (Chojnice) in 1454, Mewe (Gniew) in 1457 and 1463, Putzig (Puck) in 1464, Preußisch Stargard (Starogard) in 1464–1466, and the city of Marienburg in 1459–1460;[8]
3) keeping from 1458 a fleet of privateers that was used to fight the enemies of the Polish-Prussian party and in naval warfare against Teutonic ships.[9]

Military operations were not the only activity affecting municipal finances – the other extremely important one was cities' participation in paying ransoms for towns and fortresses; the Marienburg Castle in particular. They were controlled by garrisons serving the Teutonic Order. In order to obtain their soldier's pay, which they did not receive from the Order, the Bohemian mercenaries sold the castles to the Polish-Prussian party in 1456.[10] The agreement, however, was performed only in 1457.

The Prussian Confederation, including Gdańsk, planned to quickly take control over the lands that rose against the Teutonic Order in 1454. In the face of failures, or even defeats suffered by the troops led by Gdańsk commanders in 1454 (unsuccessful siege of Konitz and Marienburg, the loss of control over Dirschau (Tczew) and Mewe),[11] and the defiance of mercenaries who demanded the repayment of accruing debts, Gdańsk started to search for additional sources to cover war expenses. The prospect of obtaining privileges from Polish King Casimir IV Jagiellon surely increased the city's endeavours to find money for military operations.[12] It must be emphasised that apart from new taxes, loans became the second most important source of financial means for the war for Gdańsk. I shall describe three modes of contracting debts by Gdańsk during the Thirteen Years' War.

The first mode included loans from external political subjects. This way of obtaining financial means for military goals proved, however, the least effective for Gdańsk. One of the examples was a loan obtained by the Prussian estates during the stay of Prussian Confederation delegates in Kraków. After the successful uprising of February 1454 representatives of the Confederation went to King Casimir IV to agree the principles of the future legal relations between Prussia and the Crown of the Kingdom of Poland. Eventually Prussian estates were submitted under the reign of the Polish King and Prussia was incorporated into the Crown.[13] Already during their stay in Kraków, the representatives of Prussian cities (Wilhelm Jordan and Johann Meideburg on part of Gdańsk) negotiated a war loan with Polish nobles. On 9 March 1454 Prussian estates (representatives of Gdańsk and Thorn [Toruń]) contracted a loan in the amount of 2,000 Hungarian florins from Kraków Bishop Cardinal Zbigniew Oleśnicki.[14] It was guaranteed by Hans Schweidnitzer, Bartko Graudentz and Stano Gorteler, Kraków burghers strongly involved in trading relations with Prussia and other Hanseatic lands.[15] A debt note was recorded in both Kraków municipal register and Toruń debt register (on 6 April 1454). The debt was supposed to be repaid already in 1454, in two instalments: one on St. John the Baptist's Day (24 June) and the second on St. Michael's Day (29th September).[16] Gdańsk was responsible for 50% of the loan value. The letters sent between Kraków and Gdańsk inform about problems with loan repayment. Upon the expiry of the first deadline three Kraków guarantors demanded their money and suggested sending it to Kraków through Gotschalk Hitfelt.[17] Probably in July, Gdańsk handed 350 florins to Kraków burgher Nicoalus Copernicus the Elder.[18] Already on 26th July 1454 the guarantors and the Kraków Town Council once again demanded from Gdańsk the outstanding amount of 650 florins.[19] In 1457 and 1458 the delay in loan repayment made the guarantors intervene at the King's court. Letters sent by Casimir IV called the Gdańsk City Council to repay the loan.[20] The royal order of 5th October 1458 obliged Gdańsk to pay an additional 500 florins to Bartholomeus Graudentz.[21] Gdańsk stated, however, that they had paid the whole part of their debt.[22] The calls for repayment addressed to Gdańsk resulted from difficulties Toruń had with repaying their part (they did it only in 1474).[23] Moreover, Gdańsk handed all the money they owed to Bartholomeus Graudentz and thus caused conflict with other guarantors.[24] The loss suffered by merchants because of delays in loan repayment were the sources of claims submitted by them and their descants till 1498.[25]

Gdańsk also attempted to take such loans from other local subjects that possessed adequate financial means, such as Pomeranian monasteries. Already at the Congress of Toruń on the 21st February 1454 Prussian estates called on Gdańsk to try obtaining a loan from Cistercian monasteries in Oliva (Oliwa) and Karthaus (Kartuzy).[26] The call was later repeated in a letter sent to Gdańsk on 14 March 1454 by the Prussian Confederation delegates during their stay in Petrikau (Piotrków).[27] Gdańsk, however, failed to obtain a loan from the monasteries.[28] The efforts to get a loan in the amount of 100,000 Rhenish guilders from Lübeck in April and May 1454 also failed.[29] Gdańsk delegate Marquard Knake did not manage to obtain either new soldiers or money.[30] Among those who lent money to the city in 1454 there were previous members of the convent in Gdańsk. House komtur (commander) Nicolaus Poster gave the City Council 1,250 marks for a lifelong annuity in the amount of 100 marks.[31] Another Teutonic knight, Peter Steuwer, lent Gdańsk 300 marks for six years. The Council paid back the debt only in 1473.[32]

A lien was another mode by which Gdańsk contracted its debts. In this case the aim was not only to obtain financial means, but also take over some land as a tenure from which the city could draw income, and in this way cover its past and future war expenses. King's permission formulated in July 1454 was the legal basis for such activities – the King allowed big Prussian cities to take over all revenues in Prussia and have a lien on them, provided they committed themselves to cover financial claims of mercenaries.[33] The former Teutonic administrative fishing area in Putzig became an object of such operations. This time Gdańsk adopted another tactic. Already in February–March 1454, during the negotiations in Kraków, the city representatives expressed their interest in the Putzig area.[34] In June 1454 three members of the Gdańsk City Council (Mayor Herman Stargart, councillors Dietrich Oldefeld and Tiedemann Langebeke) were granted the security interest over the Putzig area in exchange for a loan to the King in the amount of 6,500 marks (Figure 9.1).[35] On 12 December 1455 Gdańsk took over the lien over this area that included also the former Gdańsk commandery and the city of Leba (Łeba).[36] At the same time, the city had to discharge the debt of the three mentioned burghers. This liability was repaid in March 1456.[37] In 1457, when the city was collecting financial means for paying to Teutonic mercenaries a ransom for Marienburg, Gdańsk passed the lien over the Putzig area to exiled from Sweden Charles VIII Knutsson Bonde in exchange for a loan in the amount of 15,000 marks.[38] Individual people also lent money to the city in exchange for liens over liturgical paraments – for example, Arnt Steinweg lent 4,550 marks in 1457.[39] Such loans are also recorded in the debt register (Schuldbuch) of 1454–1455.

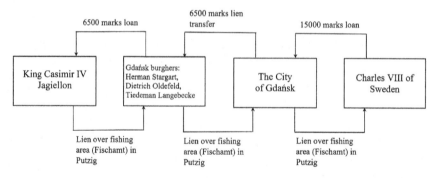

Figure 9.1. Financial operations connected with a lien over the fishing area (Fischamt) in Putzig.

Loans from Gdańsk burghers were yet another mode of increasing city financial resources. In May 1454, at the congress of Toruń, big Prussian cities committed themselves to collect silver in order to increase money minting. They also fixed the deadline for returning to burghers the value of the silver handed by them.[40] At the congress of Prussian estates in Graudenz (Grudziądz) in July 1454 Prussian cities and prelates agreed to tax themselves with the total amount of 45,000 marks (Gdańsk part: 10,000 marks).[41] The need to pay a ransom for Marienburg made Prussian cities and knights present at the congress of Elbing (Elbląg) in November 1456 take a decision to collect 82,375 florins (Gdańsk part: as much as 33,750 florins).[42] Having in mind their liabilities contracted together with Prussian estates and those concerning the maintenance of the city's own troops, Gdańsk authorities passed resolutions on compulsory loans.

The first collection had already started in September 1454. The repayment of the borrowed sums was initially planned for the next Christmas (25th December 1454).[43] In connection with the compulsory loans the Gdańsk City Council performed also various financial operations on such goods as copper, wax etc.[44] In 1454 compulsory loans were obtained from 970 people.[45] Those whose liabilities were not repaid received written confirmations, so-called promissory notes (Schuldbriefe). This financial instrument was also used later. Some of them can be found in the city archives.[46]

On 29th May 1455 municipal authorities took a decision on establishing another loan to satisfy financial claims of the Bohemian mercenaries in Preußisch Stargard and Neuenburg (Nowe).[47] The amount of this loan was fixed to be 1.5% of the property of each burgher taking part in the operation.[48] The payment was made by 149 people. Some liabilities of the second loan were secured by income on mill charges from the Great Mill and so-called pile fees. According to summative cells, in 1454–1455 altogether 74,452 marks and 6 scots were collected.[49] Another large-scale operation aiming at obtaining a loan from city burghers was performed in 1457. On 9th May 1457, on the strength of the order of municipal authorities, new taxes on goods and the "tenth pfenning" ("den zehenden pfennig") loan on burghers' properties were imposed.[50] If the loans were not repaid within one year, creditors were to be offered a rent in the amount of 1 mark for each 10 marks lent (10%). The order also provided that a 20-person committee consisting of the representatives of municipal authorities and burghers be established to make the register of contracted loans. That register has survived till today.[51] The first payments were already made on 24th April 1457 (Herman Schulte)[52], but their numbers increased after 5th May, during Casimir IV's stay in Gdańsk.[53] Altogether, about 300 people offered 60,208 marks, part in cash, part in golden rings, silver and broadcloth.[54] An additional collection of the "tenth pfenning" was performed in next months. The report of 24th June 1457 states that the loan was taken from 130 people and three guilds. The total amount they offered was 32,731 marks and 18 scots.[55]

The Thirteen Years' War generated problems with the repayment of enormous debts – problems that continued through subsequent decades. At the sejm (parliament) session held in Petrikau (Piotrków Trybunalski) in 1467, the governor of Prussia presented grievances of individual cities, including Gdańsk, about enormous debts and the poverty of their inhabitants.[56] Gdańsk pointed out that "das ewir gnoden stat Danczk wol das dritteteil wüste ist" ("the third part of the city of Gdańsk has been deserted"). After the war Gdańsk also had to renounce claims for debt repayment submitted by some mercenaries. For example, in 1472 the city refused to acknowledge the debt in the amount of 7,000 guilders for Jersigk's participation in the siege of Marienburg. Gdańsk shifted the liability onto other Prussian estates and pointed out that during the siege it was responsible for blocking one of the castle's sides.[57] Gdańsk calculated that its debts amounted to nearly 900,000 florins. Repayments proceeded slowly. Litigations between liability successors often made the process very difficult. On the basis of *in dorso* annotations on promissory notes and a new debt register made in 1478 it can be seen that the city continued to repay debts contracted during the Thirteen Years' War till 1499.[58] The analysis of available source documents shows that repayments intensified in 1471–1473. At that time the city also used to lease income on some estates from the Gdańsk patrimony. For example, in 1467 the City Council granted the lifelong usufruct of the village of Juszkowy (Gischkau) to councillor Jorgen Bock in exchange for his renouncement of claims concerning the debt of 920 marks.[59] In 1471 Peter Simon van Velßen received the right to use for 25 years Schweinewiese (Świńskie Łąki), and Alexius Schonauw the right to use for 20 years, villages Rutken (Rutki) and Zigankenberg (Suchanino). The fact that a new debt register set up in 1478 which also included outstanding debts rewritten from older ledgers shows that the City Council continued the process of redeeming its liabilities.

During the Thirteen Years' War Gdańsk tried to acquire financial means from other cities and political subjects and obtained money from compulsory internal loans imposed on its inhabitants. An increased dissatisfaction of poorer social strata and the revolt led by Martin Kogge (1456) were the side effects of the city debts contracted during the war.[60] For Gdańsk patricians, however, the Thirteen Years' War became an occasion to obtain profits on money lent to the city for conducting war operations.

Notes

1 See Bernd Roeck, *Eine Stadt in Krieg und Frieden. Studien zur Geschichte der Reichsstadt Augsburg zwischen Kalenderstreit und Parität*, vol. 2 (Göttingen: Schriftenreihe der Historischen Kommission bei der Bayerischen Akademie der Wissenschaften 37, 1989), pp. 570–603; Ulf Dirlmeier, "Die Kosten des Aufgebots der Reichsstadt Rothenburg ob der Tauber im Schweizerkrieg von 1499," in *Stadt und Krieg. 25. Arbeitstagung in Böblingen 1986*, edited by Bernhard Kirchgässner and Günter Scholz (Sigmaringen: Jan Thorbecke Verlag, 1989), pp. 27–40; Gerhard Fouquet, "Die Finanzierung von Krieg und Verteidigung in oberdeutschen Städten des späten Mittelalters (1400–1500)," in *Stadt und Krieg*, pp. 41–82; Krzysztof Kwiatkowski, "Die Teilnahme der preußischen Städte an der militärischen Aktivität der Landesherrschaft um die Wende vom 14. zum 15. Jahrhundert. Finanzielle Aspekte am Beispiel der Altstadt Elbing," in *Hansestädte im Konflikt. Krisenmanagement und bewaffnete Auseinandersetzung vom 13. bis zum 17. Jahrhundert*, edited by Ortwin Pelc (Wismar: Hansische Studien 23, 2019), pp. 29–53.

2 Eberhard Isenmann, *Die deutsche Stadt im Mittelalter 1150–1550. Stadtgestalt, Recht, Verfassung, Stadtregiment, Kirche, Gesellschaft, Wirtschaft* (Köln, Weimar and Wien: Böhlau, 2014), pp. 542–551.

3 Financial sources of Thorn (Toruń) and the Prussian Confederation settlements are better analysed – see *Księga Theudenkusa* (Fontes XXXIII), edited by Leon Koczy (Toruń: Towarzystwo Naukowe w Toruniu, 1937); *Księga długów miasta Torunia z okresu wojny trzynastoletniej* (Fontes LV), edited by Karola Ciesielska and Irena Janosz-Biskupowa (Toruń: Towarzystwo Naukowe w Toruniu, 1964); *Księga żołdu Związku Pruskiego z okresu wojny trzynastoletniej 1454–1466* (Fontes LXI), edited by Antoni Czacharowski (Toruń: Towarzystwo Naukowe w Toruniu, 1969); Irena Janosz-Biskupowa, "Przydatność badawcza 'Księgi dochodów i rozchodów nadzwyczajnych m. Torunia z okresu wojny trzynastoletniej (1454–1466)'," *Zapiski Historyczne* 34 (1969), no. 3, 155–164; Krzysztof Kopiński, "Wykazy mieszczan toruńskich pożyczających pieniądze na zapłaty dla Ulryka Czerwonki w okresie wojny trzynastoletniej," *Rocznik Toruński* 39 (2012), 137–146.

4 See Irena Janosz-Biskupowa, *Rola Torunia w Związku Pruskim i wojnie trzynastoletniej w latach 1440–1466* (Toruń: Towarzystwo Naukowe Toruń, 1965), p. 64.

5 The only researcher who analysed the finances of Gdańsk during the war was Max Foltz, *Geschichte des Danziger Stadthaushalts* (Danzig: Quellen und Darstellungen zur Geschichte Westpreussens, 1912).

6 Marian Biskup, "Załamanie się państwa krzyżackiego w XV w.", in *Dzieje zakonu krzyżackiego w Prusach. Gospodarka – Społeczeństwo – Państwo – Ideologia*, Marian Biskup and Gerard Labuda (Gdańsk: Wydawnictwo Morskie, 1988), pp. 409–415; Karol Polejowski, "Wojny zakonu krzyżackiego z Polską (XIV-XVI w.)," in *Sapientia aedificavit sibi domum. Mądrość zbudowała sobie dom...*, edited by Janusz Trupinda (Malbork: Muzeum Zamkowe w Malborku, 2019), p. 326.

7 Paul Simson, "Danzig im dreizehnjährigen Kriege 1454–1466," *Zeitschrift des Westpreussischen Geschichtsvereins* 29 (1891), 23.

8 Henryk Samsonowicz, "Gdańsk w okresie wojny trzynastoletniej," in *Historia Gdańska*, vol. 2: *1454–1633*, edited by Edmund Cieślak (Gdańsk: Wydawnictwo Morskie, 1982), pp. 54–58, 69–71; Marian Biskup, *Trzynastoletnia wojna z zakonem krzyżackim 1454–1466* (Warszawa: Wydawnictwo Ministerstwa Obrony Narodowej, 1967), pp. 172–217, 494–501, 667–694.

9 Marian Biskup, *Gdańska flota kaperska w okresie wojny trzynastoletniej 1454–1466* (Gdańsk: Biblioteka miejska. Towarzystwo przyjaciół nauki i sztuki, 1953).

10 *Die Staatsverträge des Deutschen Ordens in Preußen im 15. Jahrhundert*, vol. 2: *(1438–1467)*, edited by Erich Weise (Marburg: N.G. Elwert, 1955), no. 343; Marian Biskup, *Trzynastoletnia wojna*, pp. 424–488; idem, "Polityka zewnętrzna zakonu krzyżackiego," in *Państwo zakonu krzyżackiego w Prusach. Władza i społeczeństwo*, edited by Marian Biskup and Roman Czaja (Warszawa: Wydawnictwo Naukowe

PWN, 2008), p. 265; Wilhelm Rautenberg, "Der Verkauf der Marienburg 1454–1457. Mit Beiträgen zum zeitgenössischen Pfand- und Herrschaftsrecht sowie zur Treuepflicht im Landrecht," in *Studien zur Geschichte des Preussenlandes. Festschrift für Erich Keyser zu seinem 70. Geburtstag dargebracht von Freunden und Schülern*, edited by Ernst Bahr (Marburg: N.G. Elwert, 1963), pp. 138–139.

11 Karol Górski, *Dzieje Malborka* (Gdynia: Wydawnictwo Morskie, 1960), p. 76; Klemens Bruski, "Chojnice w średniowieczu (do roku 1466)," in *Dzieje Chojnic*, edited by Kazimierz Ostrowski (Chojnice: Urząd Miasta, 2003), p. 96; Wiesław Długokęcki, "Tczew w wojnie trzynastoletniej (1454–1466)," in *Historia Tczewa*, edited by idem (Tczew: Kociewski Kantor Edytorski, 1998), pp. 80–81; idem, "Elita władzy miasta Malborka w średniowieczu," (Malbork: Muzeum Zamkowe w Malborku, 2004), pp. 146–147; idem, "Danzigs Beziehungen zur Stadt Marienburg zur Zeit des Preußischen Bundes und des Dreizehnjährigen Krieges," in *Danzig vom 15. bis 20. Jahrhundert*, edited by Bernhart Jähnig (Marburg: Elwert, 2006), p. 97; Marian Biskup, *Polityka zewnętrzna*, p. 263.

12 Gdańsk demands concerning royal privileges – see Archiwum Państwowe w Gdańsku [hereinafter: APGd], Sign. 300, D/74, 105; *Acten der Ständetage Preussens unter der Herrschaft des Deutschen Ordens* [hereinafter: AStP], vol. 4: *August 1453 bis September 1457*, edited by Max Toeppen (Leipzig: Verlag von Duncker&Humblot, 1884), no. 237; Marian Biskup, *Stosunek Gdańska do Kazimierza Jagiellończyka w okresie wojny trzynastoletniej 1454–1466* (Toruń: Towarzystwo Naukowe w Toruniu, 1952), p. 41.

13 Marian Biskup, *Stosunek Gdańska*, pp. 41–43; idem, *U schyłku średniowiecza i w początkach odrodzenia (1454–1548)* (Toruń: Towarzystwo Naukowe w Toruniu, 1992), pp. 13–15; Adam Vetulani, "Rokowania krakowskie z r. 1454 i zjednoczenie ziem pruskich z Polską," *Przegląd Historyczny* 45 (1954), no. 2–3, 232–236.

14 See Stanisław Gawęda, "Rola finansowa duchowieństwa diecezji krakowskiej w okresie wojny trzynastoletniej," *Nasza Przeszłość* 10 (1959), 148; Zbyszko Górczak, *Podstawy gospodarcze działalności Zbigniewa Oleśnickiego biskupa krakowskiego* (Kraków: Secesja, 1999), p. 198; Jarosław Nikodem, *Zbigniew Oleśnicki w historiografii polskiej* (Kraków: Polska Akademia Umiejętności, 2001), p. 240; Marcin Grulkowski, "Korespondencja Krakowa i Wrocławia z Głównym Miastem Gdańskiem w późnym średniowieczu," *Klio* 23 (2012), no. 4, 54–58.

15 See Stanisław Kutrzeba, *Finanse i handel średniowiecznego Krakowa* (Kraków: Avalon, 2009), pp. 225–226; Marcin Starzyński, *Krakowska rada miejska w średniowieczu* (Kraków: Societas Vistulana, 2010), p. 267.

16 Archiwum Narodowe w Krakowie, Consularia Cracoviensia. Inscriptiones, rkps 429, pp. 89–90; AStP, vol. 4, no. 256; *Księga długów*, no. 25.

17 APGd, Sign. 300, D/7, 43 (letter of 27.06.1454); APGd, Sign. 300, D/7, 44 (letter of 5.09.1454).

18 The declaration of the Gdańsk Main Town Council was registered in the missive register only on 14 August 1454, see APGd, Sign. 300, 27/5, p. 249v; *Spicilegium Copernicanum. Festschrift des historischen Vereins für Ermland zum vierhundertsten Geburtstage des ermländischen Domherrn Nikolaus Kopernikus*, edited by Franz Hipler (Braunsberg: Verlag von Eduard-Peter, 1873), p. 371; Leopold Prowe, *Nicolaus Coppernicus*, vol. 1: *Das Leben*, part 1: 1473–1512 (Berlin: Weidmannsche Buchhandlung, 1883), p. 50; Marian Biskup, *Regesta Copernicana*, edited by Marian Biskup (Wrocław, Warszawa, Kraków and Gdańsk: Ossolineum. The Polish Academy of Science Press, 1973), no. 2.

19 APGd, Sign. 300, D/7, 31; APGd, Sign. 300, D/7, 42.

20 APGd, Sign. 300, D/1, 58; APGd, Sign. 300, D/1, 63; *Katalog dokumentów i listów królów polskich z Archiwum Państwowego w Gdańsku (do 1492 roku)*, edited by Marcin Grulkowski, Beata Możejko and Sobiesław Szybkowski (Gdańsk: Wydawnictwo Uniwersytetu Gdańskiego, 2014), no. 69, 74.

21 APGd, Sign. 300, 27/6, pp. 95r–v.

22 Ibidem, pp. 51v–52r, 97v–98v.

23 Księga długów, no. 25, p. 40–42.

24 *Daruf dy von Danczke bezcalet haben tausendt gulden Bartholomeo Grudentcz* (ibidem, no. 25, p. 40). See also APGd, Sign. 300, D/7, 39 (Stano Gorteler's letter to Gdańsk of 13.11.1459).

25 Marcin Grulkowski, *Korespondencja*, pp. 57–58; *Katalog dokumentów i listów królów polskich z Archiwum Państwowego w Gdańsku (Jan Olbracht i Aleksander Jagiellończyk)*, edited by Sobiesław Szybkowski (Gdańsk: Wydawnictwo Uniwersytetu Gdańskiego, 2016), no. 24, 26, 27, 70, 105, 108.

26 *Ouch liben hern, thut wol, und besucht dy monche czur Olyva, die Carthewsz und ander, das sie uns geld leyen off tage czu beczaln etc., wenne euwer libe wol weis, das wir mechtig gros geld schuldig sein czu beczalen und den soldenern alle tage vil geldes mu*ᵉ*ssen geben und wissen nicht, wo czu nemen* (AStP, vol. 4, no. 221).

27 *Hirumb so bitten wir mit allem fleisze, ir wellet bestellen eyne botschaft und senden einen vom lande und einen aws ewrem rote an die closter als Polplyn, Oliwa und Carthewser, umb 6 ader acht adir 10 tawsent gulden uns yo zcu leyhen und schicken und in so korczer czeith, wenn sie, ire gutter und kirchen von uns beschirmet sein, und wenn uns got zcu frede helfet, so wellen wir zich mit en wol vortragen* (ibidem, no. 251).

28 The Olive Chronicle contains a note that on the day of a new abbot appointment on 20 July 1454 the claims of the Olive monastery included the sum of 200 marks lent to the city of Gdańsk; *Scriptores Rerum Prussicarum. Die Geschichtsquellen der preussischen Vorzeit bis zum Untergange der Ordensherrschaft*, vol. 5, edited by Theodor Hirsch, Max Töppen and Ernst Strehlke (Leipzig: Verlag von S. Hirzel, 1874), p. 632. This debt was recorded in the debt register made upon the collection of the compulsory loan in 1454 (APGd, Sign. 300, 12/484, p. 36).

29 Max Foltz, *Geschichte*, p. 285.

30 *Hanserecesse von 1431–1476*, vol. 4, edited by Goswin Freiherr von der Ropp (Leipzig 1883), no. 270, 274; Paul Simson, *Danzig*, p. 40.

31 *Umb dieselbe zeit haben auch die Dantzker von Herrn Niclas Poster, der für diesem Kriege HausCompter zu Dantzig gewesen war, zu trewen Handen empfangen zwelff hundert und funfftzig Marck Preussisch, so das sie ime dagegen angelobet Järlich zu seinem Leben zu geben hundert Marck, und nach seinem Tode solte das Geld des Raths eigen bleiben, (…)* (Caspar Schütz, *Historia Rerum Prussicarum* (Zerbst: Bonauentur Schmid, 1592), [220v].

32 APGd, Sign. 300, D/40, 102; APGd, Sign. 300, D/40, 105; Paul Simson, *Geschichte der Stadt Danzig*, vol. 1: *Von den Anfängen bis 1517* (Danzig: A.W. Kafemann, 1913), p. 238.

33 AStP, vol. 4, no. 292; Paul Simson, *Geschichte*, vol. 1, p. 241.

34 *Item, leve herren, also gy uns utgesettet hadden to heszen dat kunteramet mit deme Lauwenborgeschen gebeyde mit Puchzk, Grebin, Subbevicz und Butow, do wy dat den landen vorleden, do wenn wy nicht de, de mit erem besten ummegingen, und hebben dat vele gemynnert* (APGd, Sign. 300, D/74, 105; AStP, vol. 4, no. 237).

35 AStP, vol. 4, no. 289; Klemens Bruski, "Puck w czasach krzyżackich (1308–1466)," in: *Historia Pucka*, edited by Andrzej Groth (Gdańsk: Wydawnictwo "Marpress", 1998), p. 86.

36 AStP, vol. 4, no. 324; Marian Biskup, *Stosunek Gdańska*, p. 101.

37 Paul Simson, *Danzig*, 124–125, no. 31; Marian Biskup, *Stosunek Gdańska*, pp. 101–102.

38 APGd, Sign. 300, D/59, 7; Kjell Kumlien, *Karl Knutsson i Preussen 1457–1464. Ett inslag i östersjöområdets historia under det 13-åriga krigets tid* (Stockholm: Wahlström & Widstrand, 1940), pp. 22–23; Marian Biskup, *Stosunek Gdańska*, p. 115; Klemens Bruski, *Puck*, p. 87.

39 APGd, Sign. 300, D/80, 54a.

40 APGd, Sign. 300, D/74, 169; Max Foltz, *Geschichte*, pp. 445–446.

41 AStP, vol. 4, no. 291, pp. 437–438; Caspar Schütz, *Historia Rerum Prussicarum*, [218r–219r].
42 AStP, vol. 4, no. 349, pp. 529–530; Caspar Schütz, *Historia Rerum Prussicarum*, DIII.
43 *Anno LIIII° in augusto. Disse na geschrevene hebben dem rade gelent, dat men en gelauet heft wedder to geven op wynnachten* (APGd, Sign. 300, 12/484, p. 3).
44 Ibidem, pp. 6, 8–9.
45 Ibidem, pp. 3–174.
46 See APGd, Sign. 300, D/80, 37; APGd, Sign. 300, D/80, 44; APGd, Sign. 300, D/80, 46; APGd, Sign. 300, D/80, 51; APGd, Sign. 300, D/80, 52; APGd, Sign. 300, D/80, 53; APGd, Sign. 300, D/80, 54; APGd, Sign. 300, D/80, 66; APGd, Sign. 300, D/80, 69.
47 *Item anno LV 29 in mey do ward over eyngedregen by rade, schepen unde gemeyn dat men solden lygen van 100 mk. 1½ mk. umme de bemen tho Stargarde, Nygenborch to betalen etc.* (APGd, Sign. 300, 12/484, p. 193).
48 Ibidem, p. 193.
49 According to Stenzel Bornbach, a 16th century Gdańsk chronicler who used many source documents that have not survived, in 1455 44 representatives of Gdańsk burghers (mainly members of the City Council and the Court of Municipal Bench) paid the total sum of 42,500 marks that was secured by income from the Great Mill (PAN Biblioteka Gdańska, Ms. Uph. fol. 113, pp. 554–555).
50 APGd, Sign. 300, D/80, 40; Max Foltz, *Geschichte*, pp. 446–448.
51 APGd, Sign. 300, 12/399.
52 APGd, Sign. 300, 12/399, p. 10.
53 APGd, 300, 12/399, pp. 3, 10.
54 Max Foltz, *Geschichte*, p. 287.
55 Ibidem, pp. 149–452.
56 *Dy herrn von Danczke sprechen also, das sie sere arm vortorben und zumole vil schuldig seyn, also das ire burger in fremden landen schulde halben warden aufgehalden und torren nicht usczihn* (Acten der Ständetage Preussens, Königlichen Antheils (Westpreußen), vol. 1: *1466–1479*, edited by Franz Thunert (Danzig: A.W. Kafemann, 1896), no. 6, p. 30.
57 Ibidem, no. 50, p. 188.
58 APGd, Sign. 300, 12/485.
59 Ewa Bojaruniec, "Georg Bock", in: *Poczet sołtysów, burmistrzów, nadburmistrzów, przewodniczących Miejskiej Rady Narodowej i prezydentów Gdańska od XIII do XXI wieku*, edited by Beata Możejko (Gdańsk: Oficyna Gdańska, 2015), p. 111.
60 Edmund Cieślak, "Rewolty gdańskie w XV w.," in *Kwartalnik Historyczny* 61 (1954), 3, 110–142; idem, *Walki ustrojowe w Gdańsku i Toruniu oraz w niektórych miastach hanzeatyckich w XV w.* (Gdańsk: Gdańskie Towarzystwo Naukowe, 1960), pp. 183–198, 221–227; Maria Bogucka, "Przemiany społeczne i walki społeczno-polityczne w XV i XVI w.," in *Historia Gdańska*, vol. 2, pp. 218–223.

Bibliography

Primary sources

Unprinted sources

Archiwum Narodowe w Krakowie – National Archives in Cracow
Consularia Cracoviensia. Inscriptiones, rkps 429.
Archiwum Państwowe w Gdańsku (APGd) – State Archive in Gdańsk
Sign. 300, 12/399.
Sign. 300, 12/484.

Sign. 300, 12/485.
Sign. 300, 27/5.
Sign. 300, 27/6.
Sign. 300, D/1, 58.
Sign. 300, D/1, 63.
Sign. 300, D/7, 31.
Sign. 300, D/7, 39.
Sign. 300, D/7, 42.
Sign. 300, D/7, 43.
Sign. 300, D/7, 44.
Sign. 300, D/40, 102.
Sign. 300, D/40, 105.
Sign. 300, D/59, 7.
Sign. 300, D/74, 105.
Sign. 300, D/74, 169.
Sign. 300, D/80, 37.
Sign. 300, D/80, 40.
Sign. 300, D/80, 44.
Sign. 300, D/80, 46.
Sign. 300, D/80, 51.
Sign. 300, D/80, 52.
Sign. 300, D/80, 53.
Sign. 300, D/80, 54.
Sign. 300, D/80, 54a.
Sign. 300, D/80, 66.
Sign. 300, D/80, 69.
PAN Biblioteka Gdańska [Polish Akademy of Sciences – Gdańsk Library]
Ms. Uph. fol. 113, p. 554–555

Printed Sources

Antoni, Czacharowski (ed.), *Księga żołdu Związku Pruskiego z okresu wojny trzynasto-letniej 1454–1466 [The register of soldiers' pay of the Prussian Confederation in the Thirteen Year'War 1454–1466], (Fontes LXI)*. Toruń: Towarzystwo Naukowe w Toruniu 1969.

Erich, Weise (ed.), *Die Staatsverträge des Deutschen Ordens in Preußen im 15. Jahrhundert*, vol. 2: (1438–1467),. Marburg: N.G. Elwert, 1955.

Franz, Hipler (ed.), *Spicilegium Copernicanum. Festschrift des historischen Vereins für Ermland zum vierhundertsten Geburtstage des ermländischen Domherrn Nikolaus Kopernikus*. Braunsberg: Verlag von Eduard-Peter, 1873.

Franz, Thunert (ed.), *Acten der Ständetage Preussens, Königlichen Antheils (Westpreußen)*, vol. 1: 1466–1479,. Danzig: A.W. Kafemann, 1896.

Karola, Ciesielska and Irena Janosz-Biskupowa (eds.), *Księga długów miasta Torunia z okresu wojny trzynastoletniej [The register of Toruń debts in the period of the Thirteen Year'War]* (Fontes LV). Toruń: Towarzystwo Naukowe w Toruniu 1964.

Leon, Koczy (ed.), *Księga Theudenkusa [Theudenkus Book], (Fontes XXXIII),.* Toruń: Towarzystwo Naukowe w Toruniu, 1937.

Marcin, Grulkowski, Beata Możejko and Sobiesław Szybkowski (eds.), *Katalog dokumentów i listów królów polskich z Archiwum Państwowego w Gdańsku (do 1492 roku) [The catalogue of documents and Polish kings' letters from the State Archives in Gdańsk]*,. Gdańsk: Wydawnictwo Uniwersytetu Gdańskiego, 2014.

Marian, Biskup (ed.), *Regesta Copernicana (Studia Copernica 8)*. Wrocław, Warszawa, Kraków and Gdańsk: Ossolineum. The Polish Academy of Science Press, 1973.

Max, Toeppen (ed.), *Acten der Ständetage Preussens unter der Herrschaft des Deutschen Ordens, vol. 4: August 1453 bis September 1457*. Leipzig: Verlag von Duncker& Humblot, 1884.

Schütz, Caspar. *Historia Rerum Prussicarum*. Zerbst: Bonauentur Schmid, 1592.

Sobiesław, Szybkowski (ed.), *Katalog dokumentów i listów królów polskich z Archiwum Państwowego w Gdańsku (Jan Olbracht i Aleksander Jagiellończyk) [The catalogue of documents and Polish kings' letters from the State Archives in Gdańsk (John I Albert and Alexander Jagiellon)]*. Gdańsk: Wydawnictwo Uniwersytetu Gdańskiego, 2016.

Theodor, Hirsch, Max Töppen and Ernst Strehlke (ed.), *Scriptores Rerum Prussicarum. Die Geschichtsquellen der preussischen Vorzeit bis zum Untergange der Ordensherrschaft*, vol. 5. Leipzig: Verlag von S. Hirzel, 1874.

von der Ropp, Goswin Freiherr (ed.), *Hanserecesse von 1431–1476*, vol. 4,. Leipzig 1883.

Secondary literature

Biskup, Marian. *Stosunek Gdańska do Kazimierza Jagiellończyka w okresie wojny trzynastoletniej 1454–1466 [Gdańsk attitude to King Casimir IV Jagiellon in the period of the Thirteen Year' War 1454–1466] (Roczniki Towarzystwa Naukowego w Toruniu 56, 1)*. Toruń: Towarzystwo Naukowe w Toruniu, 1952.

Biskup, Marian. *Gdańska flota kaperska w okresie wojny trzynastoletniej 1454–1466 [Gdańsk fleet of privateers in the period of the Thirteen Year' War 1454–1466] (Biblioteka Gdańska. Seria monografii 3)*. Gdańsk: Biblioteka miejska. Towarzystwo przyjaciół nauki i sztuki, 1953.

Biskup, Marian. *Trzynastoletnia wojna z zakonem krzyżackim 1454–1466 [The Thirteen Year'War (1454–1466) with the Teutonic Order]*. Warszawa: Wydawnictwo Ministerstwa Obrony Narodowej, 1967.

Biskup, Marian. "Załamanie się państwa krzyżackiego w XV w.," [The breakdown of the State of the Teutonic Order in the 15th c.] in *Dzieje zakonu krzyżackiego w Prusach. Gospodarka – Społeczeństwo – Państwo – Ideologia [The history of the Teutonic Order in Prussia: Economy – society – state – ideology]* edited by Marian Biskup and Gerard Labuda, pp. 353–437. Gdańsk: Wydawnictwo Morskie, 1988.

Biskup, Marian. *U schyłku średniowiecza i w początkach odrodzenia (1454–1548) [The end of the Middle Ages and the beginning of the Renaissance (1454–1548)]*. (Historia Torunia 2, 1) Toruń: Towarzystwo Naukowe w Toruniu, 1992.

Biskup, Marian. "Polityka zewnętrzna zakonu krzyżackiego," [Foreign policy of the Teutonic Order] in *Państwo zakonu krzyżackiego w Prusach. Władza i społeczeństwo [The State of the Teutonic Order in Prussia: Authorities and the society]* edited by Marian Biskup and Roman Czaja, pp. 233–331. Warszawa: Wydawnictwo Naukowe PWN, 2008.

Bogucka, Maria. "Przemiany społeczne i walki społeczno-polityczne w XV i XVI w.," [Social changes and socio-political fights in the 15th and the 16th century] in *Historia Gdańska [The history of Gdańsk]*, vol. 2: 1454–1633, edited by Edmund Cieślak, pp. 208–259. Gdańsk: Wydawnictwo Morskie, 1982.

Bojaruniec, Ewa. "Georg Bock," in *Poczet sołtysów, burmistrzów, nadburmistrzów, przewodniczących Miejskiej Rady Narodowej i prezydentów Gdańska od XIII do XXI wieku [List of sołtys (Schultheiß), mayors, high mayors (Oberbürgermeister), presidents of*

City National Council and Mayors of the City of Gdańsk from the 13th to the 21st century], edited by Beata Możejko, pp. 110–111. Gdańsk: Oficyna Gdańska, 2015.

Bruski, Klemens. "Puck w czasach krzyżackich (1308–1466)," [Puck in Teutonic times (1308–1466)] in *Historia Pucka [The history of Puck]*, edited by Andrzej Groth, pp. 68–90. Gdańsk: Wydawnictwo "Marpress", 1998.

Bruski, Klemens. "Chojnice w średniowieczu (do roku 1466)" [Chojnice in the Middle Ages (up to 1466)], in *Dzieje Chojnic [The history of Chojnice]*, edited by Kazimierz Ostrowski, pp. 46–104. Chojnice: Urząd Miasta, 2003.

Cieślak, Edmund. "Rewolty gdańskie w XV w.," [Gdańsk revolts in the 15th century] *Kwartalnik Historyczny* 61 (1954), no. 3, 110–142.

Cieślak, Edmund. *Walki ustrojowe w Gdańsku i Toruniu oraz w niektórych miastach hanzeatyckich w XV w. [Internal political struggles in Gdańsk, Toruń and some other Hanseatic towns in the 15th century]*. Gdańsk: Gdańskie Towarzystwo Naukowe, 1960.

Dirlmeier, Ulf. "Die Kosten des Aufgebots der Reichsstadt Rothenburg ob der Tauber im Schweizerkrieg von 1499," in *Stadt und Krieg. 25. Arbeitstagung in Böblingen 1986 (Stadt in der Geschichte. Veröffentlichungen des Südwestdeutschen Arbeitskreises für Stadtgeschichtsforschung 15)* edited by Bernhard Kirchgässner and Günter Scholz, pp. 27–40. Sigmaringen: Jan Thorbecke Verlag, 1989.

Długokęcki, Wiesław. "Tczew w wojnie trzynastoletniej (1454–1466)," [Tczew during the Thirteen Year' War (1454–1466)] in *Historia Tczewa [The history of Tczew]*, edited by Wiesław Długokęcki, pp. 79–84. Tczew: Kociewski Kantor Edytorski, 1998.

Długokęcki, Wiesław. *Elita władzy miasta Malborka w średniowieczu [Malbork leadership elites in the Middle Ages]*. Malbork: Muzeum Zamkowe w Malborku, 2004.

Długokęcki, Wiesław. "Danzigs Beziehungen zur Stadt Marienburg zur Zeit des Preußischen Bundes und des Dreizehnjährigen Krieges," in *Danzig vom 15. bis 20. Jahrhundert (Tagungsberichte der Historischen Kommission für ost- und westpreußische Landesforschung 19)*, edited by Bernhart Jähnig, pp. 87–107. Marburg: Elwert, 2006.

Foltz, Max. *Geschichte des Danziger Stadthaushalts*. Danzig: Quellen und Darstellungen zur Geschichte Westpreussens, 1912.

Fouquet, Gerhard. "Die Finanzierung von Krieg und Verteidigung in oberdeutschen Städten des späten Mittelalters (1400–1500)," in *Stadt und Krieg. 25. Arbeitstagung in Böblingen 1986 (Stadt in der Geschichte. Veröffentlichungen des Südwestdeutschen Arbeitskreises für Stadtgeschichtsforschung 15)*, edited by Bernhard Kirchgässner and Günter Scholz, pp. 41–82. Sigmaringen: Jan Thorbecke Verlag, 1989.

Gawęda, Stanisław. "Rola finansowa duchowieństwa diecezji krakowskiej w okresie wojny trzynastoletniej," [The financial role of the Cracow diocese clergy in the period of the Thirteen Year' War] *Nasza Przeszłość* 10 (1959), 143–158.

Górczak, Zbyszko. *Podstawy gospodarcze działalności Zbigniewa Oleśnickiego biskupa krakowskiego [Economic basis of Cracow Bishop Zbigniew Oleśnicki activities] (Biblioteka Krakowska 138)*. Kraków: Secesja, 1999.

Górski, Karol. *Dzieje Malborka [The history of Malbork]*. Gdynia: Wydawnictwo Morskie, 1960.

Grulkowski, Marcin. "Korespondencja Krakowa i Wrocławia z Głównym Miastem Gdańskiem w późnym średniowieczu," [Kraków and Wrocław's correspondence with the Main Town of Gdańsk in the late medieval period] *Klio* 23 (2012), no. 4, 35–71.

Isenmann, Eberhard. *Die deutsche Stadt im Mittelalter 1150–1550. Stadtgestalt, Recht, Verfassung, Stadtregiment, Kirche, Gesellschaft, Wirtschaft*. Köln, Weimar and Wien: Böhlau, 2014.

Janosz-Biskupowa, Irena. *Rola Torunia w Związku Pruskim i wojnie trzynastoletniej w latach 1440–1466 [Toruń's role in the Prussian Confederation and the Thirteen Year' War in 1440–1466] (Roczniki Towarzystwa Naukowego w Toruniu 70, no. 3).* Toruń: Towarzystwo Naukowe Toruń, 1965.

Janosz-Biskupowa, Irena. "Przydatność badawcza 'Księgi dochodów i rozchodów nadzwyczajnych m. Torunia z okresu wojny trzynastoletniej (1454–1466)'," [Scientific usefulness of 'The City of Toruń extraordinary revenue and expense ledger from the period of the Thirteen Year' War (1454–1466)'] *Zapiski Historyczne* 34 (1969), no. 3, 155–164.

Kopiński, Krzysztof. "Wykazy mieszczan toruńskich pożyczających pieniądze na zapłaty dla Ulryka Czerwonki w okresie wojny trzynastoletniej," [Registers of Toruń burghers lending money for payments to Ulryk Czerwonka in the period of the Thirteen Year' War] *Rocznik Toruński* 39 (2012), 137–146.

Kumlien, Kjell. *Karl Knutsson i Preussen 1457–1464. Ett inslag i östersjöområdets historia under det 13-åriga krigets tid (Kungl. Vitterhets Historie och Antikvitets Akademiens Handlingar 46, 2).* Stockholm: Wahlström & Widstrand, 1940.

Kutrzeba, Stanisław. *Finanse i handel średniowiecznego Krakowa [Finances and commerce in medieval Cracow].* Kraków: Avalon, 2009.

Kwiatkowski, Krzysztof. "Die Teilnahme der preußischen Städte an der militärischen Aktivität der Landesherrschaft um die Wende vom 14. zum 15. Jahrhundert. Finanzielle Aspekte am Beispiel der Altstadt Elbing," in *Hansestädte im Konflikt. Krisenmanagement und bewaffnete Auseinandersetzung vom 13. bis zum 17. Jahrhundert (Hansische Studien 23),* edited by Ortwin Pelc, pp. 29–53. Wismar: callidus. Verlag wissenschaftlicher Publikationen, 2019.

Nikodem, Jarosław. *Zbigniew Oleśnicki w historiografii polskiej [Zbigniew Oleśnicki in Polish historiography] (Rozprawy Wydziału Historyczno-Filozoficznego 94).* Kraków: Polską Akademia Umiejętności, 2001.

Polejowski, Karol. "Wojny zakonu krzyżackiego z Polską (XIV–XVI w.)," [Wars of the Teutonic Order against Poland (14th–16s century)] in *Sapientia aedificavit sibi domum. Mądrość zbudowała sobie dom... [Sapientia aedificavit sibi domum. Wisdom has built her house...],* edited by Janusz Trupinda, pp. 312–343. Malbork: Muzeum Zamkowe w Malborku, 2019.

Prowe, Leopold. *Nicolaus Coppernicus, vol. 1: Das Leben, part 1,* pp. 1473–1512. Berlin: Weidmannsche Buchhandlung, 1883.

Rautenberg, Wilhelm. "Der Verkauf der Marienburg 1454–1457. Mit Beiträgen zum zeitgenössischen Pfand- und Herrschaftsrecht sowie zur Treuepflicht im Landrecht," in *Studien zur Geschichte des Preussenlandes. Festschrift für Erich Keyser zu seinem 70. Geburtstag dargebracht von Freunden und Schülern,* edited by Ernst Bahr, pp. 119–150. Marburg: N.G. Elwert, 1963.

Roeck, Bernd. *Eine Stadt in Krieg und Frieden. Studien zur Geschichte der Reichsstadt Augsburg zwischen Kalenderstreit und Parität (Schriftenreihe der Historischen Kommission bei der Bayerischen Akademie der Wissenschaften 37),* vol. 2. Göttingen: Vandenhoeck & Ruprecht, 1989.

Samsonowicz, Henryk. "Gdańsk w okresie wojny trzynastoletniej," [Gdańsk in the period of the Thirteen Year' War] in *Historia Gdańska [The history of Gdańsk],* vol. 2: 1454–1633, edited by Edmund Cieślak, pp. 43–76. Gdańsk: Wydawnictwo Morskie, 1982.

Simson, Paul. "Danzig im dreizehnjährigen Kriege 1454–1466," *Zeitschrift des Westpreussischen Geschichtsvereins* 29 (1891), 1–132.

Simson, Paul. *Geschichte der Stadt Danzig, vol. 1: Von den Anfängen bis 1517.* Danzig: A.W. Kafemann, 1913.

Starzyński, Marcin. *Krakowska rada miejska w średniowieczu [Cracow City Council in the Middle Ages] (Maiestas, potestas, communitas 3)*. Kraków: Societas Vistulana, 2010.

Vetulani, Adam. "Rokowania krakowskie z r. 1454 i zjednoczenie ziem pruskich z Polską," [Cracow negotiations of 1454 and the unification of Prussian lands with Poland] *Przegląd Historyczny* 45 (1954), no. 2–3, 188–236.

Index

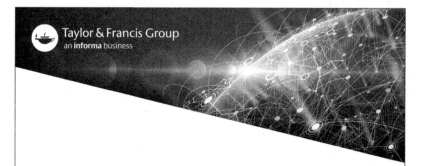